# MONKS POND

# MONKS POND

*Thomas Merton's Little Magazine*

Edited with an introduction by
ROBERT E. DAGGY

Afterword by
PATRICK HART, O.C.S.O.

THE UNIVERSITY PRESS OF KENTUCKY

Scholarly publisher for the Commonwealth,
serving Bellarmine College, Berea College, Centre
College of Kentucky, Eastern Kentucky University,
The Filson Club, Georgetown College, Kentucky
Historical Society, Kentucky State University,
Morehead State University, Murray State University,
Northern Kentucky University, Transylvania University,
University of Kentucky, University of Louisville,
and Western Kentucky University.

*Editorial and Sales Offices:* Lexington, Kentucky 40506-0336

**Library of Congress Cataloging-in-Publication Data**
Merton, Thomas, 1915-1968.
  Monks pond.

  Reprint. Originally published: Trappist, Ky.:
T. Merton, 1968.
  1. Poetry, Modern—20th century.  I. Daggy, Robert E.
II. Title.
PN6101.M44  1989     811'.5408     89-8918
ISBN 0-8131-1694-5 (alk. paper)

# CONTENTS

# ACKNOWLEDGMENTS

I AM GRATEFUL to several people who have been involved in the preparation of this facsimile edition of Thomas Merton's *Monks Pond:* to the Trustees of the Merton Legacy Trust (James Laughlin, Thomasine O'Callaghan, Robert Giroux) who granted permission for the edition; to the University Press Committee of Bellarmine College who approved the project in its early stages; to Brother Patrick Hart, Archivist at the Abbey of Gethsemani, who located Merton's original visuals for *Monks Pond;* to the original contributors to *Monks Pond* who were located and contacted and who generously gave their support to this reprinting; to Wade Hall of Bellarmine College who conceived a benefit performance of Shakespeare's *The Tempest* to help fund the project; and to Mr. and Mrs. Barry Bingham, Sr., who supported that performance through Mr. Bingham's appearance in it.

# INTRODUCTION
## Beyond Cheese and Liturgy

IN THE MID-1960s Thomas Merton, responding to the growth of the cheese industry at the Abbey of Gethsemani, wrote and pinned to the monastic bulletin board a takeoff on Joyce Kilmer's poem, "Trees." He called it, significantly, "CHEE$E." The last two lines read: "Poems are nought but warmed-up breeze, / *Dollars* are made by Trappist Cheese."[1] Merton remained suspicious and uncertain as Gethsemani mechanized to meet the demands of the twentieth century, as machines filled the bottoms and "tractors growled" in the fields, as he saw his monastery "humming with action" and filled with "high definition projects." Many of the values he held, monastic and humanistic, he feared, might be lost in the hubbub of activity.[2] He had compared Gethsemani in "Chee$e" with that prototype of meaningless activity, the Tower of Babel. Though he believed that "a completely medieval style of monastic life [was] finished," he feared that mechanization and increasing technology might bring "the injustices, the distortions, the inhumanities of the secular life" into the monastery.[3] One way to prevent this, he thought, was to have the monks' education well-grounded in the humanities, particularly in literature and more particularly in poetry. He tried in "Chee$e," not too subtly, to remind (even to persuade) his brothers that a poem was a great deal more than "warmed-up breeze."

He had tried, as novice master charged with education and formation, to give the monks exposure to literature. In a lecture on Rainer Maria Rilke, delivered 21 November 1965, he mentioned three poets the novices should know. Of Rilke himself he said: "He's certainly somebody that you need to know about if you are going to be at all educated in the humanities, see. So I suppose it is a good thing for me to keep pluggin' on him for a while." Later, he read a poem of Sidney Keyes ("I've never heard of him . . . probably nobody's ever heard of him") and, still later, discussed Robert Lowell (one of "the real good poets"). When Gethsemani purchased an offset press in 1967, Merton thought it should "put out something besides cheese ads for heavens sake."[4] So he decided to edit and produce a literary magazine, an idea with which he had perhaps been toying for some time, to take advantage of the press and, most probably, to advance his point that literature could be appreciated, even created, within a monastery. He wrote to Wendell Berry in January 1968: "I don't think a monastic press should be confined to cheese and liturgy."[5]

One reason that Merton had apparently been toying with editing a "little magazine" devoted to "poems and short prose," and one consistent with his stance as a marginal person, is that he had increasingly become disposed toward publishing in obscure places, toward "underground presses" and "little magazines." With some pride he noted in his Easter 1968 "Circular Letter": "Another question is in what out-of-the-way periodicals are my writings likely to be found these days?"[6] From the beginning the magazine, which Merton early called *Monks Pond,* was to be obscure, its circulation confined as he continually insisted "to contributors and their friends and to people who might like it."[7] There was to be no money involved, either payment to contributors or subscription charges to those who received it. To Merton's mind, money turned an underground publication into a commercial one and destroyed its marginal status. He had corresponded with a high-school student in California, Suzanne Butorovich. She and some of her friends were involved in producing an underground paper called *Clique Courier.* Merton had, at her request, contributed his poem "Prayer to the Computer" for inclusion in the paper. When she wrote that they had been approached about joining an underground press group that charged $25 for the privilege of belonging, he responded:

> You mention they want to shake you down already twenty five dollars to be in an Underground Press Syndicate. I do not understand this. The Underground is where there is no organization, no status and consequently no dues. What is the use of being in the Underground if you have to start all over again with status, organization and dues? And will somebody then start telling you what to do and what not to do? The Underground is where you tell everybody else to go jump in the lake and—if you can—charge them twenty five dollars for doing it. But honestly it is better to keep the smell of freedom, don't lose the scent or you're lost. Twenty five dollars smells bad to me.[8]

*Monks Pond* was definitely to be an underground publication and Merton made it clear from the beginning that he projected doing only four, perhaps five, issues. He wrote to Jonathan Williams: "I want to put out four offset collections of poetry-prose from all good people. Just four collections. One brief magazine flash in the air and out, but four good collections."[9] He said to Wendell Berry, "I'm only printing four issues (maybe five if overwhelmed with riches)."[10] Elsewhere he referred to it as "a temporary magazine" and one contributor, obviously convinced that Merton meant this, called it his "magazine flash-in-the-air-and-out project."[11]

Merton would do no advertising, no promotion, no sales pitch; to secure contributors, he first told a few of his friends and correspondents about the magazine—Jonathan Williams, Wendell Berry, Jonathan Greene, Keith Wilson, Margaret Randall de Mondragon—and asked them to communicate with others they might know who would be interested in such an underground, temporary project. It seems clear that *Monks Pond* reflected Merton's love of literature for its own sake. When he told Williams that he wanted contributions from "good people" (even though he later said he also wanted "good collections"), he really meant just that. He wrote to Paul C. Metcalf: "This venture is largely a matter of people getting to know people."[12] Besmilr Brigham, recruited by Keith Wilson, expressed part of Merton's plan to have unknown and "marginal" poets in *Monks Pond.* She wrote: "I do meet the requirements as Keith put it in one way: you wanted persons who hadn't 'been around much' he said. I didn't start being around until two years ago."[13] It was to be a publication by and for a small coterie of poets and writers and, in many ways, the least of Merton's concerns was that outsiders like it. Michael Mott, in his authorized biography *The Seven Mountains of Thomas Merton,* remarked that "Merton made the mistake as editor of including the work of poets who were friends and of friends who claimed to be poets."[14] Mott may interpret this as a mistake, but it was precisely what Merton intended. He solicited contributions from his friends and welcomed them from friends of friends and so on. He wrote, for instance, to his old friend and mentor, Mark Van Doren, when sending him the first issue: "What makes [life] more insane is that in my old age I decided to start a magazine (herewith). I excuse and justify myself on the ground that I intend to quit after four issues. But it is also fun, in so far as one discovers good poets hiding around in the bushes. The ones in this magazine all seem to be living in the woods or trying to. So now that you have seen it, you know I am inviting, urging you to send something if you have something—prose or verse or just a shout of some sort."[15] He wrote to Margaret Randall de Mondragon, editor of a Mexican magazine, *El Corno Emplumado,* to which he had contributed: "Need poems, prose, ideas, anything so long as it doesn't get me burned by the monks. If it is something they don't figure out ok . . . about anything that makes life have meaning. Ideas. Visions. Or just what the sun shines like. Anyone you know who is interested. Tell. It will be only four collections (4)."[16]

Merton intended *Monks Pond,* it is clear, to be more of a forum for poets and writers than a formal periodical. He did not seek, and it is fairly certain that he did not want, the usual critical apparatus—editorial and advisory boards, outside readers, referees—which one associates with "aboveground" publications. Merton used material submitted by his own friends—Mark Van Doren, Robert Lax, Czeslaw Milosz, Jonathan Williams, and others. And he relied heavily on the friends of his friends. He acknowledged in the fourth issue (Winter 1968) that Keith Wilson, Jonathan Williams, and Jonathan Greene had been especially helpful in telling other poets about *Monks Pond* and asking them to contribute. Williams, in fact, photocopied Merton's letter of 13 December 1967 (the initial letter, it seems, in which he asked for submissions from some of his friends) and sent it out to several people with the following note attached: "The above letter from Thomas Merton explains itself. I would be very pleased if you would send him a contribution for his anthology. Many thanks." Williams drew up a list of "Poets for Tom Merton's Magazine" and most of those on that list responded. Several contributors told Merton that they had been told about the project by Keith Wilson. Some told others. Marvin Cohen recruited his friends Ree Dragonette and Roberts Blossoms. He wrote to Merton: "Ree Dragonette was delighted that you took her poem . . . and was too shy to send it on her own, so it was well I did send it, I being less shy on her behalf."[17] Lindy Hough was Richard Grossinger's wife and Nels Richardson his friend. Richardson, then a precocious fifteen-year-old, had been a postulant at Gethsemani for two months in 1960. Robert David Cohen, as Margaret Randall told Merton, was the father of her fourth child. The final contributors were a network of friends and friends' friends, and that is how Merton wanted it to be. By 22 January 1968 he reported that the first issue was "now in press (i.e. about to be sten- cilled)."[18] He had received a large number of submissions and in February he said that he had "a pile of good stuff," indicating then and later that he had nearly enough material for all his issues before the first one came from the press.[19]

Merton handled the editing of *Monks Pond* by himself and said in introducing the first issue that its contents were "the first and so far only hint of a possible program." No discernible program developed and the four issues are a hodgepodge of poetry, prose, visuals, and graphics. No themes are evident and, if the order of the material in the four issues had any design behind it, it is impossible to perceive what it was. Brother Patrick Hart recalls that the ordering was arbitrary, that Merton tended to have material typed and put on stencils as he selected it. Number 4 (Winter 1968), in fact, would appear to have been a catchall for all the remaining material Merton had decided to use. He said: "There was enough material for six issues, but it got crammed into four." He himself "froze" the pond over because other projects, including his trip to Asia, preoccupied him and engrossed his attention.[20] He wrote to George Hitchcock in June, "Can't keep it up, too much work."[21]

Merton made all editorial decisions. He apparently rejected some contributions because he did not like them, others because he had received more material than he could use. He confided to Hayden Carruth as early as February: "[I] am getting so much stuff that I have to send some back even when I like it a lot."[22] On a few occasions he returned material asking that it be resubmitted later. He wrote, for instance, to Wendell Berry: "If I return the Haiku it isn't because I don't like them, but indeed would like them back. . . . This is probably a hell of a way to edit a magazine."[23] He had told Margaret Randall in December that he had to be careful not to get too far out or wild lest it offend his brother monks and cause censure and difficulty. One young poet, Geof Hewitt, submitted a poem with sexual images and questionable words. Merton sent it back with the comment: "You sense my problem: in detail, it is this: the devout young monk who runs the offset machine for me can cause trouble for me and all my pomps and works by simply refusing to cooperate, denouncing me to authorities etc etc. Now I am sure he thinks rubbers are something that go on your feet and has not sufficient experience of the world to wonder how they cost so little. But he does know that bullshit is dirty."[24] Merton may have wanted experimental, unusual, vanguard material for *Monks Pond* but he was not prepared, at least at that point, to accept greater freedom in reference to sex and anatomy in his "little magazine." In the case of Sister Therese Lentfoehr's poem, "A Hill is for Celebration," about her visit to Merton at Gethsemani, he called the poem "very lively" and seemed to feel its allusions to alcohol consumption might put him and his visitors in a bad light. But he decided to use it, saying, "after all, the only tinkling is of teacups. It can hardly shock anyone even if they figure out the 'action.' "[25]

Merton's approach to editing, if we can believe his own reports, was anything but systematic. He often worked hastily and inefficiently. In January he wrote to Jonathan Greene: "I am already full in the editorial quandary of lost letters, mss, etc. This place is a horrible mess."[26] In February he told Robert Bonazzi, himself the editor of *Latitudes:* "First number of POND is almost ready. . . . Now I know what it is like to be an editor. Lost poems. Piled up unanswered letters. Proofs. Batch of stuff for three issues ahead. Biographies of poets (lost too). Eeech."[27] In March he apologized to Ronald Anthony Punnet: "Sorry to have held up so long answering. The poems get all piled up, mixed up, lost, found, built into pyramids, birds nests, catacombs, dugouts, temples. Yours got mixed in with the ones possible for MP iii, whereas I really want them for MP ii."[28] He seems to have had no clearcut timetable and was careful not to lock himself into one. He said to June Yungblut: "Poems too, will use as many as I can, depending on space. Do you want a quick decision or can I mull them over for a while—months?"[29]

He also encountered some delays in production. He recorded in his journal that the first issue was delayed because the print shop was busy turning out liturgical texts.[30] He wrote in March to a young Jesuit, Phil Stark, that "the mimeograph people are all tied up with liturgy texts."[31] In April he told Sister Therese Lentfoehr: "I am always short of copies as I have to put it together myself."[32] In July he told June Yungblut: *"Monks Pond* III is slowly moving but we have trouble with the machinery. I hope it will be ready in a few weeks."[33] The first issue was typed on stencils by one of the monks, but Merton faced losing his typist for the subsequent issues. Stark, who had offered to do typing for him in the past, asked in April if Merton could use secretarial help during the summer.[34] Merton responded:

> Your offer to come here and help with typing. That could very well be providential as my last helper, the one I rely on for the stencils for Monks Pond, is likely to fail me. If you could just get the last two numbers of the magazine on stencils during the summer, that would be marvelous. There is going to be some fantastically good stuff—translations of the Finn Pentti Saarikovski by Anselm Hollo and all sorts goodies, with some new and exclusive Zen stuff. It could very well be worth while for all of us. By then too I might have some other work ready for you, and could keep you busy for say two or three hours a day, leaving you the rest for German, prayerlife, bird watching etc.[35]

Stark wrote of his stay, from July to September, at Gethsemani.

> It was on a July sixth that I first met Thomas Merton. . . . The essential part of my job was to turn out the last two installments of a magazine anthology of avant garde poets that Merton was editing; he called it, with typical ingenuity, *Monks Pond*. I knew nothing, again, about the quasi-underground movement in modern poetry, so the assignment looked fascinating. . . . Day by day, Merton went about a more or less predictable schedule of writing, often slipping by my room to leave a manuscript to be typed, while I worked on *Monks Pond* and some of his incidental papers and ran errands to the post office.[36]

The issues of *Monks Pond* did not appear regularly. All were printed on Gethsemani's offset press by Brother Cassian Vigna, the monastery printer. Merton selected the material for the first issue, Spring 1968, with dispatch and one of the novices began typing it on stencils in mid-January. Copies were ready by late February, when Merton began mailing them out. The second issue, Summer 1968, seems to have been ready some time in the spring, probably in late April. In the latter part of June Merton wrote that he was "getting down to editing on the next issues (2) of Pond."[37] Then Phil Stark arrived in July to help with the editing and typing of the last two issues. Three, Fall 1968, was ready for distribution by August 30.[38] Stark continued to work on the fourth issue until he left Gethsemani in September. Brother Patrick Hart remembers that he finished the typing and supervised the printing, collating, and mailing of the last issue after Merton left for the American West and Asia on September 10. Merton had thought that the third issue was the best, but he did not see the fourth before his death in Bangkok on December 10. Brother Patrick, who handled his mail in his absence, sent on "only what [was] most essential."[39]

The variety of typists and Merton's casual approach resulted in some errors in *Monks Pond,* which have not been corrected in this facsimile edition. Some of these are listed on page 348 of the fourth issue and are noted on the pages there referred to. The rarity of the original numbers of *Monks Pond* (no more than 150 to 200 copies of each issue seem to have been printed) has meant that most people have been unable to acquire it. This edition is intended to make this hard-to-obtain item more readily available. In the preparation of this edition, the original folios have been deleted and the pages have been renumbered in sequence throughout the entire volume. The contents pages have been retyped to reflect the new pagination, and all pages have been photographically reduced from the original 8½ x 11-inch size to the present format. Except for these changes, nothing in the original issues has been altered, and all the visual elements have been retained.

*Monks Pond* remains the only example of Merton's editing of a periodical or quasi-periodical, but its "underground" quality makes it difficult to assess on the level of a normal periodical. Jonathan Williams quite rightly called it an "anthology" and it is best approached as Merton intended: as the work of a group of friends and friends' friends sharing their work with each other. It should be seen as a literary forum rather than a formal literary magazine. By 1968, though Merton may always have wanted to experiment with such editing, he was far too busy, far too involved with other projects, to continue this one beyond the four issues he had said all along that he was planning. But he compiled an interesting and sometimes exciting anthology even if the arrangement seems haphazard and the quality uneven. And he made his point that a monastic press could be used for something other than cheese advertisements and liturgical texts.

# NOTES

TMSC = Thomas Merton Studies Center, Bellarmine College, Louisville, Kentucky

1. *The Collected Poems of Thomas Merton* (New York: New Directions, 1977), pp. 799-800.
2. These themes and phrases run through Thomas Merton, *Day of a Stranger,* ed. Robert E. Daggy (Salt Lake City: Peregrine Smith, 1981).
3. See "Easter Letter [April 14] 1968," TMSC. Merton's "Circular Letters" will be included in the second volume of Merton correspondence, *The Road to Joy: The Letters of Thomas Merton to New & Old Friends,* ed. Robert E. Daggy (New York: Farrar, Straus & Giroux, 1989).
4. Merton to Jonathan Williams, 13 December 1967, TMSC.
5. Merton to Wendell Berry, 31 January 1968, TMSC.
6. "Easter Letter [April 14] 1968."
7. See, for example, Merton to Besmilr Brigham, 22 January 1968, TMSC.
8. Merton to Suzanne Butorovich, 18 July 1967, TMSC.
9. Merton to Jonathan Williams, 13 December 1967, TMSC.
10. Merton to Wendell Berry, 31 January 1968, TMSC.
11. Merton to Margaret Randall, 13 December 1967; Emmett Williams to Merton, 5 January 1968, TMSC.
12. Merton to Paul C. Metcalf, 8 January 1968, TMSC.
13. Besmilr Brigham to Thomas Merton, 22 January 1968, TMSC.
14. Michael Mott, *The Seven Mountains of Thomas Merton* (Boston: Houghton Mifflin, 1984), p. 503.
15. Merton to Mark Van Doren, 12 March 1968, TMSC. Merton's letters to Mark Van Doren will be included in *The Road to Joy.*
16. Merton to Margaret Randall, 13 December 1967, TMSC.
17. Marvin Cohen to Merton, [July 1968], TMSC.
18. Merton to Geof Hewitt, 22 January 1968, TMSC.
19. Merton to Russell Edson, 24 February 1968, TMSC.

20. Mott, *Seven Mountains*, p. 526.

21. Merton to George Hitchcock, 27 June 1968, TMSC.

22. Merton to Hayden Carruth, 28 February 1968, TMSC.

23. Merton to Wendell Berry, 23 February 1968, TMSC.

24. Merton to Geof Hewitt, 1 February 1968, TMSC.

25. Merton to Sister Therese Lentfoehr, S.D.S., 20 August 1968, TMSC. Merton's letters to Sister Therese will be included in *The Road to Joy*.

26. Merton to Jonathan Greene, 22 January 1968, TMSC.

27. Merton to Robert Bonazzi, 29 February 1968, TMSC.

28. Merton to Ronald Anthony Punnett, 20 March 1968, TMSC.

29. Merton to June J. Yungblut, 23 March 1968. In *The Hidden Ground of Love: The Letters of Thomas Merton on Religious Experience & Social Concerns*, ed. William H. Shannon (New York: Farrar, Straus & Giroux, 1985), p. 642.

30. See Mott, *Seven Mountains*, p. 516.

31. Merton to Philip M. Stark, S.J., 20 March 1968, TMSC.

32. Merton to Sister Therese Lentfoehr, S.D.S., [April 1968], TMSC.

33. Merton to June J. Yungblut, 29 July 1968. *The Hidden Ground of Love*, p. 648.

34. Philip M. Stark, S.J. to Merton, 22 April 1968, TMSC.

35. Merton to Philip M. Stark, S.J., 25 April 1968, TMSC.

36. Philip M. Stark, S.J., "A Summer at Gethsemani," *Continuum* 7 (Summer 1969), pp. 306-12.

37. Merton to George Hitchcock, 27 June 1968, TMSC.

38. Merton to Jonathan Greene, 30 August 1968, TMSC.

39. *The Asian Journal of Thomas Merton;* ed. Naomi Burton Stone, Brother Patrick Hart, and James Laughlin (New York: New Directions, 1973), p. 103.

# MONKS POND

NO. I        SPRING        1968

# contents

(Photographs - Thomas Merton)

# MONKS    POND.

The purpose of this magazine is to publish a few issues devoted
to poetry and to some unusual prose and then go out of business.
At present no more than four issues are planned.  If a great deal
of good material comes in there may be a fifth or even a sixth.
The contents of this first number indicate the nature and character of the magazine and are in fact the first and so far only hint
of a possible program.  The other issues will be like this, only
different.
We have here brought together several outstanding contemporary
American poets along with a prose statement of one of the foremost
abstract artists of our time and selected dialogs of an eighth
century Chinese Zen Master, newly translated into English.  In
this variety there is nevertheless a certain consonance -- frogs
in one pond.
We hope in other issues to have some new English poetry, some translations from the best contemporary French and Spanish verse, and
perhaps also some concrete poetry: but we plan also to present
more Asian texts and perhaps even a couple articles.  We are willing to consider very short stories.
As long as there are copies of the magazine they will be given
away free to contributors and to those who ask for them.

If you want to send in a manuscript, enclose the usual stamped
and self-addressed return envelope.  Probably no more manuscripts
will be considered after Easter 1969.
If you want to receive a copy, write for one.
If you like the magazine and feel like helping defray expenses,
contributions of a few dollars will not be refused.  Large sums
of money are neither desired nor expected.


Editor:  Thomas Merton- Trappist P.O., -Kentucky- 40073.

ART - AS - ART

by

Ad Reinhardt

The one thing to say about art is that it is one thing. Art is art-as-art and everything else is everything else. Art-as-art is nothing but art. Art is not what is not art.

The one object of fifty years of abstract art is to present art-as-art and as nothing else, to make it into the one thing it is only, separating and defining it more and more, making it purer and emptier, more absolute and more exclusive, -- non-objective, non-representational, non-figurative, non-imagist, non-expressionist, non-subjective. The only and one way to say what abstract art or art-as-art is, is to say what it is not.

The one subject of a hundred years of modern art is that awareness of art of itself, of art preoccupied with its own process and means, with its own identity and distinction, art concerned with its own unique statement, art conscious of its own evolution and history and destiny, toward its own freedom, its own dignity, its own essence, its own reason, its own morality and its own conscience. Art needs no justification in our day with "realism" or "naturalism", "regionalism" or "national-ism", "individualism" or "socialism" or "mysticism", or with any other ideas.

The one content of three centuries of European or Asiatic art and the one matter of three millenium of Eastern or Western art, is the same "one significance" that runs through all the timeless art of the world. Without an art-as-art con-tinuity and art-for-art's-sake conviction and unchanging art-spirit and abstract point of view, art would be inaccessible and the "one thing" completely secret.

The one idea of art as "fine", "high", "noble", "liberal", "ideal" of the seventeenth century is to separate fine and intellectual art from manual art and craft. The one intention of the word "aesthetics of the eighteenth century is to isolate the art-experience from other things. The one declaration of all the main movements in art of the nineteenth century is of the "independence" of art. The one question, the one principle, the one crisis in art of the twentieth century centers in the uncompromising "purity" of art, and in the consciousness that art comes from art only, not from anything else.

The one meaning in art-as-art, past or present, is art-meaning. When an art-object is separated from its original time and place and use as it moves into the art-museum, it gets emptied and purified of all its meanings except one. A religious object that becomes a work of art in an art-museum loses all its religi-ous meanings. No one in his right mind goes to an art-museum to worship anything but art, or to learn about anything else.

The one place for art-as-art is the museum of fine art. The one reason for the museum of fine art is the preservation of ancient and modern art that cannot be made again and does not have to be done again. A museum of fine art should exclude everything but fine art, and be separate from museums of ethnology, geology, archaeology, history, decorative-arts, industrial-arts, military-arts, and museums of other things. A museum is a treasure-house and tomb, not a counting-house or amusement-center. A museum that becomes an art-curator's personal-monument or an art-collector-sanctifying-establishment or an art-history-manufacturing-plant or an artists market-block, is a disgrace. Any disturbance of a true museum's soundlessness, timelessness, airlessness and lifelessness is a disrespect.

6

The <u>one</u> <u>purpose</u> of the art-academy-university is the education and "correction of the artist"-as-artist, not the "enlightenment of the public" or the populariza- tion of art. The art-college should be a cloister-ivy-hall-ivory-tower-community of artists, an artists union and congress and club, not a success-school or service- station or rest-home or house of artists' ill-fame. The notion that art or an art-museum or art-university "enriches life" or fosters a "love of life" or "pro- motes understanding and love among men" is as mindless as anything in art can be. Anyone who speaks of using art to further any local, municipal, national or inter- national relations is out of his mind.

The <u>one</u> <u>thing</u> to say about art and life is that art is art and life is life. A "slice-of-life" art is no better or worse than a "slice-of-art" life. Fine art is not a "means of making a living" or a "way of living a life", and an artist who dedicates his life to his art or his art to his life, burdens his art with his life and his life with his art. Art that is a matter of life and death is neither fine nor free.

The <u>one</u> <u>assault</u> on fine art is the ceaseless attempt to subserve it as a means to some other end or value. The one fight in art is not between art and non- art but between true art and false art, between pure art and action-assemblage art, between abstract art and surrealist-expressionist-anti-art, between free art and servile art. Abstract art has its own integrity, not someone else's "integration" with something else. Any combining, mixing, adding, diluting, exploiting, vul- garizing or popularizing abstract art deprives art of its essence and depraves the artist's artistic consciousness. Art is free, but it is not a free-for-all.

The <u>one</u> <u>struggle</u> in art is the struggle of artists against artists, or artist against artist, of the artist-as-artist within and against the artist-as-man, - animal, -or-vegetable. Artists who claim that their art-work comes from nature, life, reality, earth or heaven, as "mirrors of the soul" or "reflections of con- ditions" or "instruments of the universe", who cook up "new images of man" - figures and "nature-in-abstraction" - pictures, are subjectively and objectively, rascals or rustics. The art of "figuring" or "picturing" is not a fine art. An artist who is lobbying as a "creature of circumstances" or log-rolling as a "vic- tim of fate" is not a fine master-artist. No one ever forces an artist to be pure.

The <u>one</u> <u>art</u> that is abstract and pure enough to have the one problem and possibility in our time and timelessness, of the "one single grand original problem", is pure abstract painting. Abstract painting is not just another school or movement or style but the first truly unmannered and untrammelled and unentangled, styleless universal painting. No other art or painting is detached or empty or immaterial enough.

The <u>one</u> <u>history</u> of painting progresses from the painting of a variety of ideas with a variety of subjects and objects, to one idea with a variety of subjects and objects, to one subject with a variety of objects, to one object with a variety of subjects, then to one object with one subject, to one object with no subject, and to one subject with no object, then to the idea of no object and no subject and no variety at all. There is nothing less significant in art, nothing more exhausting and immediately exhausted than "endless variety".

The <u>one</u> <u>evolution</u> of art-forms unfolds in one straight logical line of nega- tive actions and reactions, in one predestined, eternally recurrent stylistic cycle, in the same all-over pattern, in all times and places, taking different times in different places, always beginning with an "early" archaic schematization, achiev- ing a climax with a "classic" formulation, and decaying with a "late" endless variety of illusionisms and expressionisms. When late stages wash away all lines of demarcation, framework and fabric, with "anything can be art", "anybody can be an artist", "that's life", "why fight it", "anything goes", and "it makes no difference whether art is abstract or representational", the artists' world is a mannerist and primitivist art-trade and suicide-vaudeville, venal, genial, contemptible, trifling.

The one way in art comes from art-working and the more an artist works, the more there is to do. Just as artists come from artists and art-forms from art-forms, painting comes from painting. The one direction in fine or abstract art today is in the painting of the same one form over and over again. The one intensity and the one perfection comes only from long and lonely routine preparation and attention and repetition. The one originality exists only where all artists work in the same tradition and master the same convention. The one freedom is realized only through the strictest art-discipline and through the most similar studio-ritual. Only a standardized, prescribed form can be imageless, only a stereotyped image can be formless, only a formulaized art can be formulaless. A painter who does not know what or how or where to paint is not a fine artist.

The one work for the fine artist now, the one thing in painting to do, is to repeat the one-size-canvas --- the single-scheme, one color-monochrome, one linear-division in each direction, one symmetry, one texture, one formal device, one free-hand-brushing, one rhythm, one working everything into one dissolution and one indivisibility, painting everything into one overall uniformity and non-irregularity. No lines or imaginings, no shapes or composings or representings, no visions or sensations or impulses, no pleasures or pains, no accidents or ready-mades, no things, no ideas, no relations, no attributes, no qualities --- nothing that is not of the essence. Everything into irreducibility, unreproducibility, imperceptibility. Nothing "useable", "manipulatable", "saleable", "dealable", "collectable", "graspable". No art as a commodity or a jobbery. Art is not the spiritual side of business.

The one standard in art is oneness and fineness, rightness and purity, abstractness and evanescence. The one thing to say about the best art is the breathlessness, lifelessness, deathlessness, contentlessness, formlessness, spacelessness and timelessness. This is always the end of art.

EIGHT    POEMS

by

Lorine Niedecker.


1

Linnaeus in Lapland


Nothing worth noting
except an Andromeda
with quadrangular shoots -
        the boots
of the people

wet inside:  they must swim
to church thru the floods
or be taxed - the blossoms
        from the bosoms
of the leaves


2


Old man who seined
to educate his daughter
sees red Mars rise:
        What lies
behind it?

Cold water business
now starred in Fishes
of dipnet shape
        to ache
thru his arms.


9

3

You are my friend -
you bring me peaches
and the high bush cranberry
          you carry
my fishpole

you water my worms
you patch my boot
with your mending kit
        nothing in it
but my hand


4


Paul
      when the leaves
            fall

from their stems
      that lie thick
            on the walk

in the light
      of the full note
            the moon

playing
      to leaves
            when they leave

the little
      thin things
            Paul

The young ones go away to school
come home to moon

Like Frederick the Great
what was it he ate

that had to be sown
in the dark of the moon

Isn't it funny
people run their acres without a hat
figuring rain in the next moon change

while you on a stool
at numbers in a heavenly scale
know the moon changes
                    night and noon

Bird singing
ringing yellow
    green

My friend made green
        ring
- his painting -

    grass
the sweet bird
flew in

Dusk

He's spearing from a boat

How slippery is man
        in spring
            when the small fish
                    spawn

As Praiseworthy

The power of breathing (Epictetus)
while we sleep.   Add:
to move the parts of the body
without sound

and to float
on a smooth green stream
in a silent boat

FOUR    POEMS

by

Keith Wilson.


exorcism in march

ghosts ring san miguel.

they are not spanish
nor anglo it is indian
shade, dark against
the volcanoed hills
that haunts this village:

rock children, old men
mountains, trail of lava
holding prayer feathers

each day the sun
slips into an extinct cone
on the western horizon
dark clouds lie heavy
on flat prairies

the wind, when it comes,
hisses, the voices
of my neighbors singing
Mexican songs grow louder

we all know the indians are there,
pretending we are not there.

Dusk in My Backyard

      --San Miguel, N.M.


The long black night
moves over my walls:
inside a candle is lighted
by one of my daughters.

Even from here I can see
the illumined eyes, bright
face of the child before flame.

It's nearly time to go in.
The wind is cooler now,
pecans drop, rattle down--

the tin roof of our house
rivers to platinum in the early moon.
Dogs bark & in the house, wine, laughter.

# BALLAD OF A SAILOR

> . . . wave,
> interminably flowing
> --Wallace Stevens

It is because my fingers
move over these keys
compulsively
that the result

      quiets me

dark images of war,
storms, hands raised like waves
in my dreams the wind
never stops

betrayed shores
sick girls in foreign bars
children begging outside
a night that is always closed

comrades, their drowning faces
pale tourmaline, rayed with light,
open eyes and seawashed mouths

It is because my fingers
move over these keys
restlessly
that the chanty

      moves me

here, far from the sea,
this house is steady.  it does
not rock and that noise is
thunder, not gunfire.  it is
peaceful here.  say it again.
peaceful.  one has only to stay
awake, not dream, the faces of dreams
cannot touch, dreamed blood stains
only the bedsheet sails of haunted ships.

sailing, sail on, its crew of phantoms
wave, passing beyond the light, wave
& giggle among the shrouds, knowing
it is not the last goodbye nor the first
we are sharing.

Zeb

--short for Zebediah, late come
mountainman, part-time prospector
now grown stiff in the joints.
Unshaven but not bearded, bushy
eyebrows hanging over blue

At 83 the empty rifle moves smoothly
up to his shoulder, the hammer falls:
"A little stiff in the trigger, son,"
he says and looks away

                        his half-wolf dog
moves with him, flank brushing the
old man's leg, big flat head down
he watches

        Once I made the mistake
of trying to touch him; he growled
deep in his chest.  "Don't do that
boy," Zeb said calmly.  "He'll take your
hand off."  And hobbled back to his
son's house, his lame old dog beside him.


            from Some Faces for America

16

THE  LAPIDARY

by

Jonathan Greene


1


Gems spill from his hand.
Names. Inside the discordant melodies
are strung tight. Diamond name, emerald
name, tune up. Tensile strength of a structure
already there. Mere cleaving, mere cutting,
mere polishing that cluster of meaning.
Mere working the Work.

In Blake's 'Glad day' Albion rises, jewelled
earth at his feet. His energy is outward &
the cosmos uncircled. Sparks at his finger
tips, fire for hair, he is an Emanation.
Stream full of stars flowing. This giant
who sleeps in us. How many years or lives
slumbering on our own banks?

This figure, this more-than-ourselves
measures us asleep on the banks.


envoi


Words, build a creature out of air.
Bring the true powers to play


17

But don't you see (turning from
painting to engraving) the caterpillar &
bat at Albion's feet

And what of that other lapidary, the one
still at labour. His Work - a Gift to a
Beloved. Not once does she look back
to his labour. Fingers nervously
the stone aside her heart. Not
his dwelling place.


\*


Ritual on the outskirts of knowing.
Coffee ritual, newspaper ritual.
No questions to destroy
easy metaphysics of the breakfast table.

Drive in.
Look at the bright stones
in the window.
They are for the Beloved.

The lapidary should be complemented.


envoi

Collect jewels for your anthology, kind Sir.
Snatch epigram from epic & elucidate.
Show wit. Don't re-read. Be like
the child sitting at supper
waiting for ice-cream.

THREE POEMS

by

Margaret Randall

USING LOVE AS A WORD

1.

could i love you
meaning
your loving me and

i you,
could that be
quarter past five and

all the meals
without bread
on the table, is it

still warm
when the sun goes
down

2.

after breakfast
on your way to new york
you said

:your children are great.
but did you mean
you love them,

even i
don't know that

3.

you gone
i conjure the image
eyes open

the gentle pounding
here are the keys
to my house

and i come
all over conversation
turned to ice

19

4.

new york to
new mexico to
spain

to new mexico
again new york
(alone)

to mexico
finally to cuba
the window

opens.
back to mexico
where is

canada
on that map, you
have given me

that


5.

everything i have done you have done
different, everything
you have done

i have been absent in my hands
of yours, everything you breathe
i have forgotten, denied

the space you cut, the place
i move in
you, moving in me, even

the years are not the same
only the crossing, beginning
together to be

our chance at history


6.

love     :youropen mouth

THE FABRIC (not the whole cloth)

> Because if you know the measure of something
> --for yourself there is no absolute measure--
> you can find the size of something.
>                         --WILLEM DE KOONING.


the
life expectancy
how it comes on slow wheels, passes
before our eyes, hands
almost touching
called itself friction      :the two fabrics
rubbing together.

nothing, absolutely nothing
to be done
as teeth in their place, the ordered
existence.

again and again
having climbed the stairs, down the pole
like firemen
she's all right he's all right and the bread
is rising.

answer the door
it just might be, but no,
swept ordered climbed cleaned returned
to original state
                empty.

i have said four times this morning you are the one
at thirty plus
subtract those mountains those empty lots teeming
with sunrise
bent on pickings any given day.

take out viet nam the pentagon encyclical
or
her rosebush
still there is something left, still
there are skulls and apples
what
to be done with them.

YEMAYA-OKUTÉ


i am
yemaya-okuté
earth in my hands, mother
every man my son and three to give them name
:obbamoró
          jesus of nazareth
orúla
     saint frances
and shangó

lover and son, guise
of saint barbara, hair

i made my bed.
yemaya-okuté i am
fighter
open of arm to love
children and money to parcel out, refuse

to let my sons more women than one
my daughters more than one
man
i am
woman, tho i bore my children by three
i am
faithful

fertile
in one only
direction i am
yemaya-okuté, why not,
                    the roots
as well and the fruit gone out
and when they asked me

what is your color your color yemaya-okuté
i said

:blue
and green
and all the ripe between

yemaya-okuté

The fishes are going up the brooks as they open. They are
dispersing themselves through the fields and woods, imparting new life
into them. They are taking their places under the shelving banks and
in the dark swamps. The water running down meets the fishes running
up. They hear the latest news. Spring-aroused fishes are running
up our veins too.

Thoreau- Journal.

Selections from the Dialogues of the Zen Master, SHEN-HUI (8th century A.D.)

1.    Introduction    by Wei-wu-wei.

In these few introductory words I would like to point out that the readers of
these pages are having a novel experience, for they are reading a translation of the
words of one of the greatest of the early T'ang-dynasty Masters by a Chinese scholar
who understands what he is translating. Yes, this is rare indeed, for Chinese scholars in the West have not usually, if ever, had the qualification of having lived
and worked with one of the authentic great masters of Ch'an in modern China. May we
not perhaps be just a little weary of translations by scholars, sometimes brilliant,
who understand everything in question except the meaning of the text they are translating?

It is worth quoting Dr. Hu Shih here: "Chinese Zennism (American abbreviation
for "Ch'an") arose not out of Indian yoga or dhyāna but as a revolt against it.
Failure to understand this accounts for all failures on the part of European and
Japanese scholars to understand Chinese Zennism." (i)

Prof. Hu Shih maintains that the school of Ch'an, calling itself the school of
Sudden Awakening, was founded not by Bodhidharma nor by Hui Neng, the Sixth Patriarch
and master of Shen Hui, but by the great monk Tao Sheng, pupil of Hui Yüan (who founded the Pure Land Sect, d. 416), and of Kumārajiva. Little has survived of the work
of Tao Sheng; but we have valuable essays left by his brilliant young fellow-pupil
Seng Chao (384-414), and he certainly taught the essentials of Sudden Awakening,
though - as presented - sometimes intermingled with mythology and devotional practices.

The rise to prominence of the Lanka-sect claiming descent from Bodhidharma, apparently independent of the Indian tradition briefly described above, and culminating
in the 5th Patriarch Hung Jen, whose successors were Shen Hsiu and Hui Neng, remains
a mystery otherwise than as tradition asserts. All we know is that the Northern school
of Shen Hsiu, which practised purification of mind by "sitting", died out shortly after
the death of its leader, while the Southern School of Hui Neng triumphed in the person
of, and by the efforts of, Shen Hui, its 7th and last Patriarch. This latter teaching,
however, may well be called a revolt against the Indian tradition, a ruthless rejection
of mythology and devotional practices, and a reversion to Chinese practicality and
directness for the Im-mediate recognition of the enlightened condition. In this the
primacy of the Prajñāpāramitā Sūtras took the place of the Lankāvatāra Sūtra of Bodhidharma and his early successors. Neither the biographer Tao Hsuan, nor Hsuan Tsang
who spent 16 years in India, nor I Tsing who lived there for 25 years, ever mention
Bodhidharma as being the 28th Patriarch in India, nor do they mention the existence
there of a patriarch at any time. Hu Shih concludes "The myth of the 28 Patriarchs
was a sheer invention of the 8th century Zennists" (by which he means "Ch'anists" -
for 'Zen' did not come into existence until long afterwards in Japan).

It seems to follow from these historical facts that the Ch'an doctrine - and sub-
sequently the Japanese development thereof called 'Zen' - was a 'Reformation', an almost purely Chinese invention, based on Taoism, but carrying on a Buddhist tradition to
which it paid what may here be accurately called 'lip-service'. It was a revolt against
Indian 'Dhyāna', secretly approved of, perhaps, by Hung Jen, the fifth Patriarch, openly
preached by Hui Neng, the sixth Patriarch, and firmly and finally established, despite
bitter opposition and against superior numbers, by Shen Hui, the seventh and last patriarch of Ch'an. It was also the culminating point of both Buddhist and Taoist philosophy, and it constituted the purest expression of what was called the Supreme Vehicle.

_____

(i) (Development of Zen Buddhism in China, p.483, from the Chinese Social and Political
    Science Review, Vol. 15, Peiping, 1931).

## 2. From the Dialogues

translated by Ernest Moncrieff,
with notes by Wei-wu-wei and Ernest Moncrieff.

### 1 - A DIALOGUE concerning ENLIGHTENMENT

Ts'ui, the Duke of Ch'i, asks:
When Your Reverence practises 'sitting' (1) once you enter concentration, how long does it take before you emerge from it?

A.   One's mind has no definite location; how can there be concentration at all!

Q.   If you say that there is no concentration at all, then why is the 'discipline of mind' so named?

A.   Since I do not even accept 'concentration', who has taught you about discipline of mind'!

Q.   If neither mind nor concentration may be accepted, then how can one attain enlightenment?

A.   Enlightenment is just enlightenment, and there is no 'how'!

Q.   If there is no 'how' to attain enlightenment, how can one possibly 'just' attain enlightenment?

A.   I say there is 'just enlightenment' simply because you have in your mind a 'how to attain'. If there is no 'how', there will not be any 'just' either. (2)

### 2 - Concerning the "MIDDLE WAY"

The Dharma-Master Chien of Mount Lu asks:
What is meant by the 'middle way'?

A.   It means the extremes.

Q.   I am asking you about the middle way; why do you say that it means the extremes?

A.   The so-called 'middle way' is recognised just because of the extremes. If the extremes were not recognised, the middle way could not be either! (3)

---

(1)   Sometimes translated 'dhyāna'. In India the Sancrit term dhyāna could mean some form of 'meditation'; to the T'ang dynasty Masters it normally had an entirely different connotation. See Glossary.

(2)   As we might be inclined to say today "Who is there to attain What?" Later he clarifies this subject.

(3)   This dialectic approach is very important in Ch'an since it exposes the relativity of all concepts.

## 3 - Concerning VOLITION

Li Chün, the governor of Yün Chou, asks:
I saw a mountain-monk come to greet the Dhyana-master An of Sung Shan. The Master said to him: "Rice-chasing monk!" A monk of the Shou Chi Monastery also came to greet him and he said: "Rice-clinging monk"! What were these two incidents about?

A.   They mean that he rejected both. (chasing and clinging).

Q.   How, then, may one not be rejected?

A.   Just cease to want, and then you will not be rejected.

Q.   How does one cease to want?

A.   There is only ceasing to want, and there is no 'how to cease to want'.

Q.   Is it the mind which ceases to want, or is it the eye which ceases to want?

A.   There is cessation of volition only, it is neither a question of not-wanting either of the mind or of the eye.

Q.   If it is neither the mind nor the eye which sees, then one must be blind?

A.   It is only the blind who speak of blindness, those who are able to see are not blind. The sūtra says: "It is the fault of the blind (that they do not see the sun and the moon) and not that of the sun and the moon. (4)

## 4 - Concerning TRUE SEEING

The Duke of Yen, whose name is Chang, asks:
Your Reverence lectures every day on the doctrine of 'absence of discriminative thought' and advises people to follow it. May I ask you, does this 'absence of discriminative thought' itself exist or not?

A.   The 'absence of discriminative thought' can neither be said to exist nor not to exist.

Q.   Why is that?

A.   If it were said to exist, that would be likening it to worldly existence (which is the counterpart of non-existence). If it were said not to exist, that would be likening it to worldly non-existence (which is the counterpart of existence). Therefore it differs both from existence and non-existence.

Q.   What is it called?

A.   It is not called anything.

Q.   Then what can it be?

A.   There can be no 'what' in it. 'Absence of discriminative thought' is inexpressible. I am talking about it now because I am answering your questions. If no questions were asked there would be nothing to say about it. It is like a mirror; no image is reflected in it unless an object is in front of it. We say an image is reflected because an object is present.

Q.   Suppose no object is present in front of it, does it reflect at all?

A.   When I say 'it reflects' I mean it always shines irrespective of whether there is an object in front of it or not.

---

(4)   Seen by those who are not blind (the awakened) there is no difference between phenomenal blindness and seeing. But what Shen Hui is teaching here is the abolition of volition, which is the functional aspect of self-mind or egoity, the one obstacle to awakening.

Q.      On the one hand you have said 'it is formless and inexpressible'; on the other hand you said that 'it shines'; what sort of thing is 'it' which shines?
A.      When I say 'it shines', I mean that when a mirror is clean its natural characteristic is to shine.  Similarly when the mind of a living being is immaculate, the light of supreme immanence shines naturally over the whole world.
Q.      If this is the case, how can this immanence be achieved?
A.      Only when one can see no-thingness.
Q.      If there is no thing at all, then what can be seen?
A.      Though one sees, what is seen cannot be called 'things'.
Q.      If what is seen cannot be called things, then why is 'seeing' so called?
A.      Seeing that there is no 'thing' to be seen is true and permanent seeing.


## 5 - Concerning THE 'VOID'

        Dharma-Master Yüan asks:  What is voidness?  If one says that voidness exists, it would then belong to the domain of objects and obstacles.  If one says that it does not exist, on what, then, should one rely?
A.      It is for those who have not yet experienced their true nature that one speaks of void.  If one has experienced his basic nature, void would not exist either.  This is the view on which one may rely.  (5)


## 6 - Concerning NON-AFFECTIVITY

        The Deputy-Minister Miao Chin Ch'ing asks:
        How should one practise to attain deliverance?
A.      Just develop a non-adhering (non-affective) mind and you will find deliverance.
Q.      Very well, but what is non-adhering mind?
A.      In the Vajracchedikā there is a passage on this subject.
Q.      What does it say?
A.      It says: "Subhūti, Bodhisattva Mahāsattvas should develop their pure mind like this: they should put their mind in function without adhering to form, sound, smell, taste, touch or concepts.  They should let the mind arise but dwell nowhere."  Just develop a non-adhering mind and you will obtain deliverance.
Q.      How can one be aware of non-adhering?
A.      Basic insight exists in a non-adhering mind.  This basic insight is capable of knowing and putting the mind in function.

_____

(5)  Because 'void' is an objective concept to the former, and can have no objective existence at all to the latter.

## 7 - Concerning THE NECESSITY OF TOTAL NEGATION

Q.      I have often heard that your teaching is different from that of all the others. The Buddha's doctrine is one, why then this difference?

A.      It is perfectly true that Buddhism does not comprise any difference in principle, but difference exists among learners today according to the level of their views. This is why people say that there is disagreement.

Q.      Would you kindly explain this disagreement?

A.      For instance, there are people who focus the mind in order to attain concentration, others who fix it in contemplation, some who direct the mind to awareness of the external, others who converge it in order to have internal experience, some who seek to observe their mental faculties and cling to voidness, others who by bringing about awareness destroy illusion, and regard this destroying of illusion and dwelling in awareness as ultimate, some who identify the initial functioning of mind with voidness, others who destroy both awareness and illusion without penetrating basic nature, and abide in the voidness of indifference. The views of these people are too various to be stated. Our contemporaries do not understand the principle of the voidness of our basic nature, and they form views based on their own trains of thought; this is the cause of difference. Leaving aside the profane, the Tathāgata says that even the saints recognise differences in the non-phenomenal; how much less can we expect learners today to reach agreement!


## 8 - Concerning TAO and QUESTIONS THAT ARE NOT SUCH

Cheng Tsun asks:
What is the way?

A.      That which has no name is the way. (6)

Q.      Since it is that which has no name, why is it called 'the way'?

A.      It would never name itself as such. If it is called a way, that is because of answering questions.

Q.      Since 'the way' is denomination only, is that which has no name the absolute?

A.      It is not the absolute either.

Q.      Since that which has no name is not the absolute, why did you say that it is that which has no name?

A.      It is only because questions are asked that I speak of it. If no questions were asked I would not say anything. (7)

_____

(6)  This no doubt refers to the Tao Te Ching of Lao Tzu, the opening line of which says "The Tao that can be named is not the true Tao." The word 'tao' colloquially means "the way".

(7)  This formula, which occurs elsewhere in the text, implies what we would probably express by saying "You cannot conceptualise what is conceptualising, therefore the question is not a valid question."

Dharma-Master Che asks:
What is the meaning of the equivalence of concentration (dhyāna) and insight (prajnā)?

A.     The voidness of the non-arising of thought is called correct concentration. Experiencing the voidness of the non-arising of thought is called correct insight. At the moment one has concentration, the concentration is the substance of insight; and at the moment one has insight, the inseeing is the function of concentration. At the moment one has concentration, concentration is not different from insight; and at the moment one has inseeing, the insight is not different from concentration. At the moment one has concentration, concentration is equivalent to insight, and at the moment one has inseeing, insight is equivalent to concentration. Why is that? Their nature is such. This is the teaching of the equivalence of concentration and insight. (9)

---

(8)  The terms <u>dhyāna</u> and <u>prajnā</u> have been interpreted in a great many ways in both Sanskrit and Chinese. <u>Dhyāna</u> means reflection, thought or 'meditation'; <u>prajnā</u> ordinarily means wisdom, but as a technical term, it means transcendental or intuitional insight concerning the ultimate truth; Wei suggested 'inseeing'. According to one of the interpretations, <u>Dhyāna</u> implies a process or discipline, while <u>prajna</u> is something spontaneous; it seems that <u>Dhyāna</u> is the psychological aspect and <u>prajnā</u> is the metaphysical aspect of the same thing. Shen-hui himself gave quite a few different interpretations of these two terms according to the various levels of the audience.

(R.S.Y.C.)

(9)  This definition of what we are, transcendent as <u>Dhyāna</u>, immanent as <u>Prajnā</u> (functioning in space-time), may be considered as the basic doctrine of <u>Ch'an</u> and <u>Zen</u>. It could hardly be more perfectly expressed. Only the two translated terms are inevitably inadequate - though we have none better.

Prince Sse Tao inquires about thinking without conceptualising. (10)

Q.    Is the doctrine of 'Thinking without Conceptualising" intended for ordinary people or is it only intended for saints? If it is only intended for saints, then why do you encourage ordinary people to practise it?

A.    The doctrine of thinking without conceptualising applies to saints. But it it is practised by ordinary people, then they are no longer ordinary people.

Q.    When you say 'thinking without conceptualising', what does the word 'without' reject? If you do not conceptualise, of what can you think?

A.    Thinking without conceptualising means thinking without dualism. Pure thinking is being aware of suchness. (11)

Q.    Is there any distinction between so thinking and suchness?

A.    There is no distinction.

Q.    Since there is no distinction, why do you speak both of thinking and of suchness?

A.    What is meant by thinking is the dynamic aspect of suchness. What is meant by suchness is the potential aspect of thinking. For this reason I established thinking-without-conceptualising as my fundamental principle. When we can think without conceptualising, although we see, hear, feel, and know, we still remain void and tranquil.

---

(10)   The original is '<u>wu nien nien</u>' (thoughtless thought), or '<u>nien wu nien</u>' (to think that which is beyond comprehension). 'Thinking without conceptualising' is a provisional rendering, in which the word 'conceptualising' implies the false identification of a concrete mental image with an abstract concept. This is one of the terms of which I have not yet found a satisfactory rendering.

(R.S.Y.C.)

(11)   'Suchness' here implies Whole-mind, unsplit into the duality of subject and its object.

N O R T H

by

Thomas    Merton

(Based on Dr. James Laws' Journal of the Kane Relief Expedition - 1855 -
in Stefansson Collection at Dartmouth)


1

Morning came at last
The storm over we sighted
Quiet mountains green and
Silver Edens
Walls of an
Empty country - Near?
(We were deceived-- 30 miles at least)

You can tell when Sunday comes
Everything on ship-board
Quieter
            icebergs like Churches
Slow sailing gifts
                    visions
A sailor intoned
An Anglican hymn

"One iceberg on our port bow
Resembled a lady dressed in white
Before her shrine"
(Dazzling whiteness
            gemm'd with blue-green)
"In the attitude of prayer"

"As if some magician etc..."

"Gifts - visions"

A huge berg between us
And the green shore.
"As we were gazing it grounded and the shock
caused one end of it to fall over upon the other
and both burned over. A terrible sight. Crashed like
thunder.  Spray flew mast-high"

The whales came
And played around us all day.


2

Black parapets
Of Disko conjured
Out of cold rain

Something like a sentry box
On a tall summit

A boat shot out
Suddenly produced
From behind that rock
Came for us
With six eskimos
And Lieut Saxtroph
Of the Danish army.

Our pilot took over
Headed straight for the rock
A crack in the cliff
Ninety yards wide
Secret basin land-
Locked dark
All stone straight up
Two thousand feet
Into the rain
Not a spot of green
I inquir'd where to
Look for the town
He pointed to
Twelve cabins.

Then kayaks all around us
Offered fish for sale
You could obtain
A duck for a bisquit

"The Lieutenant had been in the wars between Denmark and
Schleswig Holstein; he spoke English very well and during
our stay at Lievly done everything in his power to make our
time pass pleasantly.  He was a splendid dancer and sang
the national songs of his country with much spirit."


3

We climbed to a graveyard
High on the wet rock
There bodies sleep in crevices
Covered with light earth then stones
Some were sailors from England
And America
Now asleep
In this black tower
Over Baffin's Bay
Waiting, waiting
In endless winter.

We left them to their sleep
Ran down to meet the living girls.

"I would have given almost anything for a daguerrotype of
that room. Voices soft and clear eyes light blue or hazel.
Not one bad tooth. Their hair is all combed up to the top of
the head and twisted into a knot and tied with ribbons, red
for the unmarried, blue for the married ones. Jumper or
jacket lined with finely dressed deerskin trimmed with fur
and a band of ribbon. The most beautiful part of their dress
is the pantaloons of spotted seal, very soft, with an embroidered stripe down the front which says: "ready for marriage'"

We called for a Polka.  The band
"Struck up Camptown Races we had taught them
the previous night"
Seizing our partners
We all commenced

Better dancing
I never saw at home.

"The space between the pants and boots is filled with a
legging of linen or muslin edged and lined with deerskin.
They were all scrupulously clean."


                    4

75 N.  Melville Bay
July 29.
"A conical island in a bay of ice to starboard.  It is the
Sugar Loaf island of whalers. It tells that on rounding the
headland now in sight (Wilcox Point) we shall see the far
famed Devil's Thumb the boundary of dreaded Melville Bay"

July 30.
"Toiling slowly through the leads with plenty of bear tracks
around us."

July 31.
"A good lead opening. Towed twelve miles. The much talked of
Devil's Thumb is now in sight. It appears to be a huge mass
of granite..... Here begins Melville Bay."

Bay of ice and gales
Grave of whalers
Where "in one disastrous year the whaling fleet
Lost twenty eight sail."

From the Devil's Thumb northward
Vast glacier
"One of the manufactories
From whence the huge ice bergs
Are given off"

Fifty miles wide.

8 days driven to and fro
By masses of ice.
                    Waiting
To be crushed
"All provisions on deck
Ready for a run
At a moment's warning."

The bark was thrown over on her beam ends
Our batteau lashed to the bulwark
Was ground to atoms
In a couple of minutes.

"All hands on the qui vive for a smash".

(Must we go 200 miles over ice
Dragging our boats
To Upernavik?)

Finally clear of pack ice on the 13th
We stood for Cape York
Red snow on the rocks.  Open water
Finally out
Of Melville Bay!


                    5


Cape Alexander.
Here K. promised to leave a Cairn
And a bottle with a clear account of his proceedings
To tell us his intended course
Instead
A small mound
A homeopathic vial containing a mosquito
Covered with cotton
A small piece of cartridge paper
With the letters "OK" written on it
As if with the point of a bullett.


                    6


78 N.  Cape Haterton and Etah.

Two Indians on a rock
Like an owl's cry
Signalling

"We landed and found a village of tents in a valley with
a lake of fresh water.  A large glacier over the edge of
which a cataract was pouring into the lake.  Grass almost
knee deep, full of flowers.  Indians in dogskins and the
skins of birds collected around us and examin'd our fire-
arms with the greatest attention."

"We soon found unmistakable signs of K's party having been
there. Knives and cutlery bearing the mark of the Green
River works. Pewter cups and part of a microscope. Preserved meat and pemmican cans, baking pans, forks, spoons,
a piece of a shirt with the initials H.B., spools of cotton
marked N. York, curtain material, the top rail of a berth,
red velvet and an ivory handled carving knife..."

"By signs they gave us to understand that the vessel had been
crushed in the ice. This they done by taking a clay pipe and
crushing it between their hands."

"They pointed to a child and made signs
That K was a small man
Bald and without whiskers."

O hairless Kane
Lost in ice
How long gone?
They do not understand
Time
But he cured
One of their children.

They catch birds on the rocks by means of nets
Eat the birds raw
Give anything for a knife.

That ivory handled carving knife
Probably stolen.


7


Possession Bay

"Moonlight among the ice presents a scene that none but
those who have sail'd in Arctic regions can form any
conception of. It glances from the floe ice with a
blinding glare and gives the ice bergs the appearance of
mountains of light.

"Light streaming through a tall archway in a berg
Like scenes in the showy fairy pieces
At the theaters."


8


Pond's Bay

Rookery of loons
"Greatest sight of bird doings"

Cliffs terraced notched every projection
Covered

        Thousands
Wheeling over us in moon-
Light so tame
You could knock them down with an oar

Deafening.

"We entered a cave at the foot of the cliff and found it
filled with young loons and gulls."

So we shot 500 weighing 1172 lbs.


                9

Sept 4th 1855

Midnight.  Gale.

"Get up Dr we are rushing down on an iceberg."

As I reached the deck
We crashed

A huge ice berg
Four times as high as the mast
Overhangs our ship
More of the same
Starboard
White mass
Driven head on we
Beat against it
Bows staved in jib
Boom carried away we
Recoil swing star-
Board beam smashes
Into small end of ice-
Berg quarterboat in splinters
All bulwarks driven in
Catheads bumpkins and the rest
Gone
              Wind
Swirling around angle of ice
Like a hurricane
Rush for boats driven back:
"We fired minute guns but the gale was so high the noise of
crashing ice so great the steamer could not hear us..."

(The account ends here.  Both expeditions reached safety.)

FOUR POEMS

by

Jonathan Williams.


The Yellow Peril at Moore's Grocery:


COLD
BEER
TOGO




The Traditionally Accomodating Spirit
Of the Southern Mountains Shows Up in Neon
In Franklin, NC, Once Nikwasi, a Cherokee Capital:


CAFE

A Ride in a Blue Chevy From Alum Cave Trail to FewFound Gap

goin' hikin'?
git in!

o the Smokies are ok but me
I go for Theosophy,
higher things, Hindu-type philosophy,
none of this licker and sex, I
like it
on what we call the astral plane,
I reckon I get more i-thridral
by the hour

buddy, you won't believe this but
how old you reckon the earth is?
precisely 156 trillion years old--
I got this book from headquarters in
Wheaton, Illinois
says it is!

I'll tell you somethin' else:
there are exactly 144 kinds of people on earth--
12 signs and the signs change
every two hours,
that's 144, I'm Scorpio,
with Mars over the water

here's somethin' else innerestin':
back 18 million years
people was only one sex, one sex only...
I'd like to explain that,
it's right here in this pamphlet,
50 cents...


never married, lived with my mother in Ohio,
she died, I'm over in Oak Ridge
in a machine shop, say,
what kind of place
is Denver?
think I'll sell this car, go to Denver,
set up a Center...


name's Davis,
what's yours?

## The Deracination

definition: <u>root</u>,

"a growing point,
an organ of absorption, an aerating organ,
a good reservoir, or
means of support"

<u>Vernonia glauca</u>, order <u>Compositae</u>,
"these tall perennials with
corymbose cymes of bright-purple heads of
tubular flowers
with conspicuous stigmas"

I do not know the Ironweed's root,
but I know it rules September

and where the flowers tower
in the wind there is a burr of
sound-- empyrean... the mind
glows and the wind drifts...

epiphanies pull up
from roots--

<u>epiphytic</u>, making it up

out of the air

## Osiris, From His Cave to Spring:


for the Scripture is written:
"Plants at One End, Birds at the Other!"


houseleek & garlic,
hyssop & mouse;

hawk & hepatica,
hyacinth, finch!


crawl, all
exits

from
hibernaculum!

41

POEMS FROM SALVATION ARMY

by

Alfred Starr Hamilton.


Rain

for I'll order you

a pound of rain

however this is to be done

however this is to be remembered

or I'll order you

a pound of elephants

or I'll order you

a herd of clothes

however I'll wring your gizzards

for I'll wring your hands

through a pound of golden rain

for this is the flag for freedom

for this is the flag for the poor

strike

to a ton

of bricks

that can have been left there

and never to be used by the red management


to a tummyful

of overlooking blue sky

that can have stood there

and never to have been touched by just O'Shaughnessy


for Mc Intyre's

red sky travels

to the top of the brick pile

for Mc Intyre to have been left there by O'Shaughnessy


to the curve

of the broom

to have swept John O'Shanter

back to have re-enforced that kind of a red sky management


for a red clover

for a leftover

and to have been left there

and never to have been taken by a bricklayer - leftovers

katydids

i wondered if i were restless

and katy did it

and katy did it some moreso

and all the while i did what katy did

and katy dotted my drifting i's

and crossed my bewildered t's

and katy answered all my revolutionary questions

and katy told me no lies the world over

and katy wondered for me

and katy wondered if i were restless

and katy lived in a village

and katy and you and i tilled the soil

and katy and you and i wandered

no further than the village door

## Walden House

during my Walden pencil

tall buildings followed me downstairs

upstairs the truth blossomed

the wind caught in its city branches

the blue cold glistened

on top of one cold cloud

windwards, and ever withinwards,

for I pulled my blue coat over my Subway Sleeve


## April

For we'll lift

Our golden orphans shoes

   Back on top of the morning platter


For I'll remember you

Over an April violet

   For a plate and saucer


For I'll remember you

For a springtime violet again

   On top of an empty plate and saucer

## Cinders

Why didn't you say our world

   Was full of fire and ashes as ever again?


Why didn't you say our world

   Was full of the kind of mist and sunshine

That stung in the emblazoned eye?


Why couldn't you have raised your blind thumb?

   Why couldn't you have said our world has fled to tears?


Why, that is another friend I had once,

      How did you rake your autumn rake

Over thirstier eye that once?


Why, that is a thirstier friend I had once

  Why, that is a friend of the pearl and things of that kind,

Why, that is a friend of autumn taking its chances


Why, that is a friend of an autumn rake in the sky

  Why, that is a friend of the years that have bled and gone

Why, that is a friend of here and now


Why, that is a friend of a breathing cinder,

  Why, that is a friend of a break in the misty sunshine


And yet faraway, and yet faraway,

  And yet still taking your faraway autumn chances

# FIVE POEMS

by

Simon Perchik

\*

The planes out of Newark Field
pull England through my knees : lame

I stay undressed, hug my room
with radios. It's natural

I'm loved by sound : these inter-coms,
as slow as marrow, never interrupt

: my nine radios listen in. Some crew
is placing England in the sky

and I am over and over told
pull back! pull back! pull back.

\*

No one saw.
It was a joke I planted one bare foot

and rained
fell to shave.

Soaping
I imagined myself sleeping in the faucet

flowing to a sea.
I never shaved  : my father

was once a boy of five.

I imagined myself being born.
I was born like a cloud : hot breaths
met on some mountainside
: the chance that engendered the cold
like rain
falling a garden here.

*

A summer rain complete
stares, rises in front my car
and aches, hovers
in the sudden thought
to weep. It's night
and only some rays of speed
have witnessed this collision
almost off the earth.

*

Not the lightning of roots :flowers
are falling from these clouds :the sun

has eaten everything! petals
plane that part of the berry wants gardening,
touch down where they smell
autumn needs a touch, a meal. I

am drowning the air. What's left, come quick

bend close to my arms. Here
is too much summer. Only rain, cold rain
can fill my marrow.

\*

I sit
in a room grown older, dub

the rhythm in weeds
those buds sat too. The speed

in a house grown up
drains stale walls :outside

words are remote
I

sit
with you

pronouncing villages in Vietnam
:this room pulls closed. A vase

balances on the radioed news:
the water

needs change:
ask one of the boys.

I don't need to tell you
who will be taken away.

Excerpt from PATAGONI

by

Paul C. Metcalf

ONE

a.

in the eastandean foothills, fossil lacustrine limpets are found,
and in the upland, above timberline, pliocene marine deposits -
testaceous remains . . . at the summit of the andean arch, sub-
tropical fossil floras

walled in to the east, the continent enclosed vast mediterraneans:
the amazon sea, mojos lake, the sea of the pampas

rain fell over the old mountains, preandean, and over the low
altiplano . . . the clouds refilled from titicaca, and the deserts
of gran peru flushed green

but the continent thrust to the west, against basement complex
rocks, precambrian - a resistent mass - and the young andes up-
arched - epeirogenic - overlying, truncating the old mountain
roots

b.


a man is anxious, restless, a pressure on the breast - the frame
shudders, limbs tremble

seabirds fly inland to the cordillera, dogs disappear, vicunas
descend from the mountains, mingle in the streets with indians

the sound is lowpitch, between hearing and feeling, as, remote
thunder, a groan and rattle, the crepitation of burning wood -
the earth a thinshell cavern, thumping

a man's footing is oscillatory, fluid: the desert curls, sand-
columns rising, whirling, the mountain peaks wave like reeds

the river at arequipa turned black and sulphurous

                                        near chillan
the earth bubbled and burst, hot, fetid waters swelled out

                                                  not far
from arica a number of skeletons, legs flexed on the pelvis, were
heaved from the ground

                  steam issued from pasagua bay, itself a
crater
          the ocean bubbled, smoke and bursts of flame erupting

                                                        at
callao the pacific withdrew from the shore, paused, and, foam-
capped, smooth as milk, rolled inland

lava welled out of cotopaxi, shoved blocks of ice and snow before

it, caused floods in latacunga (indians thought the crater yielded

seawater and fish

ashclouds rose, the sun turned green, the sky verdigris, copper,

bloodred, brass

at riobamba, below sangai, the land reshaped, mountains sprouted,

rivers shifted, disappeared

       cacha vanished

            near cuzco rivers sprang

in dry gullies

      a ridge thrust across the rio seco

              the shellmarked

coast lifted, uparching from the ocean, and held

c.

old stream beds and valleys - babes to the andean canyons - are

crossed, buried beneath vulcanism, intrusive granite

the cordillera blanca, uparching, cuts the trades, jungle rains

become ice sheets, and coastal gran peru, green, dries to a

desert

toxodons, camelidae vanish in the puna beds

>hot sun follows the snow, the hills groan, rocks
>split, flakes of stone and soil fall down the
>slopes

>the limestones are pitted, the porphyries sculp-
>tured - skullshape granites onionpeel, quartzite
>erodes

>young andes reshape rock wastes, reform the stream
>flows

>and the indian intrudes

TWO

a.

at the crux, the area of titicaca:

>opposite the golgo del peru, a
structural reentrant in the westward thrust of the continent

crustally unstable, subject to shallow and deepfocus vulcanism,
with thrust faults and overturned folds on the long axis of the
lake

titicaca: caught viselike between the cordilleras

        (kjopa-kjahuana is produced by blockfaulting,
        soto island may be a horst

dust is washed from the uru, as he sails in his balsa through
waterspoutcolumns, rising from titicaca

                        hailstones - chij-chi -
whiten the ground, the june snows cover koati

                          winds flash in sudden
gusts through the straits of tiquina and yampupata

                            blue winged
teal, black diver, white and black gull feed in the waters, snipe
skim the beach, white crane stalk the lakeedge shallows

                              the wind
throws a thicketful of parrots into the air, herons issue from
the yellow waterreed

        near the lake, a stunted olive, wild straw-
berry and cabbage grow

        the andes thrust up, passed an arm around pacific waters,
        cupping them from the ocean - when bottoms in the shal-
        lows are stirred, seashells foam to the surface: early
        titicaca, an inland ocean, fed by glaciermelt and rains
        from the yungas, grew and spread

the world was dark, and the sun, flameshape,

burst from wildcat rock

at tihuanacu, on the south shore, titicacatihuanacu man, lacus-

trine, andeanocean man, intruded

b.

at the centre, willka, the sun: rising over snowy cordillera,

warming the high plain, the sunvicuma, sunllama, early american

camel, sunanimal: wariwillka

world, the centre of the universe, tihuanacu, the centre of the

world - at tihuanacu, taypicala: taipiri, centre, and ccala,

worked stone: a block of andesite, worked by man - wariwillka-

stone, the sunstone:

faced full front, he stands on a socle, at the summit

of the hollow cavern, earth

(the earth is a stepped pedastal, terraced:

ocean to desert to mountain to high plain to

mountain to jungle - earth salient, reentrant

accute and obtuse

and within, the inner earth, the moonhouse: the puma,
enclosed - with longnecked condor, and wariwillka, upreaching - in the cavern, earth

>at the extreme of the sign - the ends of the
>earth - wariwillkas, the eyes winged (impreg-
>nating), head crowned, condorfeathered

and above, at the summit of the socle, the springequinox,
wariwillka, septembersun

>the head is crowned, the supreme crown: star
>signs and sunanimal heads (the necks jointed,
>moving) - condorfeathered puma at the brow,
>faced full front

around the full face, as a fillet, signs of earthsteps,
with skies superimposed

>the face human, a full nose, sight in full
>flight from the phalliceyes, winged, sun-
>animalcrowned

from the jaw, five stars (flight of the voice) and on
the chest, full centre, a birdtailed puma (the body in
motion) over the sun, with condors bordering, upreaching

>across shoulders, condors and sunsigns, and
>at the belt, sunanimals, with pumaheads, tro-
>phies, suspended

56

wariwillkas, earth and sky on the arms - from the elbow,
a trophy head faced full front: the sunthief, killed at
the solstice

      in the hands, sceptres, top and bottom con-
      dorcrowned, the female and the crested con-
      dormayku

this - the sunfigure - springsun at the year's beginning - the
indian worked in andesite

      and beneath, spreading at its feet, carved a frieze, a
      meander, with the year's other parts, the months sol-
      stice to solstice

            the world - tihuanacu - guarded from suntheft
            - june and december - the northern and south-
            ern ends of the earth - by a mighty, crested
            condor mayku


c.




the blocks quarried in the north, floated on rafts of totora reed,
across titicaca

the carving: conflation of llama, puma, fish, cougar, condor of

earth, sun, moon, sky

                    of the stepsign, stepsign with volute

                                                        chacha-

puma, pachamama

the sunfigure, rafted and carved - mounted, by andean man, on the

platform of kalasasaya

at akapana, the fortress: stone angles salient and reentrant, for

defense - as at kalasasaya, salient and reentrant stone repelled

ignorance, conserved knowledge: the southern cross, solstice and

equinox, distribution of the seasons

        in the centre of the earth, a puma, nibbling the moon -

        from full to crescent

        and letting it grow again

                and a giant wariwillka - sunanimal - stamping,

                shaking

Zen Master Pai-Chang

by

John C. H. Wu.


The most original feature of Pai-chang's (720-814 A.D.) monastic system lies in his introduction of the duty of working in the fields, a duty
which is required of all, including the abbot himself. Before Pai-chang's
time, monks were not supposed to be engaged in productive labor. They de-
pended for their livelihood entirely on alms-begging. Buddhists in India
were originally forbidden to till the ground, lest in hoeing and ploughing
they might peradventure injure and kill the worms and insects. This system
might have been workable in a tropical zone like India, where one could possibly avert starvation by feeding on fruits and dates. The practical sense
of Pai-chang revolted against the idea of exclusive dependence on alms. Why
should able-bodied monks live like parasites on the sweat and labor of lay
people? So he required all his monks to spend part of the day in reclaiming
wastelands and in tilling the fields, so that they could live primarily on
their own labor, and only secondarily on alms-begging. Furthermore, Pai-chang
insisted that the crops yielded should be subject to the assessment of taxes
on an equal basis with those of lay people. This was so revolutionary a step
that at first Pai-chang became the target of criticisms by all the conservative Buddhist monks. But like all great reformers, he had the courage of his
convictions; and he as the abbot of a large community worked hardest of all.
His favorite motto: "One day without working, one day without eating," has
become a well-known proverb among monks of all sects.

Pai-chang lived to be ninety-four. There is a touching story about his
last days. It is said that his disciples, out of respect for his age, tried
to dissuade him from continuing to work in the farms; but the old man would
not hear of it. Then they hid away his tools. As the old man sought for them
everywhere and could not find them, he stayed away from the meals, until the
tools were returned to him.

Historically, Pai-chang's healthy innovation had a vital importance which
he probably could not have foreseen. Pai-chang died in 814. In 840's, Buddhism was to suffer the worst blow in its history in China, from which it has
never fully recovered. Emperor Wu, who reigned from 814 to 847, was bent upon
wiping out this "foreign religion". The main reason for this terrible persecu-
tion was economical, as may be gathered from the following passage in the
edict of 845:

"Now, when one man does not farm, others suffer hunger, and,
when one woman does not weave, others suffer from the cold.
At present the monks and nuns of the empire are numberless,
and they all depend on agriculture for their food and on
sericulture for their clothing. The monasteries and temples
are beyond count, but they all are lofty and beautifully de-
corated, daring to rival palaces in grandeur. None other
than this was the reason for the decline in material strength
and the weakening of the morals of the Chin, Sung, Ch'i and
Liang (dynasties)."

More than 4,600 monasteries, and more than 40,000 temples and shrines throughout the empire were destroyed.  More than 260,500 monks and nuns were returned
to lay life; and 150,000 slaves were taken over by the government.

But the wonder of it is that of all the sects of Buddhism, the School of
Zen alone managed to survive the holocaust and to continue to flourish in the
succeeding dynasties as a vigorous movement.  As Dr. Kenneth Ch'en so keenly
observes, this survival of Zen might be attributed to two of its features.  "In
the first place, its lack of dependence on the external paraphernalia of the
religion, such as the scriptures, images, and so forth, enabled it to function
and carry on even after the destruction of such externals.  In the second place,
it escaped the charge of being a parasite on society, for one of the cardinal
rules of the school was that every monk must perform some productive labor every
day.  The Ch'an master responsible for the rule was Huai-hai (720-814), who even
in his old age insisted on working in the fields."

But it would be superficial to regard Pai-chang as merely a far-sighted
sociological reformer of the monastic system.  His insistence on manual labor
had a deep spiritual significance, and carried with it an intimate sense of
involvement with the common lot of mankind.  As the disciple of Ma-tsu, he had
taken to heart the utter Non-duality of the transcendent and the immanent.  To
him, a one-sided attention to the transcendent would tend to cut Reality into
two.  His vision of Reality includes the phenomenal world of causal relations,
as well as the world beyond.  In this light we can fully understand the story--
mythical though it was--of how he helped an old fox to his enlightenment.  We
are told that every time Pai-chang ascended the platform to preach, an unknown
old man followed the monks into the hall to listen.  One day, after the whole
community had retired, the old man lingered on.  Pai-chang asked him who he was.
He replied, "I am actually not a human being.  Long, long ago, in the time of
Kasyapa Buddha, I used to be an abbot on this mountain.  When a student asked if
a man of high spirituality was still subject to the law of causality, I answered, 'He is not subject to the law of causality'.  This answer caused me to fall
into the body of a wild fox for five hundred births.  Now I beseech Your Reverence to utter for me the right word that I may be rid of the body of wild fox."
Pai-chang said, "Suppose you ask me".  The old man repeated the question of his
student.  Pai-chang replied, "He does not ignore the law of causality."  The
old man was thoroughly enlightened at this word.  Doing obeisance, he told the
master, "I am already rid of the body of the wild fox.  I dwell on the other
side of the mountain.  I beg you to bury me according to the rites as a deceased monk.  Pai-chang ordered the Superintendent of his monastery to announce
to the whole community to be ready after the meal to attend the funeral of
a deceased monk.  All the monks were surprised, because they knew of no one
being sick.  After the meal, the abbot led them to a cave at the back of the
mountain.  There they found the corpse of a wild fox.  The abbot ordered it
to be cremated according to the rites.

At the evening assembly on the same day, Pai-chang related to the monks
the whole story.  Huang-po asked, "In the case of this ancient abbot, a single
erroneous answer caused his fall into the body of a wild fox for five hundred
lives.  What will happen to an abbot who gives the right answer to every question?"  Pai-chang said, "Come near me, and I will tell you."  Huang-po approached right away and gave the master a slap on the face.  The master clapped his
hands and laughed, saying, "I thought you were the red beard of a Tartar; in
fact, you are a Tartar with a red beard!"

The story of the wild fox can hardly be taken literally. But the meaning
is clear. A truly enlightened man does not ignore the phenomenal world, which
is governed by the law of causality. He sees the immutability of the transcendent, and he sees also the changes of the phenomenal world. Tao is beyond
these two spheres, and therefore comprehends both. In the words of Chuang Tzu,
"The truly wise man, considering both sides of the question without partiality,
sees them both in the light of Tao. This is called following two courses at
once." (Merton, p. 44). To follow two courses at once is the only way to rise
above monism and dualism. As Chuang Tzu puts it elsewhere,

> "Can a man cling only to heaven
> And know nothing of earth?
> They are correlative: to know one
> Is to know the other.
> To refuse one
> Is to refuse both.
> Can a man cling to the positive
> Without any negative
> In contrast to which it is seen
> To be positive?
> If he claims to do so
> He is a rogue or a madman."

The error of the wild fox is easy to detect. But if Pai-chang should cling
to his answer as the only right and sufficient explanation of the whole ineffable
Reality, his error would be just as serious if not worse. Herein is to be found
the piercing point hidden in the question of Huang-po: What would happen to an
abbot who gives the right answer to every question? In calling him to come near,
Pai-chang probably intended to give him a slap, pointing to the Ultimate Reality,
the True Self, beyond all attributes, positive as well as negative. But instead
of waiting for the master's slapping, Huang-po was quick enough to slap the
master, pointing exactly to the same Absolute. How could Pai-chang help laughing?
He had thought that his disciple might still be moving in the sphere of attributes; but he found to his greatest delight that he had moved beyond it. The
"red beard of a Tartar" is but an attribute. After all, the important thing is
not the red beard, but the Tartar!

Once a monk asked Pai-chang, "Who is the Buddha?" the master asked him in
turn, "Who are you?" It is only by being yourself that you can move freely in
and out of the world without contradictions and obstacles. Once you have found
your True Self, you are emancipated from your little ego with all its selfish
interests, because the True Self is one with Reality and embraces all beings.
In this state you can live and work in the world without being a worldling, and
you can be a contemplative and a hermit without being a self-enclosed and ego-
centric seeker of happiness.

NOTES ON CONTRIBUTORS

(We welcome information that goes beyond the mere mention of one's most recent work, and where contributors have sent in letters about what they are thinking and doing we like to quote these with their permission.)

AD REINHARDT was an abstract painter who died in August 1967 at the height of his powers, soon after an exhibition of all his most important work at the Jewish Museum in New York. Though he had made common cause with abstract expressionists like Pollock and De Kooning in the fifties he differed entirely from them. A classicist and a rigorous contemplative, he was only just beginning to be recognized as prophetic by a new generation. He was called the "black monk" of abstract art, a purist who made Mondrian look problematic, who referred to himself as a "quietist" and said: "I'm just making the last paintings which anyone can make." We reprint here his statement of 1962.

LORINE NIEDECKER has lived most of her life on Rock River in Wisconsin, where it empties into Lake Koshkoning. "My father seined for carp in the lake. Grew up smelling tarred nets, climbing thru the leaves of that lush low country fishing ...." She went to Beloit College in the thirties and started writing verse, came in contact with Louis Zukofsky when he was editor of Poetry, learned to "condense" as he did. Worked in libraries, state radio station, hospital, now lives in Milwaukee with her husband Albert Millen. Books: New Goose, 1946, My Friend Tree, (Edinburgh, Scotland, 1961 and 1962). Two new books are soon to appear. Jonathan Williams will print Tenderness and Gristle and the Fulcrum Press (London) will publish North Central. Last year the magazine Origin, edited in Japan by Cid Corman, devoted an issue to her work. Of her poems Edward Dorn writes "they attach an undistractable clarity to the word and ... they are unabashed enough to weld that word to a freely sought, beautifully random instance".

KEITH WILSON born 1927, Clovis, New Mexico, "grew up in New Mexico and the Southwest, punching cows, digging ditches, working on farms and ranches". He was appointed to the U.S. Naval Academy and graduated 1950. Five battle stars in Korea, resigned commission in 1954 to take an M.A. in literature at the University of New Mexico and has taught at Universities of Nevada, Arizona and New Mexico State where he is now assistant professor of English. He has appeared in many poetry magazines here and abroad, and published three books of verse. Two more are due in 1968, The Shadow of our Bones, and Lion's Gate, the latter to be published by Grove Press.

JONATHAN GREENE is designer and Assistant Production Manager of the University of Kentucky Press in Lexington. He has been writing prose and verse for about nine years, has one book published (the reckoning- Matter Press) and two more due to appear this spring. Since 1965 he has edited Gnomon Press, Lexington, including Gnomon magazine. He says he likes the relative solitude of Kentucky and prefers it to New York, but he hopes some time to go and live in Dublin.

MARGARET RANDALL was born in New York. She moved to Mexico, married the Mexican Poet Sergio de Mondragon and became a Mexican citizen. Together with him she founded and edits the bi-lingual El Corno Emplumado, a literary magazine of international importance. She has published more than six books of poetry.

SHEN HUI- successor to the 6th Zen Patriarch Hui Neng as leader of the "Southern School", he is a figure of decisive importance in the development of Chinese Zen.

WEI-WU-WEI who writes the notes on Shen Hui is an Irish student of Buddhism who lives in Monaco and has published several books and articles on Zen.

ERNEST MONCRIEFF, translator of Shen Hui, is the pen name of a Chinese scholar formed in Zen by a Master in Northern China before World War II and the Communist takeover. He now teaches Chinese philosophy in an American University.

THOMAS MERTON is the author of more books than necessary, the newest of which is a poetry and prose sequence Cables to the Ace (New Directions). The poem printed here is part of a long poetic work in progress The Geography of Lograire.

JONATHAN WILLIAMS- born 1929 in Asheville, North Carolina, went to St. Alban's School and Princeton, associated with the Black Mountain Group of Poets, publisher of Jargon Books since 1951, a hiker and resident of Highlands, North Carolina "until it joins the Grated Society and I opt out for Wharfedale in Yorkshire". He got a Guggenheim fellowship in 1957 "and not a damn dime since from any form of Establishment until appointment 1967 as scholar-in-residence, Aspen Institute for Humanistic Studies in Colorado". He claims to be Vice President of the Cast Iron Lawn Deer Owners of America. The selections printed here are from his forthcoming book on Appalachia Blues and Roots/Rue and Bluets.

ALFRED STARR HAMILTON is 53 years old, and lives in New Jersey. He writes: "I have been on the road during the depression. I have been through forty three states that way. I served (subservience) a year in the army. I have been a member of the socialist party ever since. I live on a budget of $80 a month today. I live in a big rooming house. I cook my own meals... Well, I don't like money. I don't like more money. What would I do with more money? ... I spend all my time with poetry." He has been published in various poetry magazines and a book of his will be printed by Jonathan Williams (Jargon Books) soon.

SIMON PERCHIK born 1923 in Paterson N.J., worked as a milkman, was a bomber pilot in World War II, returned to study law and is now a member of a New York Law firm, living on Staten Island with his wife and three children. He has published two books of poetry at the Elizabeth Press (New Rochelle).

PAUL C. METCALF lives in the Berkshires (Chester, Mass.) where he runs a real estate business which "has become quite successful and hence a problem: how do I get rid of it?" It interferes with writing. Over a period of 30 yrs.he has written poems, plays, novels. His study of historic and contemporary Cherokee, Will West, was published by Jonathan Williams. Patagoni, from which we publish an excerpt, is a manuscript on Pre-Columbian South America. He writes: "I think there is absolutely nothing substantial in the contemporary world, one treads the scene like a lumberjack walking the logs downstream. This is exciting, challenging and "fun", and a stand on dry land may at times be recalled... I'm not sure its the lumberjack's concern what happens to the logs whenever they get to wherever the hell they're going..."

JOHN C.H. WU is a noted Chines scholar and diplomat. He was Chinese ambassador to the Vatican after World War II, has published several books, including an autobiography, Beyond East and West. His latest book, The Golden Age of Zen has just been published in Taiwan and the pages presented here are an excerpt from it. Dr. Wu is Honorary Dean of the Graduate School of the College of Chinese Culture in Taiwan and Research Professor of Asian Studies at Seton Hall University. He lectured on Zen at the College of Chinese Culture in Taiwan. At Seton Hall he is teaching Oriental religion and Classical Chinese literature.

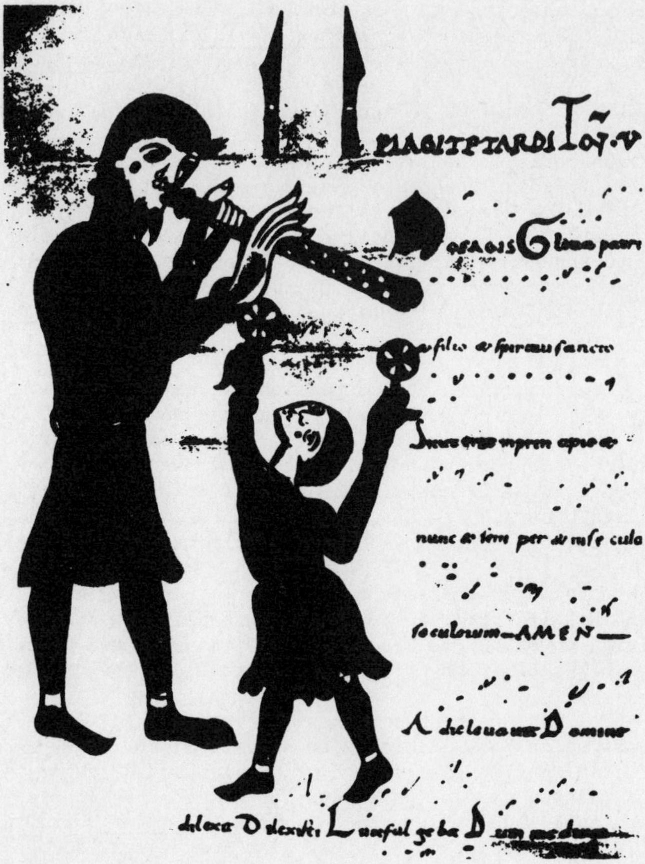
seculorum AMEN

# MONKS POND

**NO. 2**          **SUMMER**          **1968**

contents

Photographs- Ralph Eugene Meatyard
Decorations, Concrete and Antipoems -
              Robert Lax
              Thomas Merton

Louis  Zukofsky

(from Thanks to the Dictionary)


Preface

And what will the writers do then, poor things.


"A".  Quoting the dictionary.  Remembering my sawhorses, my little a.'s ab-
breviated for afternoon, perhaps for years, this afternoon.  Another acre, one, any,
some, each, aback, as aloof, till before a vowel will stand accepted, "An", active,
tho not as a vulture.  Perhaps next Ab, when the fast will not commemorate a Temple
in ruins, Aaron's rod, the serpent to blossom, will grow, goldenrod which flowers on
long stems in that vacation a part of July and of August.  David, then, on his page,
not like a slab forming the top of a capital, but not unlike an abacus, a reckoning
table telling its sums will embrace all the words of this novel.  For, David, anti-
cipated, appears when the groundhogs are not in Abad.  Abad is any cultivated city.
But David who resists all its agents is free from iridescence, and without accidenÆ
tals.  If there is iridescence, it will be at his toes.  His name, these words till
now, are almost his story.


Young  David

Not otherwise provided for, the son of Jesse stands by the water-raising wheel,
the one bucket on its rim.  On the ground, the prickly-pear is still, as before he
stood he sat still.  Type of the rule, there is neither blame nor praise for a boy's
work.

North by west, i.e. one point or $11^{\circ}$ 15' west of north, he sees the black crow
fly, the gray sparrow hop.  He knows the normal color of the crow is black, the normal
color of the sparrow is gray.  He knows, according to nature, that one is as natural
as the other.  Steady and constant himself, the birds, to him, fly, circle and fly
and are not fitful nor changeable.  If there were a deformity in them he could pick
it, but that again would be as expected as their symmetry.  As he turns the water-
wheel, he knows the birds in an assemblage of their qualities.

Follows a perpendicular of sight to a curved surface and that is a normal.  But
shifts slightly and becomes the line of his thought.  Northward is a land.  To the south
is land.  To the east is sun, which climbs to set.  To the west is sea.  He thinks
his life.  His life is not yet the present.  His future is monstrous.  In a heat he
brings to himself seven wives and the eighth is childless.  "-- David! your muscles,
cold, the pole-star, your wives oxen, your wives are stiff, your person, it turns,
as the sakkiyeks making even the beasts slaves!  You will die unable to warm yourself."
He sees a noose, the knot of which runs.  Thirsty, he subjugates peoples.  But he
stands still, the prickly-pear seems to sit.  The grief for a body, hung, repaid to
his compact boy's body before he has been responsible for its birth makes him turn
the wheel so that buckets multiply, and the winds in the twilight shifting around him,
become common to his eyes --

Item:

Joseph Deniker 1852 -- French anthropologist, not therefore a member of the
people he "so-called" nordic

-- in a series of organic isomers designating a compound in which the chain is continuous and not branched, -- his eyes, the winds in his eyes, the winds and his eyes become an ultimate substance -- identical as their composition.

TWO POEMS DEDICATED TO THOMAS MERTON

by Jack Kerouac

***

I

It's not that
everybody's trying
 to get into the act,
as Jimmy Durante
says----it's that
EVERYBODY IS
    IN THE ACT
       (from the point
        of view of
        Universality)


       Rhymes
       With
          Durante


***


II

Not oft
       the snow
             so soft
                   the holy bow


***

Besmilr Brigham

day is yellow:   ce xochitl

(debt to nahuatl)

the poet is born upon a day
embroidered with one-flower
he teaches thoughts to lie
that they may betray themselves
and for this he is humble

the good poet
looks into the center of the flower
where the unobserved seed are
that grow in his own heart
and he scatters them
with the abandonment of petals

           he asks nothing
           his body is tattooed with color
           the flower of things
           that is the destiny of his mind

but if he
hold himself above the shadow
that is in the flower
that is of all things
and in the hearts of all men

if he
considers himself
above the many-flower
that is similar
that is worked with varied threads
that blooms joyfully
he has squandered himself
he has no face or heart

he becomes a
a dissolute of his obsession
he becomes a seven-flower
he burns no incense
he makes no offering of quail
he breaks no fast
and he goes of himself into the streets

           and what is the flower
           of the one-day gift
                a rose

there is no one to say--
he dreams her petals /sleeps
in the abundance of her leaves

all yellow
I would say for some
yellow and autumn orange
that rich gold
cured and to wither
grown ripe
with the overpowering hardness
untouchable as the sun

                         for god
is truly
as the flower rich in yellow
look closely for there is
a race that has made him
coiled from the face of the flower so

a poet lives whole within a day
whose crest is the one-flower
he teaches men to speak
into the center of themselves
his hands are trained to be skillful

he lives in grace and is humble

Alfred Starr Hamilton

1.

To Father Coughlin

Do you know of a green pond?
Do you know of the mists surrounding the pond?
Do you know of the seagulls flying hither and thither?
Do you know of a cold dark lake in the midst of Ireland?
Do you remember ourselves?
Do you know of the bitter treaty between ourselves and the police dragnet?
Do you remember our subway rides here?
Do you know of our promises to a bitter sweetheart?
Do you know of our burial grounds?
Do you know of a cold stone?
Do you know where the sea washes over?
Today do you know why our best hopes are never to have been forgotten?

2.

For I'll remember you for your girlhood
For I'll remember a shining girl officer
For I'll remember one good and hard girl diamond
For I'll remember you through your red hour glass
For I'll remember you for one good scorching police whistle
For I'll remember you at your pretty desk
For I'll remember you for your black velvet claws
For I'll remember your asking for our attentive silence
For I'll remember staring at you by the hour
For I'll remember your gazing back at ourselves
For once I'll remember the dark tussle
For I'll remember your daring threats
For I'll remember you for years afterwards
For I'll remember you after dark

## Raymond Roseliep

1 - SONG OF ENGLISHBOY

Soon
as my
bloody
body
gets done
with pub-
erty,
the pub's
the turn
for me:
a hey
'n a hey,
the pub's
the turn
for me.


A wad
of bread,
a press
of verse,
bough
on my head,
no spot
of tea,
a lot
of thou:
a hey
'n a hey,
the pub's
the turn
for me.

2 - SONG

Sky
is redder
tonight
than my
suet's

little
edge
of beef
I left
for the
birds,


God is
patient
with
his
poets,


and
my song
has
no
more
words.

Emmett Williams


the red chair


i

he said it two days ago. he said it fourteen days ago. he said it two hundred
and ninety-nine days ago, to be exact. i don't know when he said it. maybe he
didn't say it at all. why don't you forget it, he said. it would be so easy to
forget, i answered, or at least i think i answered him, because i haven't the
slightest idea who he was, yes, it would be so easy to forget if only i could
remember what it is. then everything would be all right. whereupon i think he
answered, holding his hands so close to my face i could have bitten them: you
must pretend that it never happened. what never happened? ah, you have already
forgotten, he rejoiced. see, i can help you. but you must do what i tell you.
the birds, of course, the birds. the one with the black beak, the kolibri. the
swirl, the still swirl, the wingedness. the woodpecker who hammered and hammered
breathlessly. hammering. to begin with, he said, you must promise me two things.
i promise, i told him, shifting my weight from the left foot to the right foot.
first, you must never again sit in the red chair. that is too much, i protested.
it is my chair. mine. do you understand? do you promise or not? i promise. second, you must never sit on any chair except the red one. that is too much, i
protested. i hate the red chair. i hate it, i tell you. do you promise? i promise.
you're doing very well, he said warmly. cigarette? i shifted my weight from the
right foot to the left foot. as i see it, he said, but not to me, because i was-
n't listening, there isn't the slightest chance that they will return. where have
they gone, i asked in disbelief. they couldn't have gone very far, because they
haven't been gone very long. but they mustn't return! they won't, he assured me.
and then they came. but i knew, so much better than he did, that they would never
return. i bumped into them as they made their way to the red chair. you see, i
am blind. at least i think i am, because i am also deaf and can't hear what they
say about me. be that as it may, i have the advantage over them in the end. i am
dumb. when do you expect them, he asked from a far corner. they took the 5:45. but
that can't be, he said. here they come and it's only three. i'll get my sweet revenge when they come, i said softly. i sat down in the red chair to relax. i was
tired, and they would be there any minute. the woodpecker sang an octave higher.


ii

he said it two days ago. the woodpecker sang an octave higher. he said it fourteen
days ago. i was tired, and they would be there any minute. he said it two hundred
and ninety-nine days ago, to be exact. i sat down on the red chair to relax. i
don't know when he said it. i'll get my sweet revenge when they come, i said softly.
maybe he didn't say it at all. here they come and it's only three. why don't you
forget it, he said. but that can't be, he said. it would be so easy to forget, i
answered, or at least i think i answered him, because i haven't the slightest idea
who he was, yes, it would be so easy to forget if only i could remember what it is.
they took the 5:45. then everything would be all right. when do you expect them,
he asked from a far corner. whereupon i think he answered, holding his hands so close
to my face i could have bitten them: you must pretend that it never happened. i am
dumb. what never happened? be that as it may, i have the advantage over them in the
end. ah, you have already forgotten, he rejoiced. at least i think i am, because
i am also deaf and can't hear what they say about me. see, i can help you. you see,
i am blind. but you must do what i tell you. i bumped into them as they made their
way to the red chair. the birds, of course, the birds. but i knew, so much better
than he did, that they would never return. the one with the black beak, the kolibri.


75

and they came! the swirl, the still swirl, the wingedness. they won't, he assured me. the woodpecker who hammered and hammered breathlessly. but they mustn't return! hammering. they couldn't have gone very far, because they haven't been gone very long. to begin with, he said, you must promise me two things. where have they gone, i asked in disbelief. i promise, i told him, shifting my weight from the left foot to the right foot. as i see it, he said, but not to me, because i wasn't listening, there isn't the slightest chance that they will return. first, you must never again sit in the red chair. i shifted my weight from the right foot to the left foot. that is too much, i protested. cigarette? it is my chair. you're doing very well, he said warmly. mine. i promise. do you understand? do you promise? do you promise or not? i hate it, i tell you. i promise. i hate the red chair. second, you must never sit in any chair except the red one. that is too much, i protested.

iii

maybe he didn't say it at all. what never happened? the one with the black beak, the kolibri. i promise, i told him, shifting my weight from the left foot to the right foot. do you understand? i hate the red chair. cigarette? but they mustn't return. you see, i am blind. they took the 5:45. i was tired, and they would be there any minute. i don't know when he said it. whereupon i think he answered, holding his hands so close to my face i could have bitten them: you must pretend it never happened. the birds, of course, the birds. to begin with, he said, you must promise me two things. mine. that is too much, i protested. you're doing very well, he said warmly. they couldn't have gone very far, because they haven't been gone very long. i bumped into them as they made their way to the red chair. when do you expect them, he asked from a far corner. i sat down on the red chair to relax. he said it two hundred and ninety-nine days ago, to be exact. then everything would be all right. but you must do what i tell you. hammering. it is my chair. second, you must never sit on any chair except thered one. i promise. where have they gone, i asked in disbelief. but i knew, so much better than he did, that they would never return. i am dumb. i'll get my sweet revenge when they come, i said softly. he said it fourteen days ago. it would be so easy to forget, i answered, or at least i think i answered him, because i haven't the slightest idea who he was, yes, it would be so easy to forget if only i could remember what it is. see, i can help you. the woodpecker who hammered and hammered breathlessly. that is too much, i protested. i promise. do you promise? as i see it, he said, but not to me, because i wasn't listening, there isn't the slightest chance that they will return. and then they came. be that as it may, i have the advantage over them in the end. here they come and it's only three. he said it two days ago. why don't you forget it, he said. ah, you have already forgotten, he rejoiced. the swirl, the still swirl, the wingedness. first, you must never again sit in the red chair. do you promise or not? i hate it, i tell you. i shifted my weight from the right foot to the left foot. they won't, he assured me. at least i think i am, because i am also deaf and can't hear what they say about me. but that can't be, he said. the woodpecker sang an octave higher.

Paul  Klee

POEMS FROM THE NOTEBOOKS

translated from the german by anselm hollo.

True stories:

One
in great pain
grows a fine set of carnivore's teeth.

It must be something of a shipwreck when you're old
and still get excited
about things.

Tonight
the moon was a pearl
and it really signified
tears.

Small wonder.
This is sirocco country.

Once
it seemed
the heart stood still.
The brain evaporated.
No thought
but for the heart,
and that
stood still.

Don't fall, I!
With you the world would fall -
and Beethoven
survives in you -                                           (1905)


                                    *


No one need use his irony on me.
I can take care of that myself.

A dream I had:
killed a young fellow and called him an ape
as he lay dying.
He was deeply offended.
"Don't you see I'm about to draw my last breath"
he said.

"Your bad luck" I replied;
then, "you won't be able to evolve again..."

Woe to the wellfed
bourgeoisie                                                 (1906)

```
    Grandpa is riding roundabout on a peppermill.
    A thief?  Hurry - give the dog his dentures -

    Can I help you?
    A glass globe?
    How large, would you say?
    Well, full moon size, I guess -

    smiles of mutual understanding.

    Not everybody should know
    the answer to this one -
    because if they did, o my!
    all would be lost                              (1914)
```

\*

```
    To invent
    the Chorus Mysticus
    to be performed
    by a few hundred
    children's voices.

    After that
    no need to go on
    with the constant endeavor.

    The many small works
    all lead to it
    in the end.                                    (1914)
```

\*

On the night between the 30th of June and the 1st of July, 1925, I dreamt of strangely explicit things.  I saw, on the corner of two exterior walls, up underneath the eaves, a big bird's-nest, but one inhabited by a family of cats.  The young were quite big already, about four weeks old.  One in particular, a dark-furred tiger kitten, balanced recklessly on the nest's edge, its tail-end wagging in the air.  Below the nest there was a very narrow ledge which the mother cat used as her gangway to an open window.  The thought that the first outing of those kittens would have to be on such a perilous path filled me with fear, and I tried to think of ways of averting the danger.

Then I saw myself, breaking soil in a garden.  With great labor, something had been made, and out of this, something else, of a pleasurable nature, was supposed to come forth.  Suddenly a dog came running to this place and began to roll himself over it, in a destructive manner, rooting up the ground further with his snout.  I did nothing to prevent him.  This caused some surprise, but I excused myself by referring to the dog as an 'expert'.

(1925)

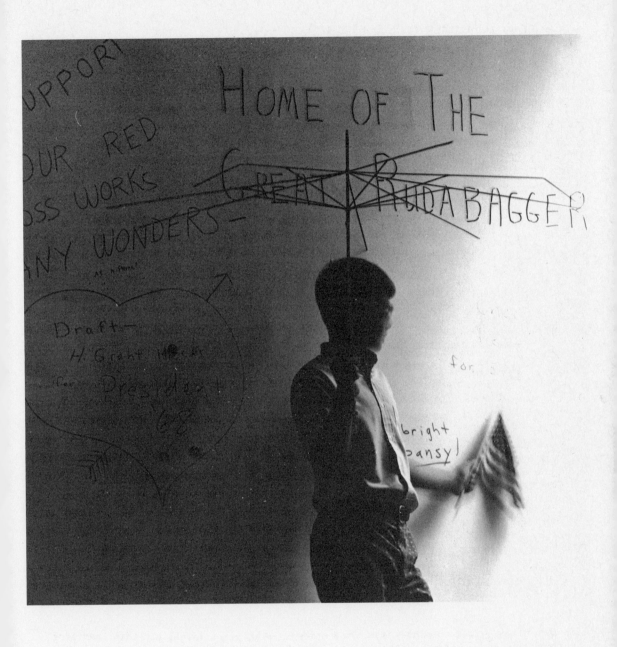

Geoff   Hewitt


THE POET WHO BECAME A POLITICIAN

His friends had made many sermons
And were killing themselves in verse
To end the war that he favored
With modest silence     his poems

Grew worse, his politics better
And someone voted him Poet
Of the Year, gave him a nice prize
That hung from his chest like a smile

Fallen from use     and he was missed
By his friends.  His poems were mourned
By all but anthologists, who
Never found out he had fallen

From favor quicker than the stale
Bread of old sandwiches goes down
To the fish who never smell first
What they eat before eating it.


CONTEMPLATING SAUSAGE

My mother has made a joke of it:
    she talks about a lady in the news
    who committed "sausage" by freeing
    her blood with a pick.

My face is too far from the water.
    I cannot see
My own reflection.
    The bridge holds
My breath, sways perceptibly.
    Life is wonderfully in
My hands.  Tonight I am the only God
    of mercy:  it is I who can cast
    the soft flesh to fish.

Where are the voices that say No, No?
    Where is my mother with her jokes designed
    to minimize fact?  Where is the wrathful
    God, whose hands tingle, helping me

Gently on the guard rail?  My balance
    fails as soon as I am up.  Falling
    back, I whack my shin and feel as if
    I'll need to limp, a wounded man forever.


81

RUMORS

A miracle!  no children
visibly harmed, the schools
having been closed
indefinitely since September.

But they hijacked his life
and crashed it against a small community
saying our mouths are empty
explaining truth is never clear.


AT THE BEAUTICIAN'S

1)  I see my anklebone
edged
between her teeth  2) her smile
is bony, she laughs so hard I cry
3)  are you coming -- Coleman writes --
early?  have the majesty to make it
late:  4) Mockingbirds At Ft McHenry
5) "Not This Pig"  I yell at her, broasting
beneath scopic eyes  6) her head settles
under air
dryers, ears up to catch the hum:  she whispers
"Yell louder"
7) "'But poetry is a figment of the imagination'"
and "go away," she alternately chants  8) "I'll put you
into the past tense" I warn
9)  "and that, my friend," she belches
"is the only favor you can do me."


* * *

Halvard Johnson

projections 4

it was cold, he felt
that his flesh was rotting

the nation trembled
on the brink of war

yesterday's newspaper
lined his shoes

& the little boy
his hand in his mother's---

    who is that funny man,
    why is he on our side of the street


projections 23

you cannot dream
you are something
inanimate, he was told

but he dreamt, he
dreamt he was a stone
lying at the bottom
of a clear, cold, swiftly flowing stream

& someone kneeling on the bank
picked him up, put him in his pocket, & carried him away

to a small town,
took him out of his pocket
polished him tenderly with a soft cloth
threw him through a window of a small house

where, on a living room carpet,
he was suddenly at home


projections 27

Bill & Joey were friends, they sat
next to each other in school,
read the same books, talked to
the same pretty girls, who couldn't
talk about either of them without
mentioning the other in the same breath,
the same breathless way

when school was over, Joey or Bill would say---
walk me home & then I'll walk <u>you</u> home

so, together they'd walk the sidewalks
between their two houses & all the girls
would envy each of them


\*\*\*              \*\*\*              \*\*\*


          Robert Zmuda


     LOVE OF THE STARS   II

     Silverfish
     spins crazy
     over the
     cement floor
     where my feet
     walk bare

     And you work
     at your life

     I go on living

     And do not say
     what becomes
     of you

     Or that bat
     trapped
     in the
     lonely
     garage


              \*\*\*

George Hitchcock

CONSIDER THE POET

who walks in a stony field behind his plow
turning up old flints
adze-heads and the bones of ptarmigan,
who lives in terror of tea-leaves
ink-blots and mendicant feathers,
who spends his tears on jujubes,
and on feast-days
pulls coins from dirty ears
to the applause of grass-blades;

whose overcoat is specked with the dandruff
of alphabets; a salamander
born in the hospitable lava, he
traffics in scoriac mysteries
and scalds the hands of those
who put trust in him:

Arbiter of waters, Nuncio of the wild iris,
Ishmaelite among the tenements of eyes,
you salute each morning the flags
which flutter in the cottonwoods
and bear in your lung the deadly flower
of recollection.

*

ON THIS FIRST DAY OF APRIL
I STARE IN WONDER

at the fountains and their agile tongues
the buds afloat in the azaleas
the larks in their circus
the eloquent pebbles moaning in the creek

at the yellow breath of the newborn acacia
the wild mustard sailing toward heaven
the stars which turn cartwheels in the sod

and your wrist sun-ringed now
with a bracelet of grace.

*

85

KEEP CLOSE TO THE BANKS
TO AVOID THE WEIR

The river ingests the reeds
the swans lead the small boats
of their young
in search of glass confections

There are cyclists on the towpath
women leaning from the stone arches
the flags of new wash
whip in the June wind

Overhead the swallows
cast their purposeful nets
in the earth underfoot the cities
of ants prosper and fall

And yet my own life here
at Iffley near Oxford a coil
of rope a bleached board
a hawser aimlessly
basking by the locks

        --

Out of profound
dissatisfaction
I make this song.

            ***

# FOUND MACARONIC ANTIPOEM

Amicorum communia sunt omnia
Main gūt ist dein gūt.
Stateram ne transgrediaris.
Hau nicht vber die schnūr.
Obermachs nit.
Trit nicht ūber das zyl.
Cor ne edito
Bekūmer dich nit zūfast.
Per publicam viam ne ambules
volg nit dem gemainen pöfel.
Aduersus solem ne loquitor
widerstreß nit dem offenbarn.
A prora & puppi perit
der verdirbt in grundt.
der ist fertig von tach an vnd von keller.

Friends have all in common
My gutt is thy gutt
Don't mess with the scales
Don't alter oder the line
Nix obermache
Don't drive through the back
Of the garage
Keep your silly ideas to yourself
Don't get in such a sweat
Don't amble down the highway
Follow not common pitfit
Don't contradict the sun
Don't deny the obvious
Wrecked from stem to stern
Rotten to the core
He's through with his
Beef and beer.

*(From an Elementary Reader, Augsburg, 1514)*

THOMAS MERTON

ACTIVE   LIFE

I   have   a   hundred   plans
that come to life in me quite gently
and yet my existence
still seems to me
monotonous.

                Goethe.

Reza Arasteh

THE ART OF REBIRTH.

Patterns and Process of Self-Liberation in Near Eastern Sufism.

This paper deals with the patterns and processes of self-liberation in the
Sufis, a group of Near Eastern mystics who analyzed the underlying realities of religion and philosophy, and unveiled the mysteries of man's psyche as a means of attaining perfection and certainty. Sufism developed the art of transcending one's
self to perfection, thereby contributing greatly to an understanding of personality
development and the discovery of self.

In essence, Sufism develops in the individual a process of continual rebirth until he attain self-liberation. The question then arises: What is this self which
the Sufis would like to realize?

According to Sufism the real self is not what environment and culture develop
in us, but it is basically the product of the universe in evolution. I shall refer
to it henceforth as cosmic self or universal self in contrast to phenomenal self, the
product of culture and environment. Cosmic self can be thought of as the image of
the universe which must be unveiled. It is wrapped in our unconscious itself, whereas the phenomenal self encompasses consciousness. In Sufism unconsciousness receives
more importance than consciousness; it possesses infinite potentialities, while consciousness is limited; and only the unconscious provides the means of attaining the
real self. The cosmic self embraces all our being while the phenomenal self designates only a part of our existence. The phenomenal self has separated us from our
origin, that of union with all of life. Having now become aware of this separation,
we can only live fully by emptying consciousness, bringing to light the unconscious,
achieving insight into our whole existence and living in a state of complete awareness.
I shall call this state cosmic existence or transcendental consciousness. The real
self can be thought of as the crown of unconsciousness, which is potentially conscious existence, the Sufi's goal.(1) To identify this psyche state is ordinarily not
easy, for its very nature is one of becoming, and when attained that is it. Persian
Sufis believe that it is self-explanatory and self-evident. Just as the sun is
proof of itself so too is the real self. Each of us has at some time experienced it.
At least once we have heard its voice, its call, and its invitation, often without
our realization. Perhaps the words "me," "he" or "it" can better identify the real
self than "I" or "we". In this sense Sufism consists of two steps:  1) the passing
away of "I", and  2) becoming wholly aware of "I". The real self exists in no place,
its very nature is intensive rather than extensive, and it can be both near us and
far removed, depending on the individual's experience. Ordinarily a flash of knowledge enlightens the consciousness, a small circle of our psyche, but when we attain
the real self a strong flash constantly illuminates the whole structure of our psyche.
Some Sufis give the heart as its site, but one may ask, "How can the heart, meaning
really an ability for intuitive experience, have a definite locus? In the following
poem Rumi designates its source, if not its location:

> Cross and Christians, from end to end,
> I surveyed; He was not on the cross.
> I went to the idol-temple, to the ancient pagoda;
> No trace was visible there.
> I went to the mountains of Herat and Candahor (2);

---

(1) At this point the Sufi is called Safi, the pure one.
(2) In Afghanistan.

89

I looked, He was not in that hill and dale.
With set purpose I fared to the summit of Mount Qaf (3)
In that place was only Anqa's habitation.
I bent the reins of search to the Ka'ba (4);
He was not in that resort of Old and Young.
I questioned Ibn Sina of His state;
He was not within Ibn Sina's range, (5)
I fared towards the scene of two bow-lengths' distance,
He was not in that exalted court
I gazed into my heart;
There I saw Him; He was nowhere else. (6)

The above poem describes the Sufi's search for the site of the real self.
Not finding it in various religions, reason or other sources, he at last discovers it within himself.

Can one achieve the state of cosmic self by being taught its principles? No,
not at all in the sense of conventional knowledge cannot transform the inner self.
Thus inner experience offers the only way. The Sufis undoubtedly rely heavily on
inner experience and accepted religious practices.

The one who seeks to transform his social self must experience at least once
that which he is seeking. He must become aware of the problems of human existence:
What are we? What is our destination and why? He must sense his origin and become aware of the fact that with all our strivings we don't know why we, like fish,
have been cast into a net allowing us endless views of the world. At this point
the individual senses that he once lived in closer harmony to nature. This awareness or insight (7) may occur suddenly, sometimes the result of a simple experience.
Sufi literature abounds with examples of individuals who suddenly perceived the
path they must follow, like Al-Ghazali, 'Attar, Rumi and others.

Sufism maintains that this sudden experience of awareness can help anyone view
himself in the perspective of evolution and change, that is, in the sense that
man was once united with Nature in the animal state, and progressively more so in
plant and mineral forms, going back ultimately to the basic composition of Nature.

Once awakened the individual realizes that the same evolutionary process which
led him to his present state is continually at work. This process may further develop his mind, make him realize his helplessness and turn him into a religious or
an intellectual man. At the next stage he becomes familiar with the idols in his
mind and attempts to break them all in order to achieve his goal. At this point
the Sufi advances to a level of being as far above the ordinary man as that of
man in relation to his earlier existence. The fully awakened one attains union
with all and helps his cosmic self come to light. He becomes a universal man remembering the entire past in the sense of evolution and seeing the whole of life
in even a small particle.

Having had an image of such a better life, the awakened person becomes a
seeker and values this image above all else. Motivated by it, he longs for it,
becomes concerned with it and directs his efforts toward attaining it so as to become one with it. He becomes competitive, but only with himself, for competition
with one's self constitutes perfection.

_____

(3) Qaf, the residence of Simurgh, who is identical with God and is the object of
    search of unification in Attar's Mantiq-al-taye, a mystical text.
(4) Exemplifies religion.
(5) Exemplifies philosophy.
(6) Insight is compared to a sword which cuts the root of the past and future
    thereby illuminating the moment. It is like a lightning flash.

Man's nature, however, does not easily bend toward perfection. While his insight may make him aware of a better life, his instincts, drives and selfish motives, or nafs, as the Sufis refer to them, may pull him down. Caught by contradictory forces in his nature, he becomes anxious. If he is lucky he stands at the threshold of two worlds: his ego stands up against his political or real self; the universal man against the social. In modern times people generally do not recognize this disharmony within themselves. When uneasy, they take a pill, a drink, or escape to an illusionary way of life. However, if an individual, like the Sufis novice, analyzes his situation and becomes critical of it he cannot exchange his ultimate certainty for temporary satisfaction. He becomes even more concerned with his existential problem. As a searcher of the truth he recognizes that he has only one heart and is potentially one entity; he cannot split into several parts. Recognizing that only the truth can save him, he concentrates solely on union, where union means identification with the desired object and disunion the heart's attachment to several objects. The object of this search consists in the realization of the real self, the state of universal man, unity with all, becoming God-like or being only the truth. To become like God means the assimilation of what God represents, that is, a beautiful creation rather than submission to the image of God; loving to save, not loving to be saved.

The removal of the self in reality means the annihilation of those experiences which bar the revealing of the real self. Sufis call the experience of removal of "I" fana, which ends in a state of ecstasy, the feeling of union; it is the beginning of baqa, the state of conscious existence.

The Sufi's goal is now clear, but how can he achieve it? First of all he must understand the limitations of his consciousness, specifically, that it contains unnecessary material and that in its development numerous veils have formed around the real self preventing it from manifesting its true nature. Once he recognizes this fact the Sufi can remove the "I" from consciousness: a state which is identical with changing and expanding consciousness to function in harmony with the unconscious.

As a first step in this direction the Sufi must inactivate nafs (the source of impulses) or more precisely, use his reason to control passion. Sufism recognizes, as does modern psychology, that this part of our being cannot be eliminated or suppressed entirely. Nafs also possesses a great negative power, a kind of force like anger or passionate love which blinds the intellect. Therefore, the Sufi seeks to satisfy nafs before bringing it under the control of intellect. Even then it will persist, just as embers glow under the ashes; nor must the seeker then ignore it, for at any time when the embers flare up, they must be quenched again. Some Sufis believe that ordinarily after the individual has satisfied nafs, in terms of both sex impulses and those relating to success and agreed, he must then gradually restrict it and bring it under the control of reason.

Because of this factor in human nature, Sufism attracts socially "successful" individuals rather than youth. The forceful nature of nafs also explains why Sufis believe that ordinary men need religious experience, even if it is only partially understood. In a positive sense the Sufis control nafs by virtuous behavior and righteous deeds. For instance when a seeker presents himself to a guide for the purpose of becoming a Sufi, he is put on probation for three years: the first year to serve people, the second to serve God and the third to observe the rise and fall of his own desires. The seeker disengages nafs from its qualities thereby directing its downward tendency thrust in the pursuit of his goal. In this process he becomes indifferent to material possession and eliminates passion-arousing desires. Now united in thought, action and feeling, he prepares to rid his mind of all conscious thoughts.

The Sufi purposely adopts a period of alienation in order to remove illusionary consciousness, that is, he adopts a method opposite to that of its development.
For the Sufi this temporary period of alienation is the most effective method of
self-analysis.  He believes that society and culture are a bridge for attaining
the real self.  Even the lives of such great prophets as Moses, Muhammad, Buddha,
of Christians like St. Francis, St. John of the Cross, of notable Sufis like
Prince Abrahim Adham and Abi Sa'id Alkhayr reveal the adoption of a similar state
in order to achieve the true self.  Through the method of alienation the Sufi tries
to rid himself of illusionary material in consciousness, which means that he has
to analyze every single experience in his mind, understand its imperfections, and
at the same time develop a thorough affection for it and see his relatedness to
it.  In this analysis the Sufi detaches himself from society, but he also develops
a receptivity and appreciation of every element in our world, relating it to its
original existence.  He becomes unaware of what he once thought perfect or knowledge he had gained, but meanwhile his immediate experiences enrich his being by
activating his insight, fostering love and developing discernment in him.   Love
becomes the vehicle which carries him forward. "Love is the drug of all drugs"
which strengthens his faith, removes his anxiety and encourages him to pass through
numerous states of mind (hal).

In the process of experiencing hals he undergoes a series of internal changes,
or if you will, he lives a multitude of lives.  Continually on guard and in love,
he guards against falling into an illusion and attaching himself to its object of
search.  According to Sufism those who are on guard and in love find no rest.  This
restlessness produces energy for further contemplation and searching of every corner of the mind in order to prepare the psyche for the appearance of the real self.
In this state he receives guidance to encourage the real self to make its appearance.  When awake he concentrates on his object of search, when asleep he begs his
real self to appear before him.  The Sufi's object of love reveals itself in
dreams and he must be ready to receive its call.  In traditional Iran the Sufi orders strongly believed that many mysteries would be unfolded in their dreams.

In essence, the Sufi's task is to break the idol of the phenomenal self, which
is the mother-idol; having achieved this aim his search ends.  Empty-handed, empty-
minded and desire-less, he is and he is not.  He has and he has not the feeling of
existence.  He knows nothing, he understands nothing.  He is in love, but with
whom he is not aware of .  His heart is at the same time both full and empty of
love.  In the process of search he removes "I" but he remains still aware of being
unconscious of consciousness.

In the next step he loses this awareness (the awareness of the absence of consciousness) in order to eliminate the subject-object relation and achieve union.
In a positive sense he assimilates all the particles of love and insight that he
has felt through the process of emptying his consciousness.  He transcends time
and place.  This state of union, the climax of the annihilation of the partial
self, is identical with ecstasy and gives the impression of a natural intoxication.
Among the Persian Sufis this painless ecstatic trance sometimes lasted for days
and weeks.  It is a state of mind which resembles sleep such that one does things
perfectly.

The individual has now experienced life first hand.  He feels no distance between himself and his object of love.  Sufis who have ended their search usually
develop this state of union through certain recollections, dances, music and auto-
hypnosis.  Having tasted it, they may again lose it.  The mystery of deep love
which flows in their lyrics like the current of the sea stems from union and disunion.  In the following lines Abi-Sa'id describes this state of union:

I am love; I am the beloved; no less am I the lover.
I am the mirror and I am the beauty.
Therefore behold me in myself.

A Sufi may stop at the stage of _fana_, which can be defined as passing from consciousness to the world of unconsciousness where reason is active. He may also pass beyond this stage and find himself in the state of _baqa_ (continuance) where he gains individuality in non-individuality, that is, infusion has taken place but the individual has entered a state of conscious existence. Whosoever achieves this state becomes a "perfect man", who relies on consciousness and is ruled by reason. Aided by intuition the perfect man functions as a totality, with spontaneity and expressiveness. Instead of studying life from afar he is life itself. In this state, indescribable and characterized by silence, the individual is now everything or nothing: everything in the sense that he is united with all, nothing in the sense that nothingness is the beginning of "everythingness". He embraces all of life, he is beyond good and bad. In a practical way he has experienced qualities embracing all of life, ordinary human existence and intellectual life; he has felt himself variously as a famous man, an ambitious one, a religious man and has passed beyond all of them, finally giving rebirth to a more comprehensive self. He feels related to all mankind, experiences a concern for all beings and tries to utilize his earlier experiences for their benefit. One can sense the same feeling in the following poem by Rumi:

> If there be any lover in the world, O Muslems, - 'tis I.
> If there be any believer, infidel, or Christian hermit - 'tis I.
> The wine-dregs, the cup-bearer, the minstrel, the harp,
>         and the music
> The beloved, the candle, the drink and the joy of the drunken -
>         'tis I.
> The two and seventy creeds and the sects in the world
> Do not really exist: I swear by God that every creed and sect -
>         'tis I.
> Earth and air, water and fire, knowest thou what they are?
> Earth and air, water and fire, nay, body and soul too - 'tis I.
> Truth and falsehood, good and evil, ease and difficulty - from
>         first to last,
> Knowledge and learning and asceticism and piety and faith - 'tis I.
> The fire of hell, be assured, with its flaming limbs,
> Yes, and paradise and the Houris - 'tis I.
> This earth and heaven with all that they hold,
> Angels, Peris, Genies and Mankind - 'tis I.  (7)

---

(7) Translated by R.A. Nicholson, The _Masnawi_.

M. Paul Vandre

I

So many children have cried
the tear
which I can not
in the bed above the bar
where I in moment exist
mention now the word of
war
of propaganda and love
for I must send forth death
accepted not, but taken
yet in the quadrangle of
burlap upon wormwood
security of verse
projects
if to view a world which is
not
red dog in cage of yellow
an entering into romantic
writings
a journey taken
upon a dream of nevermore
I and tear
have fallen

*

II

Lack of love
my brothers
I
in understanding
the oak leaf
falls
a fine garden
remains
existing unit shown
not alone
yet
without believer

*

III

Sand people
people of love sand
flowers, grass
and I exist
father is dead
yet
build me a world
of sand and rock
for in an unique
corner
lives yellow rain
captured, caught
turned on and off
to be only returned
through lonely gray
drains
yet I have the greater
uniqueness
I have the freedom
of the wind
with this
I shall live
in a world
of sand

*

IV

Love as freedom
        an uniqueness
an understanding shared
        it is lost
for you are like the dove
        I the feather
a pinion
        falls from the altitudes
to be caught by the winds
once again to return
in the fall

*

Wendell Berry


1

FEBRUARY 2, 1968

In the dark of the moon, in flying snow, in the dead of winter,
war spreading, families dying, the world in danger,
I walk the rocky hillside, sowing clover.


2

THE MAN BORN TO FARMING

The grower of trees, the gardener, the man born to farming,
whose hands reach into the ground and sprout,
to him the soil is a divine drug.  He enters into death
yearly, and comes back rejoicing.  He has seen the light lie down
in the dung heap, and rise again in the corn.
His thought passes along the row ends like a mole.
What miraculous seed has he swallowed
that the unending sentence of his love flows out of his mouth
like a vine clinging in the sunlight, and like water
descending in the dark?


3


Love, all day there has been at the edge of my mind
the wish that my life would hurry on, that my days
would pass quickly and be done with,
for I felt myself a man carrying a loose tottering bundle
along a narrow scaffold: if I could carry it
fast enough, I could hold it together to the end.

Now, leaving my perplexity and haste,
I come within the boundaries of your life, an interior
clear and calm.  You could not admit me burdened.
I approach you clean as a child of all that has been with me.
You speak to me in the dark tongue of my joy
that you do not know.  In you I know
the deep leisure of the filling moon.  May I live long.



***



96

Hayden Carruth

1.

THE GAME

    Drakes bathe
  in the brook's wide place
    where pebbles
ripple whitely beneath the water

    Preening
  stretching beating their wings
    flinging
rainbows in every direction

    Their white
  feathers a curled delicate detritus
    float and flutter
on the current's variegations

    Sunlight water
  pebbles feathers and green banks
    and then
the glistening white butterflies come

    They flutter
  close to the surface
    like feathers
inverted and reflected and imitated

    Two
  a butterfly and a feather
    almost touch and
dance downstream in a twinned fantastic dance

    Ah which
  is water which
    is air
which dancer will return which will not

    Two
  whitenesses move
    on the border
between flowing transparent worlds

    But now the drakes
  climb out on the bank
    nodding orating
looking right left and buzzing their tails

    You butterflies
  go elsewhere to play your game
    or try being serious for once--
anyway just now there'll be no more feathers.

*

THE MIST HOUR

What is it comes and
    cuts the mind in two,
the mind of things or
    more the things of mind, --
I at work with others
    in the season
when dew and mist
    come thick at six o'clock,
at work by the marsh, bending
    like the others,
still saw the things
    in which the mind delights,
harvest moon rising, soft
    in mist and silver,
the thin purple clouds,
    maples half-red half-green,
a marshland russet
    haze, russet and gray,
all in new coolness
    in which the mind delights;
but saw not wholly
    nor without distraction,
for far away some unseen
    stars exploding
in virgin magnitudes
    and planets cooling
somehow shed on my eyes
    a gaunt pathetic light,
although my friends, the others, bending
    in joy of hurting overburdened
bones, gratified in their utility,
    looked only down
like lovers into the blind
    stones of the earth;
and I cried out
    (in a way of crying out)
you, o mist-hung lavender moon, o star
    flaring in the far unseen,--
what is it comes and
    cuts the mind in two?


                    ***

Russell Edson  -  Four Moral Tales.


## 1 - DISMISSED WITHOUT A KISS

A tired cow went into her barn.
She took off her milk bag and her horns and put
them on a shelf.
She kicked off her hooves and detached her tail.
She let her ribs fall to the floor.  She dropped
her back legs. She shook her head and it fell off
...Ah, that feels good! she sighed.

When a farmer came to tuck his cow in for the night
he cried, my God, what has happened to my cow?

Oh goodnight! said the cow's milk bag.

What do you mean goodnight -are you dismissing me
without a kiss? cried the farmer.


## 2 - THE PROPHYLACTIC

He had hitched a chicken to a cart. Go chicken go,
he screamed.
Not that the chicken doesn't try, for the man pleased
is prophylactic to chicken-murder.
A woman cries from a window, what is it that the
chicken is so put to do?
It is the harness or the pot -Do you think I give
space on earth to this feathered beast other than
I milk its purpose into mine? screamed the man.
Then beat it with a whip, fool; best that it run
from pain than consider the weight of the load,
cried the woman.
No, the threat of death wins it to my will, screamed
the man, for the man pleased, as well the chicken
knows, is prophlactic to chicken-murder.

But the cart proves too heavy for the chicken. It
turns to the man and says, as you see I have tried,
but the cart proves too heavy, and I curse my ancestors for being chickens rather than horses.


## 3 - THE READING

   A fishing village. Long ago men took fish from the waters.
They saw the repeated design in the twigs of trees and in
their fishing nets. If they looked up they saw birds floating over their heads. If they looked down they saw fish
floating below their feet. The pattern more than the labor;
the shape more than the function.

99

Let us look at what we can see, said some. Look, said
one, a foot print on the beach. Soon others were able to
find many more foot prints. What does it mean? cried others.
It means our feet print themselves, cried even others. Can
other men grow out of our foot prints? It could be as we
impress our wives, so the sand impressed might yet give
rise to still another...

Look how the twigs resemble our nets!

Look, the moon is both in the sky and in the waters.
Did it daughter? Or, are they parents soon to give rise to
a hideous moon child, which drops on us like a wreath of
old man's hair?

There was an old woman which was said to know things.
And they came to her to have her read the signs.

Get out of my house, she screamed.

All right, all right, we're going, they mumbled as they
left.


4 - DURING THE TIME OF STORM

During the time of storm the good sailor finds a
certain comfort below decks in the captain's
quarters.  The captain is wont during the time of
storm to be found in the wheel-house; grown most
excited like a foolish parent.  Let this matter rest,
it speaks well of him who lets others carry the
weight of their need as preposterous concern without
help or hinder.

Are captains not like fathers who have given forth
through pleasure, more relief than joy, accidental
sons; who in the captain's ship as in the father's
house wander from one wall to another, or from
starboard to port, looking from glass areas with
little interest in an endless world made either of
water or dirt.

If the father at the end of a time of stress strikes
the son, so it is of the fatherhood that this should
be; that the father gives forth in seed a son, so
he gives forth in wrath blows against his first giving.
And that the son being something that is given so
must he take then that which is also given.


\*\*\*

Ron Seitz

AN OPEN POEM

<u>for Dad</u>, <u>the vaudeville dancer</u>

a memory of you
drug up from some depth that opened in my nighttime lonely
    musing to the ceiling
that stark image of you out of a long lost photograph clicked
    shut in the falling twenties
when you stood legs-a-spread in front of a brick wall now
    crumbled and gone too with the black dust that blew past
a torn poster of my imagination stuck ripped against the bricks
    behind and above you
a reminder of that ghost time when you tapped those skinny
    legs inside bloopy Fred Astaire pants
the gaunt white figure with cheekbones ached into your face
staring out at the street with all the dare and certainty that
    only our intelligence knows
the glint of genius beneath the black brows
letting some small part of you blow out of your brain to shoot
    a pinpoint of dark dream to the West and St. Louis and
    beyond
that selfsame small spark that lights our eye of a time when
    we were free and handsome and byGod open to anything and
    capable too
a time of white duck pants and open shirt
hair slicked black
Valentinoed to the Broadway Theatre air of a revolving crystal
    light lifting our souls before the soot and blacksmoke
    dreary pages of the thirties went up in factory stacks
    and winter hours workind the streets

that is you Dad
boneracked and white skinny in you love moods
some kind of saint all burning inside with the desire to set
    fire to you beauty for all to see
whether on a flashbulb footlight stage of clicking heels
or on streetcorner in Sunday sun with cigarette dangling white
    off an underslung scowling lip sneering hipster con kisses
    that pierced home to the heart any package of sex that
    balled by to diminish in a shift of humps the lond end
    of broadway

and what comes after is a time we can not meet
a time when the eternal panting now went up in work and was
    moneyed to exhaustion and death
a time that pinned both of us to the wheel of life

bear with me Dad I'm trying to bridge the gap
trying to reach out with words or poetry or a kiss that runs
    your ribcage through with a finger to touch the hot point
the nerve that is you and can never stop ringing

Dad let's step back across those years to when we were both

nineteen and shimmering with intelligence and cocksure
that we were beautiful
let us meet equals in our high time
no handshakes
no polite words
no fear of real contact that might send some burning shock
along our veins
let us stand both of us what we are
a white glow of pure life
that lasted only one fleeting sunny afternoon
that locked our teeth in a bitedown of proud defiance
that dared the whole world to wrest from us our own individual
personal outside-of-time immortality that no number of
years or falling hair can ever wipe away

yes Dad I walked that skinny frame with you along pavements
through dancehalls
and you too turned a leather jacket collar up and shot a
handsome glance that melted hearts in some forgotten
1954 walk through eternity with me
both of us young
and now meeting

Ronald Anthony Punnet

FORM   (For P.R.)

Underneath the
easy light/ She
exists clearly
 without contradiction/
 She could have been
  an artist/
 Just like that.
 Easily/ one of
  those women
 who have no
  close face/ No
 singular flawless
  form to look
 up close into/
  an excitement
   of eyes.
   Alice is everywhere/
   It is form after all.

THE OLD PRIEST DYING

(hands worn
   hard
  as the beads
 of his daily rosary,
  a communion of
  time and colour,
  of flesh and
   fabric, or
   the simple murder
   of self)
 cannot die easily,
 cannot practice
 escape and selfless
   prays
 a dynamite retreat,
   'Undo me God!'

WAR POEM  #2

These vagabond bullets,
   clearly a longing,
   a killers moment.
 Difficult birds
searching out god, practice
deceit.
  I am too easily
 what they say of me.
 I am driftwood in an
 ocean of blood, the
 rubbish of years.
 The Indian boy screams
   lost to all his fathers.
   "Is it a war?" My patois
 breaks him, he is drowned
 in the blood from my
 poem.  I measure my
      longing and vanish
 into thorns, tall
indian pirouettes, the
   flight of birds
      as they
 wing ass up
   at heaven.

Jonathan Greene

POEMS  FROM  THE  CHINESE


DREAMING OF LI PO

        from Tu Fu

it's all right if friends separate in death,
but when that friend still breathes-in the earth's air,
there remains this longing which the southern waters
do not answer, bring no news of you


                          & so
you're in my thoughts--  dead or alive?
how can I know:  You are distant, exiled,
by definition not here

where in the dream I saw you coming down
thru the green wood, but then fading
I lost you at the mountain pass
                         --how?
a man in prison (caught in the net of politics)
comes here?
with what-- wings?


awakening, the moon dying on the ceiling,
your face there?  deep waters, from which
waves rise (I fear) against you...



        to Tu Fu


at the top of the Mountain of Boiled Rice
I met Tu Fu wearing a bamboo hat
against the noon sun,
              but is this you
who is so thin, who writes
with such care
            that you suffer
so much
      from verse

song at the feast of the peony

          up Li Po
          and compose for the king's bidding
          tell us of the beauty of the Lady Yang

          not one
          of your old ones, for they are dead
          compared to my living lady, then Li Po

          rose out
          of the half-sleep of drink
          taking his writing brush wrote:

i/

"the clouds caught in her robe,
her face-- a soft flower,
covered with dew
I see her on the stairs
          where she stands far above earth,
far above the Mountain of Many Jewels,
she is found only
in heaven when
the moon
is high"


ii/

"perfume rises from the peony
and is watered down with dew,
and in his heart the king
dreams of her-- clouds with dawn
          and rain with dusk
sleeping in his bed
--tell me who
in all the palaces of China
has seen such beauty
except in that sleek dancer,
Flying Swallow, dressed
in her lovely robes"
                    she, who could dance
                    on the palm of
                    a hand


iii/

"they are together-- the flower
and queen, she on the stairs
lights his eyes, brings
a smile to his face,
his longing gone
with the spring
wind"

                    ***

LOUIS ZUKOFSKY is without question one of the most important poets writing in English today. Though recognized thirty five years ago by Ezra Pound he has never been accorded the kind of commercial celebration proper to "the establishment" in literature. Only recently has he begun to be published in trade editions. Two collections of short poems, All, were brought out by Norton, and recently the first half of his long autobiographical poem A 1-12 has been published by Doubleday. Zukofsky is a poet's poet, and those familiar with the little magazines and with limited editions have long known where to find and admire him. We are grateful for permission to present here a short excerpt from "Thanks to the Dictionary" which was printed in a limited edition in Japan.

JACK KEROUAC is one of the best known and most articulate voices of the Beat Generation. Author of On the Road and many other books, most recently he has published a partial autobiography, Vanity of Duluoz, (Coward McCann) which covers his Columbia days. He lives in France.

BESMILR BRIGHAM, after travelling and working in France, New York, Mexico, Central America, lives in a remote part of Arkansas with her husband. She is of French, Irish, English and Choctaw Indian blood. She has been publishing poetry in little magazines in U.S., Canada and Mexico. She writes that she is filling school notebooks with poems, and even notebooks, she says, are hard to get where she is. Bess and her husband are planning to garden, can food, get away "from all this crud of words-- to get out and go down there and dig." "Ron took the fence down and is opening it (the garden)...clear to a big tree. We can put chairs and a table down there, pick peas or corn etc., and sit in that place and prepare them, throw the debris straight back to the ground. Spring is good here..."

ALFRED STARR HAMILTON appeared in Monks Pond I, we are glad to have more of him here, and hope to present still more in the future. A book of his poems is to be published by Geof Hewitt's Kumquat Press. Lillabulero (magazine) speaks of Al as "a kind of East Coast Kenneth Patchen whose work is too little known".

RAYMOND ROSELIEP is a well known Catholic priest-poet, author of several volumes of verse. He is also published in Poetry and many other literary magazines. After teaching English for some years at Loras College, Dubuque, he is now a hospital chaplain: finds Dubuque stultifying and stifling.

EMMETT WILLIAMS returned to the U.S. this winter from Europe, bringing "piles of manuscripts from a Paris cellar." Now looking for a place to live in New York, write and carry on his work as editor of Something Else Press. His new book Sweethearts is just out, and he has edited a most impressive and important Anthology of Concrete Poetry, a dazzling book. "i wrote "the red chair" in 1958. it appeared as "der rote stuhl" in movens (dokumente und analysen zur dichtung, bildenden kunst, musik, architektur -- limes verlag, wiesbaden) in 1960, translated by daniel spoerri. the present english text is translated from spoerri's german, the original having been long ago lost."

PAUL KLEE is of course the great German painter, in whose Journals are found some poems, dreams and other literary work of high quality. We are happy to present him here in translations by the Finnish poet, ANSELM HOLLO, who lives on the Isle of Wight and is currently teaching at the University of Iowa. We hope to print some of Hollo's own poems in the next issue of MONKS POND.

GEOF HEWITT (one "F" is correct) has published in various little magazines and Lillabulero Press is bringing out a pamphlet of his poems, Waking Up Still Pickled. He is founder, editor and sole employee of Kumquat Press, which publishes Kumquat magazine, together with broadsheets and pamphlets (see Al Hamilton above). Lives in Iowa where, he says, he is: a) "striving to become apolitical" and b) "working on a definition of poetry by which I can live". ("Poetry is a figment of the imagination.") He is 24.

HALVARD JOHNSOŃ born in Newburgh, N.Y. in 1936, he grew up in the Hudson Valley, has been teaching at the University of Texas at El Paso where he says they are not rehiring him perhaps because of "wearing a beard and lowering property values". So he hopes to go to Spain. The Projections printed here are from his first book, in progress, Transparencies. (He writes: "Poems are transparent and are to be seem through ... they are also opaque, live lives of their own, are objects to be looked at, they move around, in and out of focus, they impinge on us... no poem is entirely transparent or entirely opaque... Williams is more transparent than Pound, Ashbery is more opaque than O'Hara.")

ROBERT ZMUDA is a High School senior in Pittsburgh. After graduation he plans to go into Vista. This is his first publication. He is 18.

GEORGE HITCHCOCK lives in San Francisco where he edits Kayak, one of the best poetry magazines in the country. He recently published a handsome book of poetry, The Dolphin with a Revolver in its Teeth (Unicorn Press).

REZA ARASTEH is a native of Iran, has taught and lectured at the University of Tehran, Princeton, N.Y.U., Harvard, Virginia, and now teaches at George Washington University. His articles appear in psychoanalytical and Islamic Journals. He has published several books, including a study of Rumi, the Sufist poet and mystic, and his latest, Final Integration in the Adult Personality, a remarkable application of Sufist insights to psychoanalysis. It is published in English by E. J. Brill of Leiden (Holland). Of this book Gordon Allport writes: "It deals with a problem almost totally neglected in Western thought, viz., the most comprehensive of attitude levels. How fragmented are most of our Western approaches! We look at bits and pieces of human nature, never at the final intention..." This same approach in depth marks the essay we are proud to present here.

M. PAUL VANDRE is a young unpublished poet, at present a GI in Vietnam. Lorine Niedecker brought him to our attention. He lives in Wisconsin.

WENDELL BERRY teaches English at the University of Kentucky where he is active in the Peace Movement. He lives at Port Royal, a village on the Kentucky River, where he has a farm. He publishes poetry in literary magazines everywhere (Hudson Review, etc.) and recently also a novel, A Place on Earth (Harcourt, Brace and World). He and Ralph Eugene Meatyard are working on a book about the Red River (Kentucky).

HAYDEN CARRUTH is a former editor of Poetry, author of several volumes of verse, a novel (Appendix A) a book about Camus (After the Stranger). He lives with his wife and young son on a farm in Vermont from which he wrote this winter: "Two evenings ago our duck escaped her pen, floundered through four-foot snow to the brook, went swimming in a hole in the ice. A duck, i.e. not one of the drakes in the poem; a duck named Cepanjin, of whom we are fond. I thought I could retrieve her, so I waded into the hole; but she panicked, zipped past me, and disappeared under the ice, headed downstream: 200 feet or more to the next breathing hole. We were all very sad that night. But next morning when I went down to the brook there she was, swimming contentedly in her ice-hole. Wild hurrahs. The kid danced, the wife danced, I'd have danced myself except for the arthritis. Things, especially live ones, do have a way of coming to the surface again. And long live your mag.

RUSSELL EDSON lives in Stamford, Connecticut, is an artist and writer whose prose fables appeared in a volume The Very Thing That Happens introduced by Denise Levertov and illustrated by the author (New Directions). He also publishes regularly in New Directions anthologies and in little mags. He has written, illustrated and printed another collection of fables, The Brain Kitchen, on his own press (Thing Press). It is a beautiful book.

RON SEITZ a Louisville poet and author of (unpublished) novel, Somewhere the Other Side, teaches at Bellarmine College. The best way to introduce him is in his own words: "born 1935 innocent a baby poet till after gradeschool miracle visions & highschool pole-vaulting natural handsome athlete, then Florida beach Army California Boston far west Huachuca ol Mexico to Kentucky college & out again on the road South Southwest the Coast LA to Frisco & grad school to Majorca Hollywood back in Kentucky teaching Bellarmine now-- poems along the way & grocery paperboy caddy landscape lifeguard garbageman gravedigger salesman bartender probationofficer Radio TV factory research carpenter tilesetter sewers construction executive mailman greenskeeper advertising industry warehouse teacher writer now lover at 32 & still beautiful & married a lovely girl Sally & so three boys Dylan Sean Casey". This year Ron is on sabbatical leave and will work on a new book, a biography.

RONALD ANTHONY PUNNET was born in Trinidad on New Year's Day, 1946. Though a British citizen he is in the U.S. Army at Fort Benning. He writes: "I have been in this country for 13 years... I have been messing with poetry for 5 years and was (before the Army) Poetry Editor of the Ninth Circle of Las Cruces New Mexico."

JONATHAN GREENE appeared in MONKS POND I (see notes there) is still working in Lexington (rather than Dublin) and helps a lot with MONKS POND.

RALPH EUGENE MEATYARD is one of an avant garde group of Lexington photographers who has been working through a kind of lyric and sardonic surrealism to a photographic abstract expressionism of which we show two examples here (some woods near the monastery of Gethsemani -- a New England sailing-ship-for-tourists.) The other photos include one of his son Chris in the home of the Great Rudabagga and the poet Jonathan Williams as Harvest Spirit. The cover photo is clearly political.

ROBERT LAX has been writing and publishing mostly Concrete Poetry recently, since his book Circus in the Sun. He returned from several years in Greece, this winter, and is now in Olean, N.Y.

Robert Lax

| | |
|---|---|
| one | one |
| blade | blade |
| of | of |
| green | green |
| | |
| one | one |
| blade | blade |
| of | of |
| yel- | yel- |
| low | low |
| | |
| one | one |
| blade | blade |
| of | of |
| yel- | yel- |
| low | low |
| | |
| one | one |
| blade | blade |
| of | of |
| green | green |

win-
ter

grass.

# Cratis Thebani Cynici philosophi
Ep̄lc aureis sententiis referte theologie consentanee.

Pallia non Cynicum faciunt atriqȝ cuculli
Non baculus curuus pera nec ipsa facit
Ast animus recti semper seruatoȝ et equi
Et qui fortune spernere dona potest

# MONKS POND

NO. 3   FALL   1968

# IN MEMORY OF MARTIN LUTHER KING

AS NATURALIZED US CITIZEN I AM VERY SORRY
I HAVE BEEN KILL THREATENED
GUNPOINTED ASSAULTED BATTERED INJURED
KNIFE STICKED ARM ROBBED BY BOTH WHITE AND COLORS
I LEARNED VIOLENCE DOES NOT PAY
BATTLES ARE WON IN JUSTICE COURT
SOMETIMES
PLEASE ACCEPT MY MOST SINCERE
CONDOLENCES
LONG LIVE
YOUR HUSBANDS MEMORY

(Signed)  HUMBLENESS NOBODY US LATIN.

(This telegram, one among hundreds sent to Mrs.
Coretta King, is printed here with her permission.)

MONKS POND III

Contents

[Should be Ron Seitz, 164—not Robert Bonazzi]

MONKS POND is a literary magazine specializing in new
creative work by known and unknown authors, and excluding
all forms of critical writing. Past issues have included
texts on Zen and Sufism, and the next issue will also present more of these, together with new Spanish-American,
French and Polish verse in translation. This is the third
of four planned issues. The next will be the last, and no
more contributions are being accepted. The Pond is overflowing. In fact, the body of water, barely guessed at in
the misty cover photo of this issue, is the Pacific Ocean.
Those poets who have waited months before hearing from us
about their manuscripts will understand why we do not continue publication. It involves too many letters. Nevertheless, the experience of running this magazine has been
most rewarding. You find out there are more good writers
around than you had imagined. And you make a lot of new
friends. The magazine has not been formally on sale.
Small gifts of money to help cover expenses have not been
refused, and we are grateful to those who have sent something. A few copies of the earlier issues are still available. The final issue will be sent on request.

CHRISTOPHER MEATYARD

Inner Light  No. 1

Here I meditate
above the once living, and below the ever
     moving
beside the unforgotten holders and beside
     the tightly woven cloth in which
     the flowing explorer realizes the beginning
here it is, where only a few find it.
Where it's happening,
when everything you do is bound in the inner light.


MARK VAN DOREN

St. Mary's Hermitage, Gethsemani

The monastery bells can still be heard there.
Or can they?  I don't know.  I went down once
By the winding path, and all I listened to was trees:
Not huge, but many and high, and busy
With birds; and the top leaves
Twinkled in sun, as did his eyes when he said at last,
"Here is my cell."  But it was a house,
New-built: a small one, with a porch.
And still I listened to the trees, incessant, sacred:
More than I could count.  And acorns dropped,
And squirrels scampered.  Foxes too,
He told me, played some days in the distance,
Wary of man—even of him—yet they did caper,
Lighter of foot than cats.
I must have heard the bells, but more as air, as spicy wood,
Than bronze; as sun, as shade; as silence;
As contemplation, searching an unknown tongue.

CHARLES SIMIC

The Seed

1.

I know this slow stirring.
The earth imagines its bones.
The stone is changed to blood.

Shoot up, bloom, sister!

With your newly grown teeth
Hold on
To your first breath.

2.

A secret seed
Has sprouted.
The rot it bears to the world
Is holy.

3.

Heart to its darkness
For some unknown purpose
Opens sight.

Under the closed eye-lids
The soul looks.
The grasses step out of it
And birds' voices.

4.

And suddenly!
The grain of dust
Learns its name.

When the wind blows
It will not rise.

Forest

1.

A place of twilight
Of the wind
Of the distant
Sound of the wind.

There's no one.
Nothing stirs in it.
There's only silence

With enormous eyes
Of a horse grazing.

Water, in a place
Only a bird knows,

Its scent drifting.

There's a stone
Where the fox
Sharpens its teeth,

And under it
The chill
Of the coming night;

Dry twigs, moss...

Inside my sleeping body:
Dim whiteness,
Stripped bones--
Ancient Winter!

2.

And the trees...

Dark sea twisting
Its own waves
High above the earth

Calling for what boats now,
Whose drowned sailors?

A wave plunges
Into the night
Sweeping the stars and the moon
On its way

Until it breaks
And returns

Feeble, flute-like

Bearing with it
A single
Trembling
Dark leaf.

3.

It is cold.
The earth under my body
Is old.  It draws me
To itself,

To its stones, to its salt,
To its buried forests.

My dusk dissolves
Into its huge night.

The extinct wolf
And the anchorite monk
Are restored.

In my heart
Their frost
Glitters.

WARREN LANG

sun poems

i

in the silent grass--
hung in trees
the sun

ii

swirling trees--
the sun's
the wind's eye

iii

moon's flat light--
i dream
the sun in my belly

poems of creation

1. we wind in the bowels of trees
   love  love  making a spiral of love making
   untwisting the turns of bark
   the naked flowing tree in the sun

2. the circle of our bodies seeds the sun
   the sun bursts its shell
   the moon's our birth

3. who is my body
   listens in ocean's center

4. the sun's my blood that rings my love's veins

5. earth's worms are unshelled moons
   grass's body flickers birth in our bellies
   we are circles of unborn sun


four other poems

iii
when the lights go on
the dark gets darker.

i
stars
still beads
in a pond

outside
the factory
is running itself down.

ripples
        of breath

people are meddling
with the insides
of their houses.
the houses stand
guarded by their shadows.

ii
the end of must.
trees run
in their own shadows.
feathered dogs
gods
to give hearts to.
the face you forgot
spirals in the window.

outside
strange sounds
build graves
fifty feet high.

iv
the blood's, the sun's
the river's end
the touch of small flesh

PENTTI SAARIKOSKI


Une Vie

But when Grandpa, the miner, came back from the States
spouting tales wild and woolly, his teeth
slanting backwards, his pockets empty
and said Now darling, how about building that house
Grandma picked up her scissors and struck him through
     the heart



120 miles from Leningrad

Helsinki is where I live.
Helsinki is the capital of Finland.
It lies by the sea 120 miles to the west of Leningrad.
Helsinki is an expanding city, and the rents are high.
We sit here surrounded by our forests, backs turned to the giant
 and stare at his image in a well's eye.  He wears a dark suit,
 white shirt, silver-grey tie.  In his country everything is
 quite different, there people walk on or without their heads.
We sit here in the midst of our very own forests,
but far away in the West there is a land where huge eyes float
 by the shore, and they can see us here.
Helsinki is in the process of reconstruction, according to the
 plans made by Mr. Alvar Aalto.



of pure practical intelligence

            First seek ye the kingdom of pure
          practical intelligence

        shreds of posters and headlines
            shards of gramophone records feathers

     lights shining arcs
         the well-lit borders

       when the rush-hour comes
        and the hour of the pile-up
       and the sounds of breaking steel-plate and people
              are heard in the dark


     when the journey is broken, no one is on the right road

Pope and Czar

            I have been listening
                  to my heart for a long time
                      the white screen the way
                  that discus-thrower moves
                  the tombs of Tarquinia

Pope and Czar
Metternich and Guizot
The French radicals the German police

    Which people lives the way this dead one knew

UNTO ETERNAL PEACE

     the black automobile
     the lion and no other beast

   I have been driving
   through the white screen for a long time to my heart


cold globules pass through the heart

       cold globules pass through the heart

             I want to get out from inside you
        listen
            the trees
         scratching against one another

             light and warmth in the café
                 or the certainty
           of a number or letter seen
                 from a bus window every day

             now I stand by the wall
                alone
         and the disaster cannot be averted


and goes on and has been going on

    in his famous History of the Revolution Trotsky recounts
             how Lenin
    when Lenin wore spectacles and a wig
                when it was raining
        in St. Petersburg
       Mother Russia was giving birth
           to a child
      that was to become

when they've stopped serving drinks
            the customers have been chased away
        the chairs stacked up on the tables
                and the cashier is counting the take
    when you look at it all from outside
        and business is as usual
            and goes on and has been going on

that automobile looks worth a fortune and I am sheer
                    darkness like an angel
                outflying the speed of its own light


ALLEN NEFF


Cosmic Cyclist

He suddenly wheeled his kingdom
round and reigned his vagrant blood
to shackle chassis, body, wheel
to wheel, in epicyclic chrome.

Renowned of girls, he blest their raised
meat offerings in smoke and revved
up eucharistic cans he gulped for power
gripped on handle bars of praise.

The clutch coughed, popped the pealing son
who princely left the laymen
to his blessed tracks in squealing hymns
and felt his magic levitation,

his shifting circles of ascent--
black-jacket ritual in gear
with sharpened fortune--skid and slip
in orbited abandonment.

The isle of death
Where wander figures in the noontime sun.
One stops to look at his watch, dissolves.
Another weeps and the third,
Wandering alone in woods,
Becomes the trees.  High birds are silent
Looking down, and the noon frowns.
A man perchance comes by and looks.
Night's upon us, say the birds and fly
Away.  The men—or ghosts—for what are they
Who wander in the Isle of Dead?
Walk on, not one moment sped
Beyond their mournful walk.  No sooner than
The dew is rent than they fall
Into the fathomless earth where birds,
Tender birds, have birth, and the noon calls.


America lover machine

Cupolas and anxiety

Lick my tongue

The palms blush

Lick Harlem

Oh wind

&

Song rise timid-

powerful like sea

in this boat

and sink us

into our blood

JUNE J. YUNGBLUT

Beckett:  Art As Impasse

In a dialogue some twenty years ago with Georges Duthuit on the
painter Tal Coat, Beckett claimed that "the only thing disturbed by the
revolutionaries Matisse and Tal Coat is a certain order on the plane of
the feasible." Duthuit, who has stated elsewhere that he was under the
impression that a painter's function was to express, by means of paint,
asks Beckett what other plane there can be "for the maker." The dialogue continues:

> B.  Logically none.  Yet I speak of an art turning from it in
> disgust, weary of its puny exploits, weary of pretending
> to be able, of being able, of doing a little better the
> same old thing, of going a little further along a dreary
> road.
>
> D.  And preferring what?
>
> B.  The expression that there is nothing to express, nothing
> with which to express, nothing from which to express, no
> power to express, no desire to express, together with the
> obligation to express.
>
> D.  But that is a violently extreme and personal point of
> view, of no help to us in the matter of Tal Coat.

Beckett's "violently extreme and personal point of view" has continued to dominate his work.  It is the point of view which gives a
perverse kind of hermeneutics to his work which allows meaning to e-
merge through the act of submerging all possible statements of meaning.  Beckett's continuing analysis culminates in the statement on art
as failure in Dialogue III:

126

There are many ways in which the thing I am trying in
vain to say may be tried in vain to be said....The pathetic
antithesis possession-poverty was perhaps not the most tedious. But we begin to weary of it, do we not? The real-
isation that art has always been bourgeois, though it may
dull our pain before the achievements of the socially pro-
gressive, is finally of scant interest. The analysis of
the relation between the artist and his occasion, a relation always regarded as indispensable, does not seem to
have been very productive either, the reason being perhaps
that it lost its way in disquisitions on the nature of occasion. It is obvious that for the artist obsessed with
his expressive vocation, anything and everything is doomed
to become occasion....But if the occasion appears as an
unstable term of relation, the artist, who is the other
term, is hardly less so, thanks to his warren of modes
and attitudes.

Nearly twenty years before the dialogue on painting took place,

Beckett had written about the instability of relation because of the

effect on the self of time as he saw it worked out in Proust's A la

recherche du temps perdu. According to Beckett we cannot escape from

yesterday because we have deformed yesterday or been deformed by it.

It is irremediably part of us, within us, "heavy and dangerous." Be-

cause of this yesterday within us, "we are other, no longer what we

were before the calamity of yesterday."

Beckett is not referring to the content of yesterday. Whether

good or evil, he says, it has no reality or significance; the only

world that has reality and significance is the "world of our own latent

consciousness, and its cosmography has suffered a dislocation." Aspira-

tions of yesterday do not have validity for today's ego; therefore at-

tainment, which Beckett defines as "the identification of the subject

with the object of his desire," is impossible. In fact, "the subject

has died—and perhaps many times—on the way."

The occasion of art as an unstable term of relation plus the artist as the other unstable term of relation give us, in Beckett's analysis as he continues the dialogue with Duthuit, a dualistic view of the creative process. All that should concern us, according to Beckett,

> is the acute and increasing anxiety of the relation itself, as though shadowed more and more darkly by a sense of invalidity, of inadequacy, of existence at the expense of all that it excludes, all that it blinds to...(we should) submit wholly to the incoercible absence of relation, in the absence of terms or, if you like, in the presence of unavailable terms, admit that to be an artist is to fail, as no other dare fail, that failure is his world...

The problem of the relationship between the interior and the exterior for the artist is the Sisyphus stone the artist must continue to roll up the hill—without yet reaching the top where there might be rest. The artist, perhaps "innocent" as Beckett felt himself to be, has inherited the aftermath of a broken world order. On the linear plane of history we can no longer discover an analogy to the cosmological order of the gods. In effect, the breakdown between the two worlds has left us in the situation of Sisyphus; tortured criminals, as Miss Jane Harrison puts it in her classic study, <u>Prolegomena to the Study of Greek Religion</u>, are all offenders against Olympian Zeus. We infer that we have been rebels because we know we are under sentence. It is the theme of Camus' <u>Myth of Sisyphus</u>; Kafka's <u>The Trial</u>, "In a Penal Colony"; and much of modern existentialist writing.

Malone's Sisyphus-stone moves in a horizontal direction, but it is the same journey without end; it is the journey of a writer who has nothing to write because there is nothing to write about but is under compulsion, nevertheless, to continue to write.

> My little finger glides before my pencil across the page and
> gives warning, falling over the edge, that the end of the line
> is near. But in the other direction, I mean of course ver-
> tically, I have nothing to guide me. I did not want to write,
> but I had to resign myself to it in the end.

Martin Esslin, in his introduction to a collection of essays on
Beckett, describes this paradox of the artist who finds himself in a
world where there is not satisfactory metaphysical explanation (certainly
to the artist, if not to others) that can direct or give meaning to his
work. Esslin concludes:

> If, in happier periods of history the artist could have no
> doubt that by his work he was exalting the glory of the Crea-
> tor, that he was striving to capture a glow of those eternal
> canons of the beautiful that remained pristine and unchange-
> able forever in some celestial sphere beyond the physical uni-
> verse; today, if he has lost the faith, religious or secular,
> of his predecessors, he is left to fend for himself, without
> intelligible purpose in a world devoid of meaning. And yet
> the urge, the inescapable compulsion to express—but what?—
> remains embedded, as strongly as ever, in the artist's nature.
> A situation that is as absurd as it is tragic, yet for all
> that, a brave, an heroic position, challenging as it does
> the ultimate nothingness...

As a mystic deprived of the vision of God, Beckett may have to
await the neo-Barthian word of God breaking through from the other
side. Or, as a mystic, only momentarily in history deprived of the
vision of God, he may find the "journey" is parallel to a "dark night
of the soul" and that emergence beyond the impasse will become possible
through the union of Word with word and Self with self, if the self remains open to faith while discarding worn-out words and hollow tradition.

129

There is an alternative to these possibilities. Perhaps Beckett is best described as already having chosen it. It would be characterized as contentment at remaining on this side of the impasse because of finding aesthetic fulfillment in shaping the content and form of failure in expression. Jean-Jacques Mayoux is trying to render this alternative visible in his description of "The Theatre of Samuel Beckett":

> Beckett's theater turns in upon itself, seeks to coincide with itself in a pure theatrical reality, much as three generations of symbolists sought, successively, a pure poetic reality, a pure pictorial reality, a pure fictional reality....This quest for an artistic truth that is both immediate and necessary, that is divorced from all social preoccupation, is the evidence of honest pessimism. When all fabrications of what we call civilization, all collective structures, are rejected as illusory, when all worldly activity is viewed as vain, useless, ridiculous; nothing remains but the consciousness of ourselves, and the forms of expression which we can given (sic) to that consciousness. This kind of theater, turning in upon itself, turns back also to its beginnings in the medieval Christian world: an Everyman in which the stripping bare and final nakedness of man would be relieved neither by reward nor comfort, in which all such alleviation would appear only as a kind of thinking void, and where this awareness would spin round and round in self-declared abjection.

The seeming perversity which causes Beckett to continue to refuse to succour his characters and his audience with a new metaphysic, has both a rational and a moral explanation and justification at its core. In one of the few interviews he has allowed about his work, he referred to the "confusion" and "mess" all around us and concluded that

> our only chance now is to let it in. The only chance of renovation is to open our eyes and see the mess....One cannot speak any more of being, one must speak only of the mess. When Heidegger and Sartre speak of a contrast between being and existence, they may be right. I don't know, but I am not a philosopher. One can only speak of what is in front of him, and that now is simply the mess.

Therefore, according to Beckett's view, it is not possible to speak of a metaphysical framework which might give meaning to existence or shape to the chaos. His characters are in the mess, taking it in, quite literally, in Comment c'est:

> the tongue gets clogged with mud that can happen too only one
> remedy then pull it in and suck it swallow the mud or spit it
> out it's one or the other...I fill my mouth with it...it's
> another of my resources...question if swallowed would it
> nourish and opening up of vistas they are good moments...

Beckett's characters continue to crawl through the labyrinthine mud seeking the way out of the impasse, which is not yet possible, or death, which is not yet possible, or silence, which is not yet possible. "There are enormous pressures in our world that seek to induce mankind to bear the loss of faith and moral certainties," says Esslin, "by being drugged into oblivion." Against these pressures, he continues, the need to confront man with the reality of his situation is greater than ever, for it is this confrontation which gives man dignity if he is able to face reality "in all its senselessness; to accept it freely, without fear, without illusions--and to laugh at it." This is the stubborn morality at the heart of Beckett's perverseness. A critical assessment must accept his metaphysic of the work of art, then analyze what goes on within it, before bringing to bear on his work the perspective from differing world-views.

This approach indicates continued research along the line of what Artaud means by "essential drama," what Beckett, writing about Proust, means by "the essential Idea," and what implicit and not yet discovered structures of thought lurk in the shadows of Beckett's universe. His work should be watched for any emerging breakthrough of what he himself has termed his "impasse." If this occurs, we may see an ensuing wave of creative writing in which the verbal terms of Nothingness force the universe through its meshes like a sieve. Perhaps when that has run its course, at least in the metaphysical world of Beckett's work of art, the "I" will at last say "me," or the death of all writing will ensue—or Godot will finally come, not tomorrow or yesterday, but today.

ALFRED STARR HAMILTON

### best wishes

supposing you poured forth
your noodle in this manner
supposing that's all you could do
presupposing and positive enough
to have added that kind of a preposition
and made your best wishes out of noodle soup
supposing that's all you could do
supposing you added nothing else that was savory
like they all do
supposing you never went fishing in the bowl
supposing you guarded this little with your spoon
supposing your name were Williams
supposing any of this fizzled
supposing you were an outcast
supposing you were a paleface
supposing you came to these conclusions
supposing you knew of oodles too
supposing you were a somnambulist
supposing anywheres else you lost
your noodle in this manner

## Lucky

I could say
Seven comes eleven
Hoodlums
I could have paved the road
For miles ahead
I could add the blocks up
To Providence


## Goldhunter

I know this is an anthill
I know this has lion's claws
I know there is no end to this
I know this is over a golden coin
I know this is my living room for relatives
I know I have given my veins to the vain and sultry climbers
I am the lame earth


## Cotton

Look at that blue woven blanket
Look at what the sun did today
Look at the ink
Look at our penmanship
Look at an essay from here to the fields
Look at those hospital sheets
Look at the irk through our fingertips
Look at the irk that is left behind the clouds


## Dawn

I'd like the yellow pencil that comes out of those night clouds
I'll come to the bright Japanese maple vine
I'd like a red Japanese jewel
I'd like a scarlet jewel
I'd like a shawl to put over its shoulders
I'd like a shawl to put over the voice of the poor

## Club Steak Dinner

I wondered once
If I considered
Cauliflower leaves
That are shaped
Like clubs

I wondered once
If I considered
The sterling sauce
To have been
For a cloud

I wondered once
If I considered
The blue sky
To have been
For a policeman

I wondered once
If I considered
The gold wings
Slanting off of
The windowpane
To have been
For the guiliflower of gold

I wondered once
If I considered
The brass buttons
On military coats
To have been
For the yellow beans

I wondered once
If I considered
The hand of a soldier
To have been
For the slaughter

I wondered once
If I considered
The rain on the platter
And whatever was the matter
To have been for the juice
Off of the fat of the hand

I wondered once
If I considered
The blue sky
To have been
For a policeman
At the dumbfounded doorway


## Black Widow Spider

For I'll remember you for your girlhood
For I'll remember a shining girl officer
For I'll remember one good and hard girl diamond
For I'll remember you through your red hour glass
For I'll remember you for one good scorching police whistle
For I'll remember you at your pretty desk
For I'll remember you for your black velvet claws
For I'll remember your asking for our attentive silence
For I'll remember staring at you by the hour
For I'll remember your gazing back at ourselves
For once I'll remember the dark tussle
For I'll remember your daring threats
For I'll remember you for years afterwards
For I'll remember you after dark

134

OTTO RENE CASTILLO

(translated by Margaret Randall)


Something More Than Force

<u>for you, who must feel the pain</u>
<u>of this absence too</u>

I

It's a sharp august dusk
and I say to you all,
now I am sadder than ever.
Perhaps nobody knows
as you do, my love,
no that I'm only
a long succession of cries
                            within you.
Far away,
with blows they have broken my joy
inside you,
still they can't understand my hands
that so suddenly ripped
the dark wind from your face.


II

They don't want
                my rivers
to flow to you.
                They don't like
your wings
        to fly to me.

They want to ignore
the gesture of your lips
and they've put a dark cross
on the name you love
to repeat.

But, love,
they cannot erase your heart
in the far away depths of your breast
as it beats my tenderness.

They can't, love,
tear you from the heights
you live in my eyes.

They can't, my love,
rip you out of my life
because, like the sea,
I too keep something of your name
in me.

135

projections 1

there were things he could speak of
to no one
           & having no confessor
he would write them in narrow-lined notebooks,
locking them first in a drawer of his desk,
then piling them on a closet shelf,
burning them finally & stirring the ashes with a stick

one night, on a bus to Montreal,
he unburdened himself to the wife of a man he didn't know,
who listened in the darkness
& carried it away
with her


projections 8

in Juarez
one Pedro Morales, a civil servant
roams the streets, throwing poisoned meat
to the dogs, flinging
their deflated carcasses
onto the back of his truck

farther south
the Federales burn marijuana patches
& poppy fields

in many parts of the world
men stoop to the doors of ovens & furnaces
banking the coals, faces the color of fire

Pedro Morales watches
the burning of his dogs, the firing
of the oven, the flaming village

behind him
his shadow
takes on heroic proportions

projections 14

the female animal-tamer
reclining on leopard-skin pillows
surrounded by an all-male, animal cast

      the problem, he finds, is achieving
      incident, without detracting
      at the same time from the central voluptuary

teeth bared, breasts prominent, hips
curving toward oblivion
               whip in her hand


projections 40

    coming across trees
    parched & angry
    deciding that she
    deserves whatever happens
    to her now, finding
    water in the shadow--

        to sleep then & wake
        conscious perhaps
        that some things were
        not as bad as they'd seemed

     relaxing, forgetting
     shooting a rabbit for supper


CZESLAW MILOSZ

(translated by Czeslaw Milosz and Peter Dale Scott)


Sentences

What constitutes the training of the hand?
I shall tell what constitutes the training of the hand.
One suspects that something is wrong with transcribing signs.
But the hand transcribes such signs as it has learned.
Then it is sent to the school of blots and scrawls
Till it forgets what's graceful. For even the sign of a butterfly
Is a well with a coiled poisonous smoke inside.
Perhaps we should have represented him otherwise
Than in the form of a dove. As fire, yes, but that is beyond us.
For even when it consumes logs on a hearth

We search in it for eyes and hands.  Let him then be green,
All blades of calamus, on footbridges over meadows
Running, stumping his bare feet.  Or in the air
Blowing a birchbark trumpet so strongly that further down
There tumbles from its blast a crowd of petty officials,
Their uniforms unbuttoned and their women's combs
Flying like chips when the axe strikes.

And yet it's too great responsibility to lure the souls
From where they lived together with the idea of the hummingbird,
The chair and the star.
To imprison them within either-or: male sex, female sex,
So that they wake up in the blood of childbirth, weeping.


LINDY HOUGH


The Coin Game

Insulates
each throw is important
brings us to the fore
before we're ready, ready communication to each other
breathing heavily—
tossed, out of doors
which hold us in, a bell
which rings, the dizziness of
hitting it at the same time, first
you, then very quickly me, our
own style, the crack it sits on, those
dizzying moments of pleasure, then settle
back, hum your own tune and
go again, each to his fore
always before we are ready.

These things sit on the back yard space.
A divider from a box of cookies, your hair
which i raked in a pretext of raking
the long grasses to see whether there was
spring grass underneath yet, and spawned
again the confusion between a pseudo-
Christian concern for keeping the yard nice
for the others who live here also/ and
essential lack of genuine feeling, since i
hate our neighbors here, deplore almost
everything they do as immoral and careless;
a bookcase you made sits there also: originally
a place for the bottle of cider filmed to sit on
i think and then a place for aaron to put his cookies
now the cats sit in it and are weighty tomes

# ADULT LEARNING

une synthèse
des connaissances
actuelles

OOOOOOOOOOOOOOOOOOOOOOOOOOOOOO
OOOOOOOOOOOOOOOOOOOOOOOOOOOO
OOOOOOOOOOOOOOOOOOOOOOOOOO
OOOOOOOOOOOOOOOOOOOOOOOO
OOOOOOOOOOOOOOOOOOOOOO
OOOOOOOOOOOOOOOOOOOO
OOOOOOOOOOOOOOOOOO
OOOOOOOOOOOOOOOO
OOOOOOOOOOOOOO
OOOOOOOOOOOO
OOOOOOOOOO
OOOOOOOO
OOOOOO
OOOO
OO
O

O
OOO
OOOOO
OOOOOOO
OOOOOOOOO
OOOOOOOOOOO
OOOOOOOOOOOOO
OOOOOOOOOOOOOOO
OOOOOOOOOOOOOOOOO
OOOOOOOOOOOOOOOOOOO
OOOOOOOOOOOOOOOOOOOOO
OOOOOOOOOOOOOOOOOOOOOOO
OOOOOOOOOOOOOOOOOOOOOOOOO
OOOOOOOOOOOOOOOOOOOOOOOOOOO
OOOOOOOOOOOOOOOOOOOOOOOOOOOOO

EMMETT WILLIAMS

**SENSE SOUND**

**SONSE SEUND**

**SOUSE SENND**

**SOUNE SENSD**

**SOUND SENSE**

| | | | |
|---|---|---|---|
| black | black | white | black |
| black | black | white | black |
| black | black | white | black |
| black | black | white | black |
| black | black | white | black |
| | | white | |
| | | white | |
| white | white | | white |
| white | white | | white |
| white | white | white | white |
| white | white | white | white |
| white | white | white | white |
| | | white | |
| | | white | |
| black | black | | black |
| black | black | white | black |
| black | black | white | black |
| | | white | |
| white | white | | white |
| white | white | | white |
| white | white | | white |
| | | | |
| black | black | | black |
| black | black | | black |
| black | black | | black |
| black | black | | black |
| black | black | | black |

lustig
luslustigtig
lusluslustigtigtig
luslusluslustigtigtigtig
lusluslusluslustigtigtigtigtig
luslusluslusluslustigtigtigtigtigtig
lusluslusluslusluslustigtigtigtigtigtigtig
luslusluslusluslusluslustigtigtigtigtigtigtigtig

ERNST JANDL

ROBERT LAX

| | |
|---|---|
| OVID | DIVO |
| VOID | DIOV |
| IDOV | IOVD |
| VIDO | OVID |

| | |
|---|---|
| VOID | DIOV |
| DVOI | OIVD |
| IDVO | OVID |
| OIDV | VOID |

| | |
|---|---|
| IVOD | DOVI |
| VIDO | OVID |
| OVID | VIDO |
| DOVI | IVOD |

| | |
|---|---|
| DVOI | VOID |
| IDVO | VIDO |
| OIDV | IDOV |
| VOID | DIVO |

| | |
|---|---|
| OVID | DIVO |
| VOID | DIOV |
| IDOV | IOVD |
| VIDO | OVID |

G 16

**beba coca cola**
**babe        cola**
**beba coca**
**babe cola  caco**
**caco**
**cola**

**cloaca**

DECIO PIGNATARI

to us drinking our tea in the sunshine,
all this we know;
what do we not know.  The insides of things.
The juxtaposition of grain and wheat to flour,
the river carrying sticks and leaves and oil
in lazy flotilla, what is and what can be seen,
and what we make and what is made as by-product.
The juices we spew out      and our aim, if
we are concerned, and the effect, if
we are not concerned.


### The Days

Had it been right, had it been wrong
days of conception and rhythm
dancing to the days, the days enfolding all the movements
the music enfolds the movements, carries them,
without the movements the music still focuses them—
the involuntary stare on the center figure
by the powdered madam in a high white box on the side

the house swells by its movements, breathing
lying on its side
belly too full to lie on, where are we going,
into what power
and what encumbrance of ourselves do we lead our own heads


### ELAINE KNIGHT


### Observation

Change is the color of dawn.
Morning rhythms melt the darkness.
Light is a slow invader.


### Reflection

Gathering thorns,
We missed the roses.
Harvests are the harvesters.

BESMILR BRIGHAM

## The Tiger-God Legend

Tigre Mejoran

led a man to the dead forest
the forest of dead tress, all
dead in a dead land, and he--
the man,
went of his own will going
for the beauty of the Mejoran

for the Mejoran
was without compare beautiful
in her dew-sun striped fur--
luminous yellow of corn life,
broken through blending with
the black blue-fire war paint--;
her head cut clean in shadows
as the moon cuts through the heavens
and her jade eyes
lay like two stones
deep-washed in the underground
rivers to the sacrificial
priests' ponds of zenotes.

the yellow of her hair
was of a color
flung from the corn-maidens' hair
among the blue flesh paint
deep below in the dull of water

and the young man
without fear followed her;
though her cry
was such a going-down cry
from the open spaces
lingering of itself in air
as the bush-girl made--
she of the rare red hair,
caught sleeping under the arch of
a dead tree log and thrown
into the jade fire-eyes,
strangled in unbelief screaming.

but the Mejoran
turned the man not into a god
as his wild feet
running for shadows

sang to him over the
crackling sounds dead brush
makes, but only
into another of the dead trees;
and his arms
fell out stiff from the trunk
his stiff body made,
all without sap or leaves

young men
sleep after--afraid
to go into the road at night;
yet how often
the Mejoran calls at their window,
though the forest of dead
belief
has been burned by a fire
caused by the lightning


tiger and dancer

                        in the wood
"I see all there is," the tiger said

stalking shape in shadow, I
see dancing bird
                    (wings of falcon
in the sky

"I see leaping tiger," said the bird
light-ness of cloud
I sail in the sun's eye

I come down into man and dance he said

"when man dances it is I"--
said the tiger in her lair


        The Tigre Can Be a Thought

        For thought
        is a thing hunted down
        like the tigre
        Mejoran.

He springs
in the night
and no one
can know from where;

his dark shape
covers the body
in rush of fur
before the kill
and not one
can catch the sight of him.

'Dance'
the heart says;
and great is the dance,
intense and without bounds wild
of one
caught in the will of the Mejoran.

Blood burns
fierce with desire,
but there is no fire
like that
that burns in the eyes of the Mejoran,
or pulses
in leap of starlight,
caught in darkness,
against his shallow flank:
no fire
that burns so clean in death.
His massive paws,
strung with thorns, are
daggers--death for death.

Only the
most
fearsome or brave
dare

search for
or follow him;
and still--
and rare,
is the silence of the Mejoran.

Conquistador


      following banner the holy cross
 i    desire for conquest a very natural
      thing

      not to be blamed
      perilous
      imposition of religion as
      empire in faith--to govern
      (an art toward God

      Cristos and Madonnas
      living presence--
      personal
      against the subjectors' rage
      cruel hand a wounded scattered world
      cannon-shot
      animal with thigh broken
      that limps in service of the
      altar
                        sword and axe
      brutal
      fanatic face the devil's
      armor hairy men--flayed
      in skin of beasts    who hold back
      their held-up clubs:  heads under
      heel the subdued slave


      cutters in wood who cut
 ii   their own stark faces
      (for life is excellent)
      'sangre limpia' made clean with
      pain
      --a transposed
                        Moreno saint
                        whose robe
                        folds on fold
                        the pyramid mountain

151

```
        workmen
iii     strange penitentes
        tools bound to the wrists
        making on their knees

        shapes of rest and glory

        mixed beliefs in poignant skin
        Xipe) shed-horn and snake
        holy bird a cross, the bleeding crucifix
        soldier-friars masters at masonry
        —and most old books
        shield of gold-torn will
        sending souls to Paradise

        to re-make a world in that hard joy
        they 'lay it in ruins'
        that rose up its varied forms
        spontaneous interior belief—
        quick to the lash of suffering
        a race of
                            humid apostles
        the earth accessible
        who arrive at that near grace:

        between gates of the sun
                            Aleijadinho
        tiger and quetzal!
        conquerors of the master race's
        perpetual cross


                            to lay the abstract
iv                          in no surer destruction
        from the snake's mouth
        beneath their tongues
        they wore the shape—

        (they were already...builders in stone



            najua woman

            the rain
            has washed the mud of the earth against her
            the wind
            has blown all the birds from her hair
            and still she keeps walking
            carrying the load of roots on her back
```

MARTIN TUCKER

Threads

I leave my clothing with my lovers,
a memory to be sent to the cleaners,
hoping because never hopeful a goodbye
will skirt issues improperly addressed.

Oh love and lovers if you would know
I have saved my clothing beyond tears to give—
My nakedness I lost some years ago
and style shelters my multitude of dreams.

Listen, a garment rustles in the wind:
catch me, before the thread binds a pattern.


What Whitman Would Have Seen Sunday

He was wearing bare feet on the Brooklyn Bridge
reading the New York Times.
Sleek as an arrow his green chino pants
pointed at the heart of style.

Like a long day's summer
he swallowed the sunshine
never missing a flick
of the cinema section.

He made one world into two,
not noticing the addition:
Brooklyn, Manhattan, city, fields,
either way he turned
he seized both legs of a journey.

He did not embrace people with a look,
yet Whitman would have known:
A man reading on the Brooklyn Bridge alone
with toes naked to the air
is sharing, is part of the human affair.

## Brooklyn Landscape

Six pairs of jeans stretched their loins on a line
the line ran right into an iron ladder
the ladder reached as high as the neighboring steeple
the steeple thrust gray and smooth in the blue sphere
while leaves lay round bellies of trees.

The woman who washed her family's denim
went next door to church at the proper time,
with her sons she knelt in pressed black woolens,
and amid the words they forgot their line
shouting with good works all the way to heaven.


## JULES TELLIER

(translated by Don Devereux)


### Nocturne

We left Gaul aboard a vessel that sailed from Massilia one autumn

evening, just at nightfall.

And that night and the next I remained awake and alone on deck,

soon listening to the wind moan over the sea and dreaming of things

that I regretted, then contemplating the nocturnal waves and losing

myself in other reveries.

For this is the sacred sea, the mysterious sea that thirty cen-

turies ago the subtle and unfortunate Ulysses stirred in his long

search; the subtle Ulysses who, delivered from marine perils, accord-

ing to Tiresias, was yet to wander numerous lands bearing an oar on

his shoulder, until he should encounter men so ignorant of navigation

that they would take this burden for a winnowing tool.

It is the sea that the old poets and old sages ploughed in their galleys and triremes; and as they stood on upper decks in the midst of attentive sailors, the sea, itself attentive, heard on such nights the songs of Homer and the sayings of Solon.

And this also is the sea where, in the first centuries of the Christian error, when the reign of holy nature was ending and that of cruel asceticism was beginning, the master of an African barque heard voices in the darkness, and one of them called him by name and said to him: "Great Pan is dead! Go forth among men and announce to them that great Pan is dead!"

And in the mysterious starless night, above the black chaos of the sea and beneath the black chaos of the sky, there was something sad and strange in dreaming that perhaps the nameless, shifting, and obscure place which our vessel was crossing had seen all those phantoms pass, and had kept nothing of them.

And it is because this thought came to me, and because it seemed strange and sad to me, and because it troubled my weary rhetorician's heart for a long time, that it still is possible for me, amid so many forgotten hours, to evoke those distant dark ones when I remained alone on the deck of a ship that sailed from Massilia one autumn evening, just at nightfall.

DAVID KILBURN


Numbers Ten Thru Zero

Prelude:

Thorpe, a young psychiatrist, using projective techniques to investigate
the identical suicides of three returning astronauts, tours Europe on a
brief vacation.  He meets and falls in love with a young French girl,
they arrange to meet, but she fails to turn up and he never sees her
again.  Two days later he is killed in a car accident.


10.  Outer Space

Thorpe turned to Control:
"Break hard with the retro-jets as we enter the atmosphere, I leave the
timing to you."
Behind, Lunar 1, its rockwinds of falling meteors.  He looked towards
the distant spiral of the blue-green nebula.
"Next time I'll sing for you," he whispered
and, aloud,
"Toledo next stop."


9.  Radio Silence

Whistling "Lili Marlene," he crossed the hotel portico and headed through
the cobbled streets to the empty square before the cathedral.  This was
the centre of the town, but where was the bronzed Aphroditine he had come
so far to meet?

                    it's reasonable
                    (to lie)
                    it's reasonable
                    (to cry)
                    it's reasonable
                    (at times)
                    to die

A nun passed close to him (yes, all her bones had Latin names).  "Tomorrow, tomorrow, if only then I can tell you my name."  He looked up
to see a squadron of SAC B52's making for the delta.

8.  Stalag 17

He slipped, and such was the spacing of the barbed wire that
            (I feel and you feel)
his body, trapped at the thighs, projected outwards from the fence
            (You feel and I feel)
head downwards, face outwards, arms stretched.  With the last burst
            (I know and you know)
of gunfire, she turned to see blood and brains spurt through his eyes
            (You know and I know)
90 percent on her side of the fence, by rights, he too had escaped
            (Goodbye, but no regrets)
But who could quibble with these grey emissaries of dawn?


7.  Immediate Landscape (Commitment replaced by psychedelia)

non-seasonal
temperature control.
humidity regulated
instant data transmission.
technological
non-natural selection.
desacralized
mass media.
rapid intercontinental
artificial light.
mood controlled
megapolis.
retro-actively legislated
learning theory.
dodecophonic
dawn chorus.


6.  Szondi Test

He thought of his days as a boundary-fence rider in the Australian
outback.  The vast cycles of the sun and stars, wind and rain.  Kan-
garoos, difficult to believe they still had such things nowadays.
The jury returned, he stood erect to face them.  A quick glance con-
firmed the eight were a homosexual, a sadistic murderer, an epileptic,
a hysteric, a paranoid schizophrenic, a catatonic schizophrenic, a
depressive, and a manic.  The proceedings were conducted in an archaic
legal language, from what little he gathered, it seemed his crime was
in connection with a radio transmitter he had left locked in the boot
of his Mercedes near the Cathedral, and that he was guilty.  Behind
him, the tattered banners of Aldermaston hung like antimacassars on
the barbed wire of the deserted set.

157

## 5. Photographic precursors

Assassination of Mayor Gaynor in New York, Warnecke, USA 1910.
Execution of Weiderman, Versailles, Paris Match, France 1938.
Marinus van der Lubbe, Dallas, Texas; Haroun Tazieff, USA November 1963.


## 4. Ganser Syndrome

"Nothing to say, Dr. Thorpe? Remember the laser guns washing helicop-
ters from the ash-grey sky of North Vietnam? The magazine with the
photographs of toy soldiers, luminous flags against the torn sky, heavy
weapons, shock troops, thermo-nuclear parity agreements, dead stars,
post-card messages, the enemy task force intercepted over New York?
Just what was the code tune we used to end radio silence?"
"I can't whistle it. Perhaps we were together, a place we did not know,
nor each other. I can remember the wind, the falling rain, birds in the
sunlight and, above all, your smile (no more do people die)."


## 3. Tesselated Epiphanies

1. Claude Eatherly: flying dutchman of the stratosphere.
Overhead, B52, winged angel of the Strategic Air Command. Its womb
nurtures the time-frozen deaths of the unborn. Here too decisions
are made, electronic positives of transistorized synapses. Decisions,
decisions, always decisions. His washed brain is desiccated by a warm
breeze of ionized blood, but the tears remain, immortalized in the
fused films of a billion negatives.

2. Casino Royale: meta-dream of the new sensibility.
It was all duty and fireworks, tempered by love and red tape.
Potted dreams, paper flowers that grew in nuclear ashes. Machines
analogized to minds, diode decisions and it's all play, play, play.
A carnival of polythene kisses round someone else's admass grave.
One-way tickets to a purple sunset thermoset at 1 million centigrade.


## 2. Cargo Cult

Black hairs fell from the wasted pale concavities of his chest. An
apocalyptic stutter necessitated ostensive communication.
He passed his time cutting out photographs, adverts, areas of print,
typing out film titles, the names of stars (often modifying with
colored washes) and uses them to construct a three-dimensional Latin
square that would intersect the modalities of his consciousness.
Any day now, he expects the victorious General LaSalle, the walls of
his prison will rush back, once again a fellow man will grasp his hand.

1. Inner Time

In the brief interval that remained, he thought of many things, and
finally of Joseph's coat of many colors which, it seemed, could be
of any color or no color at all.  Was this the paradox he sought?
But now, in his rapidly blurring speech, words gradually lacked con-
sonants.  Symbols slid from him.  He seemed to melt into the chiar-
oscuroed corners of his cell, as once again he felt a wholeness in
the world about him.  Even the texture of his dreams was now too thin
to bear the timelessness of the amniotic return he now awaited.


0. The Everlasting Motorcade

As the steering column erected through his chest, his body exploded
into the dying fireworks of a retreating carnival, unraveling coils
to the metering devices that were to transmit the profane language
by which he mediated the deaths of Jayne Mansfield and François
Dorleac with the deserted Dealey Plaza.  For now he was to regain
the cosmos.


PAUL C. METCALF


Excerpt from Apalache, a Work in Progress

accokeek       acquack

up the susquehanna and juniata, across the mountains at kit-hanne

sasquesahanock, patowomek, chesepiook

choccoloco,

chockolog

fakahatchee, loxahatchee

meddybumps, saukatunk-

arunk

out of the valley of menaun-gehilla to the mouth of little kenawha chaubuqueduck, messatsoosec...twada-alahala

machaquamagansett...the kenogamishish...conno-

harriegoharrie

near egunk hill, the upper part of moosup's: peagwompsh

a branch to the forks of youghiogheny

chinklamoose askiminikonson kaskaskank  across the north

and east forks of quemehoning aggamogin rippogenus quin-

nehtukqut across the nipnet and between the breast-shaped hills sisquisie

taghkanick wyalusing wyomissing at quabaug six trails converged mobjack

coinjock the big bone blue lick trail skunkscut nipsic chipchug scantic

from the head of clinch to the fork of tug nisquitianxet gungywamps

scitico woxodawa the licking route sankety unkety nausset the north

prong of nickajack scusset

the black fox trail began at the cherokee towns along the hiwassee,

passed rattlesnake springs, crossed the hiwassee and followed down-

stream along the north side, crossed the tennessee at hiwassee island,

and continued west to the mounds in sequatchie valley

       sopchoppy chequepee quaddic

       capawack cotuit quidnic

       sebec naugus obscob

       moxie nissitisset wisconk

       stissing catsjajock

hackinkasacky hobocan nayack picipsi sinsink

                chenango    cheningo

                (cheningo chenango)

from the lower towns of the cherokee to babahatchie

        ochriskeny lackawack        from cisca, by the

        ruttawoo ocitoc             black fox spring, to

        naivsink goynish            the great lick


        catawissa shantituck        by way of tioga, lycoming

        santuit tatnuck             creek, to tuscarora valley


        tellico jellico             through auchquick, the

        chopmist popsic             kusk kusks, to hockhockon


        shagwango congamuck         over stony hills, across

        snipsic boxet               sholola creek at the falls


        sneeksuck yawgobby          on the border of the hard

        sunquams passquesit         land, and up to the great rocks


        minisink appoquinimink      portage at pemaquid,

        succabonk pagganck          thence up the damariscotta

        machepaconaponsuck          to sheepscot waters


            moose                       scook

                    sneech                      sag

        sip

```
                                                    scug

              tug                       tist

                                                       slank

                   puss cuss


                   _____


left the river beyond the openings, to a spring that issued from a ra-
vine--up the mohawk, across schoharie & canajoharie, through oneida
country, across oriskany, oneida, canawawga & chittenango, thence to
the deep spring on the onondaga boundary, and onondaga villages on the
river--across owasco outlet, into land of the cayugas, and the lake--
to the seneca river, the territory of the senecas: canandaigua, and the
genesee--across tonawanda, to the tuscaroras, and niagara


euchee nacoochee elloree sewee
wateree sugaree santee tybee
congaree sautee yemassee wimbee


                              otsego owego otsquaga otsdawa
                              otseningo oghwaga otego otstungo


           passadumkeag mattawamkeag kassanunganumkeag
           nahumkeag maskeag amoskeag kenduskeag


from pontegwa, the river falls, past watanic and ko-iss, to namaskik
for the fishing--thence to penikook, past lake winnisquam, lake opeechee
and aquadoctan, to chenayok: the mouro-mak--win-nebis-aki trail
```

naumkeag okfuskee ochenana    meduxnekeag withlacoochee oswegatchie

   penobskeag hatchechubbee owasco    on the east bank of the sus-

quehanna, the paxtang path    transquaking rockawalking    by the

great pond from high land aslant to the lower part of the great plain

   pissepunk podpis    owego to susquehanna: the lake-to-lake middle

trail    sunsicke arrowsic    from the long calm to the falls of

patapsco    bigbee lublub tashmoo tombigbee    across the mauromak,

following the ocean sand, reaching the penobscot, and upstream

nipscop tickfaw moodus    trails on both sides of the genesee    bash

bish shickshock    across fishing creek to shickshinny    anacostia

anticosti    between the alarka and the tuckasegee, with a stone cairn

on the ridge    quassaconkanuck    to allaquapy's gap    yawgunsk

 

    great salted standing water

    where the sun shines out

    at the bushy place

    at the place of mud

    first or oldest planted ground

    the dancing place

    at the pine spring

    a long straight river

    a meadow

    bull thistle

    tidewater covered with froth

    the place where clams are found

the sprucy stream

at the sweating place

at the sweet land

the place of fear

the place where deer are shy


beginning at conestoga, the trail crossed the susquehanna at connejohola,

crossed the headwaters of conewago creek, crossed catoctin creek, the

monockissey and the potomac, and extended on to opequon


zinnodowanha


ROBERT BONAZZI


Sea Poem

      washing shoreward
the fog's fingers probe
      recovering death's keep
      (eyes staring from still deep)
the funeral dirge
full moon


Morning

waking dreams
of yellow slants of light
and
crow caws

in starlight (through the trees)
one chicken
strutting the fencerail

this morning


[Poems by RON SEITZ—not ROBERT BONAZZI]

164

Face

opening (onto rooftops)
    the upstairs window
the mystery of distance in the whistles
There! the side of the house!
the still white glow of wood
shining into the night

head back
arms spread
my (nailed by the moon
    held by its light) face
crucified in whiteness


Generation

sunken cheek and blue-jawed they
galloped through dives damning
Buddha a pregnant
book Zen

my Apocalypse howling
generation now
old and
spent


Carnival

    to cross the Gulf for Mardi gras
fat Tuesday's wine mask & dance
    to collapse Ash Wednesday
underwear drunk & tickertape
stoned raw the First Station of the Cross
    to rise once more in Holy Week
Voodoo boned in Creole Light
    to clash cymbals & the River
tug wails dying
amen

THOMAS MERTON

The Geography of Lograire

Prologue: The Endless Inscription

1 - Long note one wood thrush hear him low in waste pine places
    slow doors all ways of ables open late
    Tarhead unshaven the captain signals
    Should they wait?

2 - Down wind and down rain and down mist the stranger.

3 - In holy ways there is never so much must

4 - Should Wales dark Wales slow ways sea coal tar
    Green tar sea stronghold is Wales my grand
    Dark my Wales land father it was green
    With all harps played over and bells
    Should Wales slow Wales dark maps home
    Come go green slow dark maps green late home
    Should long beach death night ever come
    And welcome to dark father-mother land
    Simple white wall house square rock hill
    Green there low water hill rock square
    White home in dark bituminous con-
    Crete ways to plain of fates ways
    Fathers hill and green maps memory plain
    In holy green Wales there is never staying

5 - Plain plan is Anglia so must angel father mother Wales
    Battle grand opposites in my blood fight hills
    Plains marshes mountains and fight
    Two seas in my self Irish and German
    Celt blood washes in twin seagreen people
    German Tristram is all mates' Grammer
    I had a toy called Tristram and Gurton's
    Needle in another sensitive place
    What Channel bard's boarder house next sweet
    Pub smell on cliff of winds Cliff was
    A welshest player on the ruggy green at Clare
    Away next New Wood Forest fool on hunter map
    Ship of forests masts Spain masts in Beaulieu wood
    Minster in the New Wood Minster Frater in the grassy
    Summer sun I lie me down in woods amid the
    Stone borders of bards.

6 - In holy walks there is never an order
    Never burden

7 - Lay down last burden in green Wales seas end firs larches
Wales all my Wales a ship of green fires
A wall wails wide beside some other sex
Gone old stone home on Brecon hill or Tenby harbor
Where was Grandmother with Welsh Birds
My family ancestor the Lieutenant in the hated navy
From the square deck cursed
Pale-eyed Albion without stop.

8 - In holy seas there is never so much religion.

9 - On a run late hold one won
Tarhead slaver captain selling the sables
To Cain and Abel by design

10 - Design desire O sign of ire
O Ira Dei
Wrath late will run a rush under the
Funnel come snow or deadly sign
Design of ire rather I'd dare it not dare
It not the ire run late hold strong Wales to a mast
Young siren sexes of the green sea wash
Hold captain home to Ithaca in a pattern of getaway
Hold passion portion siren swinging porter
Gutt bundle and funk gone
Down slow mission done as possible
And another child of Wales
Is born of sea's Celts
Won rock weeds dragon designs
Missions capable defenders

11 - In frail pines should they sometimes wait
Or ponds said one space cotton in captain design
Trace a dark pine fret way work walks
In soft South Pine house eroded away
Sweet-smelling Virginia night and mint
Should they wet those cotton patches
Wash out a whole town

12 - Wash ocean crim cram crimson sea's
Son Jim's son standing on the frigate
Jim Son Crow's ocean crosses a span
Dare heart die Spanish ram or Lamb Son's Blood
Crimson's well for oceans carnate sin sign
Ira water Ira will not wash in blood
Dear slain son lies only capable
Pain and Abel lay down red designs
Civil is slain brother sacred wall wood pine
Sacred black brother is beaten to the wall
The other gone down star's spaces home way plain

13 - Dahomey pine tar small wood bench bucket
     Under shadow there wait snake
     There coil ire design father of Africa pattern
     Lies all eyes awake crowded night
     Traces gone tire far traces of dawn's fire
     Dead rope hand cotton over captain branch

14 - The willing night hides everything
     Wills it tar face fret work wash out all chain
     Saving all one country slave
     Snake and tarheel minister and bat
     And blood and ram and Isaac done in a dare.

15 - Plain Savior crosses heaven on a pipe

16 - Hay Abraham fennel and grass rain ram under span's star
     Red grow the razors in the Spanish hollow

17 - Hallow my Savior the workless sparrow
     Closes my old gate on dead tar's ire slam
     Gone far summer too far fret work blood
     Work blood and tire tar under light wood
     Night way plain home to wear death down hard
     Ire hard down on anger heel grind home down
     Wary is smashed cotton-head beaten down mouth
     When will they all go where those white Cains are dead?

18 - Sign Redeemer's "R"
     Buys Mars his last war.


FRANCIS PONGE

(translated by Cid Corman)


The New Spider

Instead of killing all the Caribs, it would
have behooved us perhaps to seduce them with
spectacles, acrobats, hunts and music.

                                    --Voltaire

From the moment day breaks it is obvious in
France—although it unwinds in corners—and
marvellously confused in the language, that
spider and web can only be one.
　　So much so—when the star of silence pales in
our little backyards as on our bushes—
　　That the least dew, to speak distinctly,
　　Can make it sparkling to us.

　　This animal which, like a ship's anchor, first
casts off in the void,
　　So as to—even upside down—maintain itself
there suddenly
　　—Suspended without context by its own decisions—
　　In expectation of a place of its own,
　　—As it does not dispose, however, any employee
at its edge, when it wants to reascend must swallow
its rope:
　　Strumming unsuccessfully above the abyss,
　　Once it has understood must change tactics.

　　As light as the beast may be, it cannot really
fly,
　　And though no more terrestrial robber is known,
it is determined to run only to heaven.
　　So it has to climb up into the rafters to—as
aerially as it can—extend its entanglements, to
set up its obstacles, like any bandit in the
streets.

　　Radiating, it spins and weaves, but in no way
embroiders,
　　Taking every short cut;
　　And no doubt it must proportion its work to the
speed of its course as to the weight of its body,
　　To be able to get to any one point with always
less delay than the most ready game animal,
endowed with the most extraordinary restlessness,
to extricate itself from this net:
　　This is what is called the range,
　　Which each knows instinctively.

　　According to the situation and the species—
and the power as well of the wind—,
　　The result is:
　　Either fine vertical rigging, a sort of very
taut brise-bise,
　　Or autoist veils as in the heroic days of the
sport,
　　Or costumes from second-hand shops,

Or even hammocks or shrouds rather like those
in classical funerary settings.

Up above it moves like some boding funambulist:
Alone too, it must be said, in connecting these
two ideas,
The one deriving from the cord and the other,
evoking obsequies, signifying tainted by death.

In the sensitive memory all is confused.
And that's good,
For in the end, what is the spider? If not
the entelechy, the immediate spirit, common to
bobbin, thread and web,
To huntress and to her shroud.

However, the sensitive memory is also the
cause of reason,
And so it is that, from <u>funus</u> to <u>funis</u>,
It is necessary to reascend,
From the point of this amalgam,
To the first cause.

But a reason which would not leave the sensitive
by the wayside,
Wouldn't this be it, poetry:

A sort of <u>syl-lab-logism</u>?
Let's pick up again.

The spider, constantly
At its murderous and funereal toilette,
Makes it in corners;
For strolling,
To stretch its legs.

Dead, indeed, it is when it has its legs
crumpled up under and looks like only a
net shopping bag,
A discarded sack of malice.

Alas! What should we do with the shadow of
a star,
When the star itself has bent its knees?

Reply is mute,
Decision mute:

(The spider then sweeps itself away...)
While in the dim sky rises the same star—
which brings us to day.

any news from alpha centauri

i

the dog suddenly punched the back of his knee with its snout
short snap of teeth he stopped shouted hey your dog bit me
in the dark street the other man swayed and will go on swaying
thick weed in the sea of remembered nights
                                    an event of no consequence
but for the small marks on his skin in two days they faded
not as persistent as cigarette burns on his hand and arm
the previous summer he'd stayed so drunk he believed himself Orpheus
many a man before him     delusions of a like nature
well dogs never gave him no trouble did Kerberos know the good dead
by their smell was he blind as most of them are did cat people ever
enter Hades
          a little of that goes a long way he thought
walking on in the frosty night with the stars as stately
as ever up there any news from Alpha Centauri
they have their own scene there pretty small pretty quiet
a fortnightly newsletter printed on green gas


ii

the muse

jumped up and down       in the radar forest
to attract her attention

sorry sir no message for you

zap zap the day was over

sometimes
he had his doubts


iii

laughing all over her face her body swung
into it too she was telling him something
she was such a joy he didn't know where to look the cat
came in he looked at the cat but it did not enter this moment
how years had changed them     how they had taken his memory
sometimes he thought his mind away

every instant of waking a new start often so slow
he made many mistakes per hour
the cat lay down in front of the fire
and she had already turned into another
lovesong worksong
                    dark soon in the winter
there was hardly any time to stay
awake to think out a sentence like that
one movement
                she gathered all objects in out of the light
where they hung in the room about him
how 'years' stood in the air in his place a dumb idol misnamed


iv

mythology
            's a fat momma
she sits in a chair and talks
long threads of story
                        take care not to get them
round your head there's no one will come unwind you

birds out the window kept flying this way and that
it was hard to keep up
from the other window he saw the football game
if only they'd been allowed to use their fists maybe spears
much happier homegoings        long ships
pushing off Troy shore

the cat came in he looked at the cat it had a bird in its mouth
there had always been a great deal of dying all over the place


v

the drive to the citadel

                        cornering well and zooming along the straight
they were there in no time
the musical back projection had stopped
                                it was hard to remember
at any moment it could be wound back to the sequence where fire
fell from the sky rose out of the ground
tearing time out of bodies
                    their time


176

a few minutes had passed since he saw some red flowers
tulips he thought in a window across the street
now they are gone
                     there was still some green left the stalks
most probably
well he said I give you the stalks
and saw her holding them smiling
again he had trouble looking

they were in bed murmuring up into our another
the world she was twisting and turning on his stalk


PAULA ELIASOPH


Phenomenon

It is strange!  There was
a time when I was
writing, and I wanted to

say what I thought was
a message.  I found
there were no words that express

the feeling of thoughts.
I became an artist.
Now I find that when I

wish to show the inner
depth of formless
responses, innervating

me---the colors fade
from primary to
delicate shades, into a

sort of nothingness--
almost a colorless
presentation in the

atmospheric space.
Where does this lead?
Words are too harsh, colors too bright.

Only the intangibility
of living existence
remains.


177

TED ENSLIN

Aurum Genetrix

Whatever made the fire
sinks
            degree
                on
            degree
set    fragile
                    collapses.
The heat does not.
                        It
                returns
voyage
    on
voyage
            to the sun.


You will do
    only
what you will do---
I suppose this
is what I must expect
        yet
in the doing there is that
which is undoing.
    I
am not prepared
for it.  You are you
    ---yourself-
beyond anything
that moves or says
        or does.
The light comes shyly
after many days of rain.


From the Maine Journal

July 14.  I spend a good deal of each day mowing the roads and the
large field behind the house, fighting a never-ending battle against the
encroachments of poplar and alder clumps.  Today I uncovered a great flat
rock, a magnificent seat from which to look through the notch below.  It
is directly behind the house, but I had never suspected its presence un-

til I bent my scythe point against it.

July 17. On my return walk this evening, I encountered what I at first took to be a large black dog, dark enough so that I could see only the outlines. But as it scampered away, I sensed my mistake and lit a match. A bear cub, fairsized from the tracks. And in a moment I heard a crashing in the underbrush--probably its mother. A few moments of trepidation, but nothing further occurred.

July 19. Everywhere this year the men are haying in the right season for it--apparently stirred into more than usual action by the hot dry season. Stopping by Mary Dalrymple's to see whether she would like to go on an early berrying expedition, or perhaps had some wood to be split, she tells me of a young girl just married to a seventy year old pensioner "to save her name." Mary thinks very little of the match or of those involved. Going on to tell of the other woman's shiftlessness, she says, "Why she don't know nothin! She wouldn't know beans if the bag was opened." In her shed I saw a handmade wooden fork for pulling hot clothes from a washtub. Another of those well-worn, completely utilitarian objects, beautifully simple and clean-edged which make her life the admirable thing it is.

July 24. Tansy in bloom. Early this year, due no doubt to the protracted spell of heat and dry weather. A bloom which never fails to excite me--the naked simplicity of its rudimentary "button" form and the aromatic pungency of the crushed leaves. Old Mary, seeing the bunch I had picked today, spoke of the old wives' custom of making "tansy bags" to be worn either around one's neck or waist as a cure for bad colds-- also of its use in a tea for abortive purposes. This latter use was one with which I had long been familiar. She seems to make no special note

179

of the plant, but I see that she has planted two clumps of it in her dooryard. She says that fireweed (the great willow herb) has been similarly used. Unbearable heat today. At one point I lay down in the woods to take a nap, but I was closer to a clearing than I had realized. I woke to hear a young woman singing a semi-religious folksong with some conviction and much spirit. Looking through the edge of the woods, I saw a farmhouse which I have seen from many other angles. Something in this awakening which makes up for a great deal. A tonic to send me on my way again.

July 30. Almost before daybreak, Mary and I left on a long hike across the back intervale in the direction of Porter Hill in search of blueberries. This is a section with which I am not at all familiar, although Mary knows it well. She points out fields which she and her husband scythed by hand years ago, many of them grown up to groves of young trees now—the old Blanchard place, falling in, as so many others, a clearing where there was once a log cabin. Mary remembers having walked by there one time when the young woman who lived there was digging a grave for a newborn child. "I didn't stop, I can tell you." She tells me of the plants which she knows, many of them the same that I do, but with different names, and there is usually a use connected with each one—the fruits of a humble "make-do" economy which is enviable, and which is dying out—more each year. A walk filled with lore, and I hardly care whether or not we find berries—though I imagine it would offend Mary's practical nature in such things if she knew of my carelessness. Finally, after having gone beyond the road to a path so grown up with swale grass and bushes in places that it was almost impossible to fight our way through, we come to a young forest where she had thought we would find blueberries. "It was a field, leastways a cutdown, the last time I come here. Course that was three years ago." I think of so many similar experiences which I have had—trying to find old roads marked on the section maps. Finally we come to a flat stone bridge in a swamp—magnificent flat stones left there how many generations ago? I would imagine there are few living whose grandfathers would have remembered it, and then a dry stream bed which we follow uphill to a clearing where the berries do begin. Such a profusion that we forget that we are not really certain of where we are, but working up the hill I find that it is in back of the abandoned Larcom place, and that we have come out exactly where we had intended. After filling our buckets, we went into the dooryard, found the well—a deep clear one—washed down our "dinner" with water and berries and returned by the road. I have no idea of how my neighbors employed themselves today, but I doubt if it was in any way better spent for most of them.

August 2. A conversation with old Mary about her latest blueberrying expedition: "I walked up there by the white house berryin' along the road as I went. There's that Finn in charge of it now. I saw him comin' down the road, and all them signs! But I didn't hurry none, just stood and waved, and he did. When he come up I asked him if it was all right to walk down the road, and he said he didn't know why it warn't. I thought I might get a bawlin' out. 'You're Mrs. Dalrymple, aren't you?' he says, and I says, 'Yes, sir.' 'You live down by the red schoolhouse?' 'Yes, sir.' 'Well, I don't know why it isn't all right for you to walk down this road all you want to!'"

August 19. My one vervain spike keeps its blossoms after forty days of continuous blooming. As I went out to look at it, I found a number of sticks across the road. Of course! Old Mary told me that she might come up here today, blackberrying, and if she saw that I was busy she'd leave signs so that I might know that she had been here without disturbing me—a thoughtfulness with which I can't credit many.

August 20. Eating lunch with Mary after our latest berrying expedition, I thoughtlessly took two biscuits instead of one. She laughed and told me that the old people used to say that to take more than one wants in that way means that someone else is coming—hungry.

August 21. After having heard another of Johnny Grant's tooth stories, perhaps it is worthwhile to recall some of the best of them. The people who live a backwoods life such as this rarely attend to such matters with any regularity, and a dentist's job is still to pull decayed snags rather than to attempt to save them. Usually the stories I hear are told with grim humor, but a great deal of suffering must lie behind them, for those who were too poor to have proper attention, or holed up in a lumber camp in winter, miles from the nearest village: "One winter I was up back of Rangeley, cutting pulp. Got down to the village about once in two weeks for supplies, but not too regular at that. I started to get a hell of a toothache—swelled up and then began to jump. Didn't make too much difference what I did, it just got more miserable all the time. Did get in to Rangeley, but found the dentist had gone to Florida for the winter. Good and handy, I'd say. So back up to camp I asked the cook what to do. Told me to try carbolic acid. I did—for about six weeks. Got so my gums was burnt and numb, and I didn't feel nothin' in them, but the pain was there, all right—deep in my jaw. Finally the dentist did get back. I got down there late one night and roused him out of bed. He took one look at me, asked me what I'd been usin' and told me I oughta be dead

182

after that treatment. But he pulled it right there and then, no an-
aesthetic or nothin', and I told him I'd live to dance on his grave.
I could, too; he's been dead for ten years. Another time I was stayin'
with my father. Tooth started to ache, and I asked him about it. He
tells me to take a mouthful of water and sit up on the cookstove 'til
it boils. Well, like a damn fool I took him serious. 'Bout the time
I was ready to climb up on the stove, I come to. I was so mad I spit
water all over the place, an' he just sat there and laughed! One time
I had a feller workin' for me in the woods. He come in one day and <u>he</u>
had a toothache. Said it hurt something awful. I asked him if the
tooth was hollow and he said it was. I told him to take a shotgun
shell apart, pack the tooth with black powder and touch her off. "Will
that help?" he says. "Damn right, 'twill," I answered, just waitin'
to see what he'd do. Well, he gets himself a shell and does just what
I told him. He was just strikin' a match when he spies me laughin'.
God, was he mad. But you know, funny thing: after he cooled down, he
didn't have any more toothache; didn't bother him for the rest of the
winter.

"My grandmother lived to be pretty close to a hundred. When she
was ninety-odd, little nephew of mine used to like to rock in her lap.
Poor old lady only had one tooth left in her head, a front one, and it
was loose. Kid-fashion, little Ralph used to like to play with it.
Sort of tickled the old lady, and she'd say she'd like for him to have
it on some sort of watch charm when she died. And you know, he does
have it, right to this day."

DAVID IGNATOW

It Sets Them Free

There is someone smiling at me from behind
and someone holding out a hand in front
to say hello
and either side are persons unfamiliar
with familiar ways to put me at my ease
I should despair, I do despair
Where are the stones I much prefer
to carry I collect and string
around my neck.  I am on my hands
and knees and people are trying to lift me
by my shoulders and rid me of my necklace.
They do not understand that without it
I am just a person like themselves,
unhappy, going out of their way
to help others in the illusion
that it sets them free.


Conversation for One

In the supermarket of the white clerk
I ask the negro in the rear
behind a screen peeling rotten leaves
off cabbages. He says, Yes sir
to my question. Them riots
are by sabages.  I don't like em one bit
No reason for dem to happen
Somebody's gonna get hit
I'm pleased to hear
and move on to pick my fruit.
I hear him sigh behind me.

Lucky the leaves feel nothing
as they fall or we'd have howling
to fill space as far back as the birth of God
who would be awakening
to a world of screams.

Like a woman is my soul
crying for peace and love
bound to me in marriage
neither of us can dissolve,
unhappy soul I torment
with my doubts of its value.

Country Poem

Now I understand myself running back
to the city, out of breath and happy
to have escaped the sight of green vomit
and the groaning power lawn-mower--
this advertised peace.  I wanted truly
undisguised faces of boredom, swirling
about me in the street and my own grim hail
to traffic jams and subway panic
to death by cops' crossfire
to racial riots
to dope addiction
to strikes and water shortages
to married life in Queens overlooking the cemeteries
to the top kid schools among the wealthy professionals
on the East Side uptown
and to the crumbling beer can-littered schoolyards
of Harlem.  Nothing is hidden
Nobody lies or covers up
A low gas cloud covers the city
on which the people slowly choke in bed
but not one's own green vomit to walk on
in silence.  It hands a curtain from the trees.
Scream and yell and pound the walls here in the city
to be ignored or beaten down
Speak of the bitter with your last breath
and sweep the whole city into the sea
with a gesture or drive your car off the dock,
taking with you the city's death
but none of the green vomit
of those who spill their guts
and stand on it in silence like trees
that hide their birds from one another
and live for hundreds of years
without comment.


MARVIN COHEN


The Ideal Business Man

Hello!  What are you doing here?!

What do you mean by here?

The world!  I never expected to find you in the world!

Why not?  The number of guests it entertains is _infinite_, so why


185

shouldn't I be numbered among them if it includes such various—

But it's strange to find you here, you being such a notorious idealist that people are gossiping that the world is not the place for you!

Let them gossip their damndest! The world is an ideal laboratory for conducting my investigations in; since it so stubbornly resists my ideals that it imposes the most rigorous discipline on my experiments! It would be easy, and lazy, and simple, to be an idealist in some ideal place. But where's the glory in that? It's only invited conformity. But it's difficult being an idealist in the world! Almost tragically so! Therefore my struggle is heroic, to spite the world's opposition and establish an underground movement of rumblingly revolutionary ideals. Success in that is really commendable! The odds—they're so fantastically great!

And what are your ideals?

Well, personally, my ideals are to make a lot of money.

But isn't that worldly ambition?

But I told you that the world must be taken into account and included in my ideal transactions.

You're not a utopian, you're a businessman?

Sure: making the disguise complete.


A Fat Man's Unboasting Proclamation of a Bless'd Inner State

Nature has three rates of speed: Slow, Faster and Invisible.

Which rate have you been slaughtered by?

Since I'm fat and stately, it's been by the Slow.

Being sluggish and sedate, you've been comforted by the Faster.

186

Being dull and slothful, given to vague lumps of appetite, I've been appeased, and deliriously liberated, by that rapid foe of thick stillness, Invisibility.

Yet have you recorded that adventure? By that I mean, its presumed Grace seems to have left no at least apparent mark on you, whereby dignity is added to your carriage, or mystery enhances the parts and mobility of your unimproved person. Your appearance lacks the mystical state of change.

Because spiritually, I remain Nature's property, her dutiful, lumbering, cumbersome, oafish and buffoon-like slave, an opaque dolt, dumb and deficient of grace. For what sign tokens inward to the soul? Ignobly on the outside, I'm just the same. The Invisibility, granted me by Nature in witness of her feats, is concealed from view, so that physically I'm still mocked.

Do you feel cheated?

No. My fame in men's eyes is unrecognizable. I'm clumsy and ill-assembled. But privately, I'm stamped with Nature's reward. In secret dignity, I dwell impeccable.

To be mocked by your outside declaimers, and scorned laughing fit!

Let me endure these stones. Slow, faster, or invisible, Nature rates me as her own; dark in my depth, untestified by a stature to correspond for show in the fair of men's semblance, is something unassailable: a diploma by nature, as her loyal graduate.

But you're not dead yet!

Yet it's within my depth, you know. A debt I pay, on pain of all else!

Then you are a dependent of nature?

Yes, and it's my solo, independent strength. My most individual claim. My loftiest distinction.


## A Flimsy Explanation of an Amazing Transformation

A thin man came into a room where a fat man had been.

Did the thin man <u>replace</u> the fat man, or had the fat man already left before that?

Neither. The new thin man <u>was</u> the former fat man.

Then what accounted for the difference?

What difference?

Obviously, thin and fat.

Don't be superficial. The soul is beyond such distinctions.


## The Beast's Holy Skin

You're a big beast.

I'll kill you for calling me that!

That's what I mean: your impulsive reaction was that of a beast: I've just tested it.

The idea of your "testing" me is even <u>more</u> infuriating. My desire to kill you is still stronger. But now that I'm <u>talking</u> about it, you're saved. I've delayed my real beast impulse, and from reflex it's been reflected into reflection, as act hesitates into its diversion, and verbal analysis substitutes for your death.

I see that far from being merely a beast, you're also a man: the heir of thought, the son of delay, the wide-eyed offspring of regret and introspection.

As a man, humanely, I bid you live.

I will, you big beast.

Don't rile me, or tempt my savagery.

I appeal to your tender sentiments, to your high reason and benign intellect.

Oh; by invoking them, you do subdue the beast. Your appeal is doubly strong, so I bid you live twice; but for that to happen, I must kill you once.

Don't! My first death may get fond of itself and linger past habit into perpetuity.

Such foresight is beyond mortal reach. For one reason, I won't have you die: I would be imprisoned and kept from society. Why should I endure punishment, just to rid the world of your lively pricks and thorns? So "beast" me and "beast" me and "beast" me: but I'll resist insult and great injury with restraint: for our double mercy.

Your manhood has gloriously covered your beast. And for the froth to crown it all, an angel has appeared. Your true beast requires fakery of elaborate theology! Such an endless beast it must be, and hideous beyond belief, for an angelic facade to reinforce the human concealment of it! It took a god to keep your beast in check! A god that you have become! In awe I back away (Does so) and supplicate your interior beastliness whose supreme repression is in the God you are: or if you aren't the god, the appearance behaves as such. I worship what keeps the beast in! (Genuflects or prostrates himself before the other, in tremors of submission, devout beyond sincerity.)

ANDREA PFEIFFENBERGER

## Waiting for News

The leaves are dropping
from the vine.  For weeks,
this plant has grown here,
drinking the water I fed it,
digging deep with its roots,
seemingly healthy.
Today its leaves, pale and
weak, began
to drop
from the vine;
having given up hope
of hearing from you,
this transplant failed.

In the carrying of dirt,
the watering, the turning to and
away from the sun,
I made
a mistake.


## A Lot of Good

A lot of good it does the dead
to be buried today,
down under the earth,
not seeing the air white and blank,
green wood under a thickening shroud.

Some of us ride in a bus past a churchyard
full of snowed-in stone benches,
and hope to fall with the snow
and not to be buried by it,
when we die.

JONATHAN GREENE

The gods 'at work'
                        to be read in or with
                        different voices


A: Split open once again:

B: Does the leg twitch
   touched by electricity?
C: Yes.
B: Well, then is it alive?
C: No.
A: Such nonsense for serious matter.

D: Thinking you could breathe easy?
E: For once, yes. Or
   at last.
D: Split him open again, boys.
   Hate to do this but you gotta learn
   somehow.

E: Look at that, I still get up in the
   morning, put on the eggs.
D: Boys, he thinks he's alive.
E: Well, a little belly comfort
   never hurt. Or it's better than
   being too sick from hurt.

D: Crack him harder this time, boys.

A: One more gone.


---

Suggested voices:

A: Poet's voice, in obvious sympathy with Everyman.
B: Could be T.S. Eliot. Or German professor's accent.
C: Flat, as monosyllabic answers coming from a dull one.
D: Gangster-type voice or with irony of villain in a Western.
E: De-humanized Everyman. Or straight out of the last scene
   of an unknown earnest Eugene O'Neill.

NANCY-LOU PATTERSON


Calling the Great Barred Owl

(Waterloo County Bush-10t, St. Thomas' Night, 1967)


Entering your country
we can see
by some exact inversion
darkness falling
white among the trees
and feel the light against our cheeks
in soft black touches.

Shouting a counterfeit call
against the silence
we await you, each in his own
blood's clamor
while the distant farm-dogs
signal in chorus
and the far fox coughs.

When you speak
the dark-veined branches
mesh to an echoing heart,
a crystal chamber;
booming your answer
we and the trees and the night
become your voice.


For Mother Teresa

(Carmel of St. Joseph, St. Agatha, Ontario)


Coming to see you
in your February death
    I drove through land enshrouded
    under a stinging veil.

Now as I kneel and count
my city-fingered aves
    I can see your face, cold
    as a snowy landscape.

White wax lilies, candles
gesture victorian ceremonies;
    near you a young novice
    kneels, an unwavering flame.

Hands as sharp as lilies grip
your paper of promises
        fulfilled in the serge you wear,
        in your plank-and-trestle bed.

You are no longer native
to the wind, to conversation;
        silence is your country:
        death, your vocation.


The Ausschteier*

With her white fingers she worked the needles,
bone of her bones, knitting up her hopes
in tight white loops, to lay a table of future,
to fall like snow on a mountainous bed.

She filled up eyes of silver with thread
new as the latest catalogue, out of the
cushioning papers, stitching in time,
and now the nine she saved sew up
her cold and empty bed, and the snow
of years fades down the leafy bower
of her quilts.  Crow red: that's
for kisses, color of hearts; indigo:
the eyes of an unknown suitor; gold:
the band for her empty finger.

                              Now,
fold her down, lay her needle bones
in their rustling papers, leaves over,
stone under, pierced by the pins of
death, closed in the basketing earth.

———————————
*Pennsylvania German word for trousseau.

193

TEO SAVORY

Sunken Bell

The bell sounds in the temple
one strike to mark the last
of the five divisions of night
chant hope for another day
Light strikes the gold-bright
spire birds wheel and fly
away  Their song makes dawn
The poem flies upward praising
the day

The bell is sunken
under the lake water
it is dumb and scummed
In the room many are
seated around one
Outside the drenched man
green-scummed has forgot
how to walk heavy limbs
water-logged trunk  two
others dry as the earth
must drag this dredged
one between them close
to the wide glass door
In the room the chant is
low there is no bell
The door cannot be opened
fingers slither on glass
and sink  The poem has flown
away

At the last of five divisions
voices rise in the dark
birds wheel in the dark
the poem seeks the day
In the lake the sunken
bell throbs and strikes
one muffled note  The earth
trembles at its stroke
The voices chant in praise
of night

194

Brown into Green

(to Nhat Hanh)


After five months of drought

   the rain

hills burnt brown soil lost heart
trees in a wind danced macabre
skeletal out of season their leaves
clacking around their feet like
knuckle-bones our eyes ached for green
hands for a clod of damped earth

Now the rain
   it falls gently
      beginning at dawn
         darkening daylight
   sluicing the roof-tiles
      drumming off eaves
         gorging the ground

the rain
   falling gently outside
      lulling safe dreamers to lateness
   falling in puddles for birds
      in splashes for children walking to school
         slanting its writing on window-panes
   turning hollowed-out herb-stalks
      to quintessence of green

(the rain)

   into the deep green of our country
      where only the willow turns tender as rice

the rain

   brown into green
      will it rain
(names we'd never known before now)
        on Huế and Tra Quong?

HAYDEN CARRUTH


November in the Woods

Autumn going, a broken
    radiance

ferns rusting, birches scarred and white
a balsam's
    downsweeping rough dark boughs

powders of crystalline faint snow
    like dust of silence

    but how the
axe-bit nips bright wedges out
    scattering
the woodcutter's song of satisfaction
    chips of incantation
    on delicate ground

and now so soon
    the whitefooted mouse hath run
printed faint vigorous rows of tracks
older music, a plainsong in and out
among the balsam's
    dark downsweeping boughs.


CARLOS REYES

Pane

    rounded & brown, smooth like
    the loma, the birth-
    place of humanity: Maria

    Kuna (cradle) Indian
    exiled from her
    people, full of white-
    man's child, big
    eyes staring at me

    Black straight hair still
    in bangs      --the gold ring
    is missing
                barely
    visible are the marks
    she tries to hide.
    No line down the nose
    marks of beauty, according
    to their customs

Only in dreams
does she wear the bright colors
of the mola, appliquéd blouse
& three yards of material;
her ankles have grown fat
almost gone the marks
of wrappings

She is pure, of a pure race
her sons will not be
(in their eyes) will not see
the mortal cayuco, carved out
canoe of the body, of the soul

Pane, tomorrow, does not exist
for those suns, for her
only motichi, night
& wagala gualu: white faces
foolish moon-children out in the sun, always


      Dancing Paper Dolls

Outline, charcoaled
      on     some     space
of paper
        ((maybe it flutters))
if there is a breeze: movement
suggests life

(Cast yr fate to the wind: song

          I need you
the wind, perhaps, or flame
to burn at my edges
darkening, forcing some reaction
on my part
      How can the paper-
man be expected to do any thing
      any way, with
out
the breath
    A.
      matter
of chemistry
      Crumpled
I do not make it
to the waste
basket
    but ricochet off
the wall

                    thrown
there by hands
unknown
            B. -
                physics
explains it,
                tidy-
ly
        -ing

I exist therefore I am
(on paper at least)

I have a name
typed
at the bottom of this
page

In the beginning God created
paper
            form-
less

Oh!  I know it
my mexican friends might
disagree & say
it all began with corn;

Or my religious friends, that we are all of
clay

                    Paper does not come
                    from earth-
en clay) never has
reproduced its-
self

Other hands turn the crank
                            Despised by Susan Sptless
            "dirty old paper-
man"  don't you know "every litter bit hurts..."

If I have
        pores, they are for the benefit
    of ink, seeping
thru.
            "Smoking is prohibited"

The soul burns easily.

Carlos Reyes

THOMAS MERTON

The Conquest of France: Speech and Testimonials, 1941

Abbeville is like a landscape in the moon. I am in a labyrinth of walls,
with wide, cleared spaces in between and, here and there, a complete building.
I see the spire of a church, through a stage set of bombed houses. In the
middle of a block of spick and span ruins stands a hotel, intact, as if nothing had happened at all in the world. Some German soldiers are sitting at
tables, in front of it, under an awning, looking at the empty street.

They are like children playing house. There is nothing on the tables.
But they are sitting there, I suppose, to enjoy the shade of the awning.

In another window further down, a German soldier, an old man, leans,
smoking a cigar and blinking at the street, in his undershirt.

I hesitate, on this corner, and finally turn back and put down my lug-
gage under the awning of the hotel, walk into the café where a lady in a
black dress sits behind the counter, in the big empty room, with her hands
folded, and as still as a statue.

I realize she is listening to the radio, through the loud speaker of
which now comes the Beer Barrel Polka, sung in German and frequently inter-
rupted by the coughing of static.

All around her the walls are covered with the old familiar signs: Amer
Picon, Pernod, Dubonnet, Cassis. There is a big, red Byrrh calendar, which
has not been changed since August 19, 1940, nearly a year ago.

I ask for the railway timetables. Without a word, the lady points
sternly to the rack on the other side of the room. The railway timetable
is also a year out of date.

Before I discover that, a voice begins to talk on the radio, exhorting the conquered French in some kind of esperanto.

"Caro populi inferior:

Ben mas favorable beginnen unser speeches mit dem Puppels conquist, pueblos massacrat, humilissimo, abajo; nous vous tendrement lieben, pero nous vous sehr streng (suddenly) beat up, mes pauvres amis! That goes to show the moral lesson from the survival of the victuals, or should I say the revival of the biggest?

Franzos, massacrat, canaille, humilie toi. Meminisse, pobrecit, nuestro formidabili conquistu, y te tais! Our soldaten kommen at youse last May a year ago up out of the spring flowers, mighty fast, before you was aware. Give us your scraps of bread and your dregs of wine, give us your Picasso pictures and your Third Empire furniture, as if we knew the difference. Conquisti: we are the most well-bred and humane of Caesars, we smokken de cigarre, we likken de cigarretten, huffen te puffen de gud burgerliken meer-schaum pipe, scrape our clean heads every once in a while with our manicured nails, jouer le violon, singen de Wagner, muy religios, besides, because our army is a perpetual Sunday school.

Now let us recall, O Franzos conquisti, los circunstancios di su late-recent massacri from pleasant memory.

Our humane boys come raging up out of the ground like country gods with flowers all over their hats, and the flammenwerfers all concealed in delicate blooms. Oh, wassn't we a lovely bevy of tanks, tan bellos como praticos, to come busting out of the elaborate cages of trees which our Furrier themself planned, in his gardenhouse imagination?

Let's look at the record, then, boys: and here is how we standen. Maginot linie: gross metallico concreti, inquassato, horribili.

The whole earth murmurs with machinery deep in the tunnels. Hills come

200

to life. Huge silent mushrooms of cement come up out of the ground and point here and point there de kanonen: schreck! schrack! The silent mushrooms sink back into the earth. Underneath the tons of loam the trains of your soldiers go ringing along the military railways, transportat from here to there in the crinkling of an augenblick. Die Ganze Erde iss full from elevators, telephonen, hospitalization plans, free insurance, sewage disposal, collective bargaining, proces verb aux, dental clinics, y todos los milagros de la tecnologia moderna. That's what you think!

Alors: Nous. Tanken, Schlafwagen, Flammenwerfer, Glockenspiel, Abort, Stuka, everything besser. Besser Glockenspiels, more horrible tanks, big rubber boats, not to mention a monopoly on Tom Swift's electric rifle.

Oh yes, gentlemen: Our Leader, Alfred Hitler, I think, has proved himself a jump or two ahead of you French gentlemen. The romantics, or should I say the romantically inclined, among us, believe that our leader, Alfred Hitler, borrowed the notion of the flammenwerfer from that Ancient German concept of Fafnir the dragon. You think so? You are entitled to think so. Have your delicious thoughts.

But allow me to utter a discrete hatful of German breath in warning to you French gentlemen: I advise you, with an outburst of particularly heavy and inept and irritating sarcasm fretting in every pore of my big, red, gleaming, sweaty body, that our Furrier, Alfred Hitler, quite definitely meant business and means it still, as our dastardly Russian allies are finding out this minute. So put down those spoons with which you intend to menace us and meditate a while on what happened to you who think you are so famous, so well-known and so heard of throughout the world. Resign yourselves to the fact that you are Alfred Hitler's long-lost little brother,

Edgar.  Believe me, my French friends, you scarcely realize that for our
Fewer to show sutch gnadigkeit, sudge bonhomie in his puffy, moustached coun-
tenance towards youse, is some favor for an Aryan to demonstrate towards the
bunch of Jews that youse happen to be.

Now to return to the cursus belli and to your singularly insulting de-
feat, o unhappy Franzosen, which we now temper with all kinds of proffers of
kindness (because, of course, from the first nobody meant anything but the
sheerest, mildest and most affectionate form of kindness.)

Krieg.  Stark positiv:  Krieg.  We sitzen in the Sigsfreed Line with our
feelings hurt to the point of intense agony, for one whole winter.  German
feelings smart like sunburn.  Oh, Wow!  Insufferable!  The Generals scream
and beat their heads against the walls of forts in an attempt to restrain
their delicate feelings.  O noble rage tudesque!  Hundreds of infantry ser-
geants weep like bulls, they are so offended at the injustice of the whole
world.  German feeling rises quick as the mercury in a big, inaccurate ther-
mometer.  Even the little children cannot stand the insults to the nation:
they take their dolls by the foots and crash them against the side of the
house.  German honor begins to rage like a big out-of-date locomotive.  It
is too late.  Feeling is too high.  Teach the world a lesson.

German honor explodes, everything goes black.  Too bad for youse, you
flippant, artistic Franzosen: now every German soldier is turned into a merci-
less Arminius with firecrackers going off continuously in every part of his
head, with drums and rattles clattering in his chest, with his big lungs
heaving like bellows in a forge, his arms moving like the sails of mills,
his teeth hopping about like the keys of mechanical pianos and his eyes
flashing like electric signs.  This is the terrible moment, for the whole
world: every German's skull is a big wide hall full of Wagner, every German's

breath hisses like the fuse of an explosive charge. This is the glorious moment. Somebody blows a whistle. A million unbelievable Siegfrieds, all exactly alike, rush headfirst at the enemy, from every possible direction, like madmen, like football players, like drunks.

In every part of Belgium, Holland and Northern France, the early morning air fills with clouds of parachutes  floating down as silently and gently as portuguese men-of-war in the warm, shallow water of a southern beach.

Hanging under every parachute is a Siegfried, holding in his hand a small, framed portrait of Hitler, reciting with tears in his eyes the German irregular verbs or the multiplication tables.

Shrapnel flowers all over the rivers and canals like a garden of white flowers that instantaneously disappear. The sides of the houses fall down, and tanks come rushing out into the open, shooting in more than one direction.

Teams of Siegfrieds, like tumblers, leap instantly upon one another's shoulders at the edges of the concrete fortresses before the men inside have had time to drop their novels, and the acrobat on the top has in one hand a flame-thrower and in the other a small swastika flag.

The war is already over before it has begun. The German army is everywhere.

Pour makken a longue story raccourci, nous voulons vous régaler with the exquisite pleasure of some interesting testimonials which we have received from all quarters in conquered countries testifying to the enthusiastic admiration of the conquered for us, their conquerors and, incidentally, throwing some light upon our truly remarkable and never-before-seen military tactics whose swiftness and deadly efficacy surprised everyone but our Führer, Arthur Hitler, who doubtless foreknows and foresees everything. First testimonial: Lettra autentica di un fantassin Frencesi.

"Cher Führer.

I thinks youse is vraiment remarquable. On the morning of May --, 1940, I was working the vacuum cleaner in Blockhouse 864 of Sedan when I heard somebody monkeying with the general's icebox. Très peu méfiant, d'ordinaire, I must have sensed some new événement. En totto casu, poking my head around the door, what was my surprise to see the blockhouse was full of Germans, some with their helmets on, some with their helmets off, sitting in the easy chairs, reading the newspapers, eating the officers' cold chicken, drinking the wine, using the toothpicks, combs, hair oil, talcum powder, and taking pictures of the whole proceedings with expensive Leica cameras. Thus I knew that the conquest of France had taken place. I turned off the vacuum cleaner, changed into civilian clothes and made off at once without further ado."

Second testimonial: Same crummy outfit: Offizier.

"Dear Sirs:

I have no doubt the textbooks of history will be at a loss to describe your interesting invasion of the --th inst. A few days ago, taking advantage of the early sun, I had set up my easel within a half-mile of Blockhouse x561, in the Metz sector, and had begun to sketch, when I noticed several dozen joueurs de football (association) approaching, vêtus de caleçons bleu-blanc-ruges and carrying with them their football. Their captain asked me, politely enough, if it would inconvenience me to have them indulge in une petite partie de foot' in the midst of the landscape I was sketching, and only after I had replied that it was no inconvenience at all (thinking of perhaps enlivening the landscape with the figures of ces sportifs) did I realize that the man had addressed me in German. I leapt to my feet and began to dismantle my easel, but it was too late: with a loud shout, the men in football suits had rushed upon the nearest blockhouse and, with the football (which contained a charge of an unbelievably powerful explosive), demolished the entire blockhouse before my very eyes. I slipped away while they were posing for the cameras of the cinemas and escaped to Marseilles, where I now eke out a precarious living selling postcards."

Troisième lettre: Capitaine d'artillerie Belge..."

But while the voice on the radio goes on, I get up again and go outside the café under the awning, where the tables are still occupied by German soldiers, but now probably all different individuals, although they all look alike. All playing house.

I take up my suitcase and glance around, hesitating, looking for the sign I saw a moment before, saying Bahnhof. While I hesitate, one of the soldiers approaches me and stands sadly by for a moment. He has something to say.

What will it be? He is a musician? He is very happy? The German Army is everlastingly young? What is it now?

As soon as I glance at him, he steps forward and takes the suitcase and typewriter from me, straightens up and says:

"Alles fertig, Herr Korrespondent!"

Still not quite sure whether I am being arrested or what, I say something brusque, the first thing that comes into my head:

"Wo gehen wir hin?"

I get an immediate answer:

"The car is waiting around the corner in the shade; if you don't mind walking that far."

"Very good."

"Bitte schön."

I let him precede me, we goose-step smartly away from the terrace of the café and around the corner to a big Mercedes-Benz, open.  I get in.

"Anything else, sir?" says the soldier.

I give him some money and say:

"You have been very prompt."

He grins knowingly.

"You can thank the captain for that," he says.  "He was very sore when he found out you were wandering around alone out there in the country."

"Well," I exclaim in a rage, "it was his fault, wasn't it?"

"Yes, sir," says the soldier in confusion.  We exchange brisk salutes, and the driver comes running out of the hotel like a hare, looking at me wild-eyed and pulling on his gloves.

"Nach Paris!" I roar.  "As fast as you can go."

And we leave the ruins of Abbeville in a cloud of dust.

Notes on Contributors

Owing to the size of the present issue, the notes will have to be
shorter. See MONKS POND I and II for HAMILTON, RANDALL, JOHNSON, WILLIAMS,
LAX, MERTON, BRIGHAM, METCALF, HOLLO, GREENE and CARRUTH. HALVARD JOHNSON
has moved to Puerto Rico; otherwise there is nothing special to record here.

CHRISTOPHER MEATYARD is thirteen years old and lives in Lexington, Kentucky.
His father is the photographer Ralph Eugene Meatyard whose work appeared in
the last issue.

MARK VAN DOREN needs no introduction. He is one of the major American poets
of the century, still actively writing while in retirement in the Berkshires.

CHARLES SIMIC grew up in Chicago, has lived in New York since 1958 and has
published one volume of poetry, What the Grass Says (Kayak).

WARREN LANG has been writing poetry and practicing Zen for some years. He
studied at M.I.T., changed over to literature in graduate school in Indiana
University, where he also teaches Freshman English.

PENTTI SAARIKOSKI is one of the best new poets writing in Finland today.
We give a representative selection from the translations of Anselm Hollo,
published in England.

ALLEN NEFF teaches at Eastern Illinois University and publishes verse in
American Weave, CEA Critic, Karamu and Cats Magazine.

ROBERTS BLOSSOM is an actor and playwright who has also published two books
of verse. He lives in New York.

JUNE J. YUNGBLUT helps her husband run Quaker House in Atlanta. She is
active in the peace and civil rights movements. A close friend of Dr.
King's family, she has also recently completed a study of Beckett, of
which we offer an excerpt here.

OTTO RENE CASTILLO, a young Guatemalan poet, joined the guerillas in his
country, was captured by the government army, tortured and burned alive on
March 19, 1967. A book of his poems in English translation is being prepared by Margaret Randall.

CZESLAW MILOSZ is one of the most important Polish poets and critics of the
twentieth century. Though he broke with the Marxists and left Poland, he
is still very much in contact with the literary and intellectual life of his
country. He has edited an anthology of Polish poetry, and his best-known
work in English is The Captive Mind. He lives in Berkeley, California.

LINDY HOUGH founded the magazine Io with her husband, Richard Grossinger,
when he was at Amherst and she at Smith. She teaches English at Eastern
Michigan University. Quixote (Madison, Wisconsin) is bringing out a book
of poems by her and her husband.

ELAINE KNIGHT, born in Los Angeles, was for a while active in the New York
theater. She has lived in New Mexico since 1962 and has published poetry
in The Christian Century and Ante.

The CONCRETE POETRY section gives sample experiments of work done in this
field. Three items have already become famous in EMMETT WILLIAMS' Anthology
of Concrete Poetry. They are the work of Williams himself and of well-known
concrete poets JANDL (Austria) and PIGNATARI (Brazil). LAX has also been
very active in this international movement.

MARTIN TUCKER lives in Brooklyn. He has published verse and non-fiction in
New Republic, Nation, Saturday Review, Commonweal, Epoch, Coastlines and
other magazines.

JULES TELLIER, born in Le Havre in 1863, was a minor French poet. His early
death in 1889 was not particularly marked. A few close friends published a
small memorial volume of his work entitled Reliques de Jules Tellier, and in
1891 Anatole France devoted one of his regular "La Vie Littéraire" columns
for Le Temps of Paris to a mild, if belated, eulogy. Only one prior effort
at an English translation of "Nocturne"—an obscure and occasionally inaccurate attempt in 1924—is known to have been published. DON DEVEREUX,
who translated this section, lives in Santa Fe and is affiliated with the
Museum of New Mexico and with an OEO program for New Mexico migrant workers.
He has published articles on Southwestern history and ethnology and has also
written for The Christian Century.

DAVID KILBURN edited a literary magazine when he was studying chemistry at
Birmingham University, England. He now lives and works in London and is in
with the people who run Ambit, which accounts for the Ballard-like style
and irony of his story.

ROBERT BONAZZI is editor of Latitudes (Houston, Texas) and has two volumes
of poetry about to be published in New York.

FRANCIS PONGE is one of the major contemporary French poets. Those who do
not yet know his work can find examples in English in the Penguin Book of
French Verse, Volume 4. CID CORMAN, who did this translation, is an American poet living in Kyoto, Japan, where he edits an important and distinguished
magazine, Origin. Origin recently devoted an issue to Ponge.

PAULA ELIASOPH is an artist who for many years taught art in New York
schools. She lives in Jamaica, New York.

TED ENSLIN is a hermit and poet well-known to readers of literary magazines.
He lives in the Maine woods. His Journals, he says, "...as I first conceived them, were written as a storehouse of material which I might use
later, but I soon found this a very tenuous excuse. Most of the things
which I really wanted to use in other forms I could remember without fac-
tual writing. They were written in spite of myself, and often to spite
myself, to try to find some sort of continuity in a life. Usually I did
not find much pleasure in re-reading them, but the act had freed me. So
I find that in organization of some of that material, the dullest and most
prosaic recording of weather patterns, conversations with people whom I

found interesting in their own search for continuity, even though they might not know the word, is as rewarding as any quasi-brilliant accident. It does not matter chronologically whether season follows season, nor that dates do more than signify whether a snowstorm or a mosquito can be expected. It is a part of a life as I have pleased and been pleased to live it."

DAVID IGNATOW is a well-known poet whose most recent book, Rescue the Dead, has been published by Wesleyan University Press. He teaches at Vassar.

MARVIN COHEN was born in Brooklyn and has lived in New York and London. He has published in New Directions anthologies, and his book, The Self Devoted Friend, was brought out by New Directions this year.

ANDREA PFEIFFENBERGER graduated from Vassar this year and is going on to study at the University of York, England.

NANCY-LOU PATTERSON is director of art at the University of Waterloo, Canada. She is a liturgical artist as well as poet and mother of six children. Her verse has appeared in Beloit Poetry Journal, Prairie Schooner and elsewhere.

TEO SAVORY edits the new Unicorn Review (Santa Barbara) and publishes fine books and broadsides at The Unicorn Press. Her latest collection of poems is Snow Vole.

CARLOS REYES writes, teaches and edits poetry (The Wine Press) in Portland, Oregon.

Mit Keyserlicher Mayestat Gnad vnd Priuilegio. ℭ Gedruckt zů Augspurg durch Heynrich Steyner

M. D. XXXI.

# MONKS POND

NO. 4          WINTER          1968

ENVOI

     So the Pond has frozen over--as planned.  There was enough material for
six issues, but it got crammed into four.  The problem of losing good poems,
of failing to answer letters, of forgetting to send copies, of not notifying
poets for months that they had been accepted: all this is the hell of editors.
But it was good experience.  The magazine was, we believe, a good one.  This
was due largely to the enthusiastic help of those who liked it and wanted to
be in it and who told other poets about it.  From the beginning: Keith Wilson,
Jonathan Williams and Jonathan Greene, especially.  The last two issues would
never have been possible without the layout work and typing of Phil Stark, a
Jesuit scholastic from Woodstock who spent the summer here to do this.  The
consistent good looks of the magazine are due to Brother Cassian, the monastery printer.  Help like this has made MONKS POND something unusual in little
magazines.  This is now the final issue; we have completed our four seasons.
If you have all four, good.  Number One is already out of print, unfortunately,
but the others can still be obtained, free, for a brief time.  Write to

MONKS POND   Trappist P.O., Kentucky   40073

Table of Authors

[Should be Matthias Gill, 271, and Augustine Wulff, 323]

WENDELL BERRY


On the Hill Late at Night


The ripe grassheads bend in the starlight
in the soft wind, beneath them the darkness
of the grass, fathomless, the long blades
rising out of the well of time.  Cars
travel the valley roads below me, their lights
finding the dark, and racing on.  Above
their roar is a silence I have suddenly heard,
and felt the country turn under the stars
toward dawn.  I am wholly willing to be here
between the bright silent thousands of stars
and the life of the grass pouring out of the ground.
The hill has grown to me like a foot.
Until I lift the earth I cannot move.


WILLIAM WITHERUP


A Day of Scattered Rains


It is a day of scattered rains.
A wind, blowing from the direction
of the Sangre de Cristos,
carries the scents of wet cedar and juniper,
of damp earth and sand,
and mixes it with the perfumes
of blossoming apricot, cherry and peach.

A thousand miles and two months away
and I am still disturbed
by these metaphors of your skin.
My nose, my pores, my heart
are overloaded with memories of your smell;
I have become a cloud
swollen with blossoms and moisture--
the pain of left-over love.

*Take me, wind, over the mountains
and let me break open!*


215

### After Talking to You Long Distance

#### 1

I put the white enamel coffee pot on the stove
light a Pall Mall
and a stick of Six Roses incense
and then walk out of the cabin
to look at the stars.

The night is clear and warm,
the air smelling of young willows
and spring water, of apple blows
and wildflowers, of cedar and pine,
of horse droppings and soil
and of cooling rocks and stones.

The stars are profuse tonight
and give off a faint light
that seems to flow out of the earth itself.
Below in the valley
the small stream, swollen from melting snow,
rushes through the willows
and sounds like wind.

The crickets are thick in the weeds
and grasses around the cabin.
Each one is a small black mirror
to a star--microcosm to macrocosm;
the distance between each male
and its lover
is as great, in the scheme of things,
as between star and star,
as between you and me.

I think of the rasping of their wings
as the humming of telephone wires--
the desire to touch
across a long distance.

#### 2

You said my drunken letters hurt.
Forgive me.  My bragging of other women
was a mask for my own suffering,
and in my drunkenness I didn't consider *your* pain.

We lie to cover our own inadequacies
and too easily forget that another's heart,
for all its energy and power,
is a delicate thing.

3

Your voice
though traveling a long distance
was warm in my ear.
Your pain passed into my ear as sound
and the sound dissolved in my blood
as wordless pain
and the pain moved to sound again
in the pulse of a poem
and the next morning
the poem moved me to running--
dropping down from the cabin
through prickly pear and yucca
across sandy arroyos
and through fields of cedar
where thousands of katydids
in the bark and branches
shrilled like telephone wires.
O I ran a long distance
from my cabin to Tesuque
to send you in a white envelope
a holy wafer
pressed from the dough
of our mutual pain.

4

You said my suffering was beautiful.
Your suffering is beautiful to me.
The odor of your pain is that
of a lilac cluster torn from its bush.

DOROTHY BECK

Two Zen Stories

### 1 Rules

A novice who had undertaken the study of various religions asked his superior why there were so many different orders.

"It would be so much simpler and easier if there were the same rules for everyone."

"What rules do you suggest?" asked the Father.

"That isn't for me to say," replied the monk. "Someone much wiser than I am would have to decide."

"Who is to decide who is wise enough? You would have to make up a rule before you made a rule. If we understood why we make one rule, then we could understand why there are so many."

### 2 Explanations

Wuntu was a great lover of music. He could play a number of instruments but none of them very well. He liked to sing but was never good enough to sing solo. Wuntu went through half his life lamenting the fact that he could not do justice to his muse. Little tunes would come into his head and he would record a phrase or two, hoping they would grow into big thematic pieces to be played in the future. But he was always left with the fragments of something great unexpressed.

At last, in his middle years, Wuntu was enlightened. One evening, after contemplating the sound of one hand clapping, he decided to give up being a musician and a composer. For he had discovered that he himself was music.


There are no words.
There are no words.
Even eyes censor
the exquisite sight.
There are no eyes,
only exquisite sight.

Union

(Written after witnessing the outcome
of a collision between two horses in
Pelham Bay Park; a white horse and a
black horse were lying head-to-head
on the bridle path, both of them dead.)

White horse black horse
galloping, each
to run his course
that soon must reach

an end.  Between
their foreheads white
and black unseen
the ghost of light

that softens death
when stallions meet
in hardened breath,
the end so neat

that quiet screams
"The sun is dark!"
and Nothing seems
to be a park.

Thank You

When you swooped down on me
I was already lower than the dragon
slain by St. George,
as large as death on Gothic structures.

What I wonder at is how you dragged the beast
as far as you did,
weathered the scaly surfaces,
planted your palms so deep.

219

ROBERT DAVID COHEN

1

This begins where others are likely to leave off; this begins
at the end
the invisible door opens and I step into a room without a ceiling
I have permission to fold my hands and put them in my lap
I've got to live here

People aren't practiced-on here
If I do whatever I want, will you do whatever *you* want?
Some current explanations won't do
Here are the five so-called senses:  they enter a room
What do THEY want?

Ever since, I haven't listened for harmony
if there was harmony, ok; if not, ok
That's harmony

At the age of 108, I saw the depth of my own superstition
At 22, the stupid waste of a thousand years

2

Baby Night and Baby Day
babies of the dusk and babies of the dawn
the early-baby gets the worm; the worm gets the early-baby
I already know that; but do you think I could intuit it?
The thing that suicides don't seem to realize is that when you kill
yourself you don't die, you just fling yourself into another cycle
of birth, into one infinitely more miserable than the last, the one
that seemed so impossible to deal with (exclude men who commit suicide
rather than betray comrades)
I don't know what I'm talking about
The police and sirens watching the night, making the circuit
mysterious and morbid superstition
My father owns the Pentagon, he can't help it
but they are so few, and they are so weak and exposed
HELIOPHAGE tells the truth; HELIOPHAGE can't help it

Nature is a myth, at best; a habit, at worst
We talked about this before, no?  About the man-on-the-mountain
(hermit) being the least capable of clarity
You warned me not to be seduced by an image
I'm only beginning to learn from you

Read the last stanza again, then come back to this
I feel that waiting for issues to become "clear" isn't all that
rational, and in some people waiting can become pathological

*Robert David Cohen*

What would clarity consist of
But impatience isn't a bad thing, is it
we shouldn't try to fool each other

Here I am, nothing new, words, punctuation marks, smears
a large animate lump of matter dropped from the blue
and wondering what to do next
The last year of the life

There are already too many people who talk only to themselves
Then I will be longing to see you
in the complete wreckage of the wind
Everything is different; almost nobody realizes this
It's hard to know if one isn't simply walking in one's sleep or
exchanging one dream for another
I wasn't *born*; all I know is that somewhere along the line I came to
consciousness
What's all this about being born?
I was dropped here
"What a fine golden-haired lion!"
We know things with our own knowledge, or else we don't know anything;
I'm growing tusks, horns, antlers
tired of dark, ignorant knowing...

3

I was making tea, I was feeling cynical
I saw a Naga, and it was me

Henri Bergson (1859-1941) "spoke with absolutely no gestures, without
notes, his hands folded in front of him"
Pandora's Box, the policeman in my dream, watch me, to make sure that
no one sees me, the hero, the appendix, suffocation, we cannot exist,
ask Headquarters, jumble of information, bad analogy, frustrating the
wish, breaking the hymen, the man who bluffs his way, intuitive likes
and dislikes often "wrong," my lameness in a daydream, letters from
another world, self-mutilation, sleepwalking, ask Headquarters, who
will give us this package, what's the address, where is the hotel, I had
a high fever and dreamt of turkeys pecking my father's face, cold night
wind, put in strait jacket, erotic light coming from everything, don't
lie, you won't be missed for long, the grapes looked so real the birds
tried to eat them, who cares, I closed the book and threw it away, he
thought he was going to die, how do you spell "cat"

I was making tea
I saw a Naga, and it was me

Chiclero

in mud he sloshes
alligator hide a rough skin
fish swimming the
trees chicozapote
                        for
chewing gum

bandido of woods
he boils white sap
wax
thick melts it
into dirty balls his
mules haul out to rivers

the mules
sink their bodies in--
rain time) monsoon slicks
                        hura-kahn
black swamp
snake of the Antilles
sliding sticky gum
beast-drivers            eating
                         heart of the palm
                         white ant's nests
                         where little bees
                         deposit their hunger
out of the law:

and lie
dead on the trail
mute before the machete
hunters who haul down the knife!
bog on loaded (through jungle
lianas
with the rich honey
                        a tree-christ snow
from wood so hard when dry
the nail of the cross
bends under blows and will not
enter it
though hard rain blunts
and tears its leaves with

                        a fiercer wind

the intensity of (art

loco
witch

who carries a great pod
full of ripe
                        poppy seed
- -

she
scatters

her little dried
scents of
                    opium
freely
          as
sunflakes
blizzards of snow


- -

she
shakes
                them
not watching to see

which
one
comes up




                bañero

at the bath pavilion
white sun stone
                    still pool
the white ducks swim

flay up their wings
shaking the hot air
to a spray of feathers and
                            flurry
and dive--
their thick necks under

223

and two little girls
babies
with round faces
sit on the polished stone
steps that go
                    down
and watch--
the court of the white princess...
bathing

shaking their clothes off

in the white clouds
reflecting against the transparent
                                    water


        they got wet (mojada

crossing at Del Rio the river
washed
up deep as their hearts

their hearts in the river

they walked
nine days and nine nights
picked nuts like the squirrels
hid with the animals

following the monte
indians
camped on rabbit hunts
indians and coyotes

bows and arrows held above the water

arms extended the border patrol
didn't see them
they walked into (through the
country
still as the animals
moved strange deer hunting water holes
a hide of surplus clothes; and it was easy
they looked

a part of the earth
they walked on

look at me my mother

just once come off the little dance
is there nothing left but words
the flow-off from a jangle box your
voice
not connected with the strings anymore
the sweet harmony
of touch /of thought
of touching with the voice simplicity
sounds even an animal can make

a bird
trained to a mechanism of speech
where are the woods you came from
the woods of tenderness
speak to me my strange little
bird
in your own root tongue
look at me
with the eyes of morning still in your face

let your hands let your small feet
once (reach out to
stand still and in all this passing
let me at last be able to touch you


involved with things

how are all the things left at the house
pictures of loved ones the pictures are
loved beyond flesh past
                    love
yes,
they are where you can get to them
taken each from the frame in an order
exact as words

the dishes
set apart stacked in relationship
your coat
the soft dead fur that touched your face
hangs safe tight with
gowns and blouses, the weave of thread
patterned still against their colors
all is in place all is at rest

in the chifforobe
waiting for your hand waiting for
your breath to wake them, waiting
for one day when far from the sky
I go out
with loaded arms
and take each little ghost
and stifle its screams in the heat of fire
waiting for Christ to raise them


PHILIP GARRISON


Two Songs for the "Other Wild Man"

*--Makah: the Wolf Dance*

Water boils in a woven pot under
stiff hanging pine boughs--
loneliness is a man.
*Hear their voices?*
Cedar bark for hair
ragged on the hard shoulders
& sniffing one hand--
the human smell.

Throat clumsy with words
for things low on the ground
        "twinflower"
        "kinnikinnick"

the stiff-legged walk in
smoke rhythms

people stand in the hills
dew gleaming on stiff arms
            (a bark groove is a fingerprint)

sky over miles of pine!


--


Fog crosses Neah Bay.
I glide into a long-house.

The people listen to my feet.
Flames beat a dry log
--our drum

shadows flick on the ceiling--
now they wear wolf shapes, they

dance hard
& I am already gone.


The Stories

1

A small rain
a thin cold rain

clicks on the shake roof &
on miles & miles of valley.

They came to the pine forest hills:
"What a wonderful tree!
"Look, it has eyes & hair!
"Look, here is a quiver and a bow"
& he followed them home.

We sit by the living room woodstove
& tell stories, dry
& warm in the high dark
Columbia Plateau winter.

And step outside only
to throw in more wood
the rough bark, tight grain
clattering into flame.


2

The people'd been hungry weeks
& a mangy old bull wandered by:
"Ah, don't kill him.
"Rub his back with firewood."

Next day a few buffalo
walked right into the traps:
"For a little while we are saved.
"We have a little meat."

Those people were Blackfeet
400 miles east, over
the Columbia River cliffs
                            --the plains

snowed-in tonight
the buffalo killed off
& people gone into cities.

That is the story
we were telling.


                    3

Back outside
no moon.
I pick up the kindling.
Hooves scrape nearby
through snow, on wide
stiff frozen grassland.

A shape lurches into the firelight.
A weight falls from my hands.
The fire turns & tosses.


                HALVARD JOHNSON


                around about

    pushing aside
    the thick branches,
    branches thick with
    tender & green leaves,
    pushing aside the green
    tender leaves, moving
    into sunshine, looking
    for yellow sunshine
    from blue sky,
    sniffing a wet breeze,
    pushing aside the thick
    leaves, moving into
    sunshine, looking for
    berries?

dead man's float

milwaukee, wisconsin.  some time
near the beginning of the war.
a 4th of july parade, amid news
paper reports of bodies found
dismembered, dumped in trashcans
along the lake michigan beaches.

      we decorate our tricycles
      with fireproof red white & blue
      streamers. we pump along the route,
      waving our flags, grinning
      at patriot parents. later

that summer i fell in a lake
& survived. my too-old-for-the-war
uncle began to teach me to swim.
arms out. legs out. face
in the water, holding my breath:
learning to live, practicing death.

ROBERT BONAZZI

Searching for a Lost Cause

:in an abandoned tunnel
with a camel on your back

its humps are balanced on your spine
and its legs
are askew and floundering

you deposit the camel midway
with no regard
for the dignity of darkness
and travel on alone

:you come upon
a camel vendor
with a flashlight

      he tells you
you've made a mistake

*Robert Bonazzi*

## Hardhat

He is put out of my mind, edged
out because his life is so well.

No problems
save his knees which ache.  Nothing awry
in his mind or heart: half a century
gone
and his love has never been lighted by GE.

Today my father says he's been fired or laid off--
whole crew sent home.  He tells of one
Negro man there twenty years who would not
hand in his hard hat.  It was his: man bought
it ten years before.

They took it from him
and his job
and forty-three others.

But this hard hat bothered my old man
more than anything.

Out in the other room he is napping on the couch.
There seems no way to have that
irretrievable hard hat.

Even in dreams.


## Waiting for a Train

so early freight makes
no effort to clear the track
backs up     moves forward
i switch off my engine.

boxcars crab claw     artificial
lights stammer a beacon
between them     again &
once more and i smell bread
at nabisco.

when the trackshoulders empty
  caboose shrinks to black.

a horn sounds
buick behind me     must
smell bread too

WHISKE

WHI  SK

WHISSS

KE  E    Y

SHKEEY

WHISKW

HISKWY

WHISKY


whisk  EY

EYW   hisky

WHISKW

aaaa s h ky

w h I S key

h i S K y

YK e h w ik


WHISKI

hseykW

I s k e y

WISHKI

THOMAS MERTON

THOMAS MERTON

## Semiotic Poem from Racine's *Iphigénie*

```
c e s        m o r t s
c e t t e    l e s b o s
c e s        c e n d r e s
c e t t e    f l a m m e

     C E S
     C E T T E
     C E S
     C E T T E
   M O R T S
   L E S B O S
   C E N D R E S
   F L A M M E
     C E S
     C E T T E
     L E S

     b o s
     e e e e
     o e e l
     s t s t
     r s n a
       t t
       e e
     s o r m
     l e s b o
     m o r f a
     f l a m m a
   M O R S

     L E S B O S
     C C C C C C
     E E E E E E
     S T S T S T
C E S M O R T S C E T T E
     L E S B O S

     c e n d r e s
```

DAVID M. COLLINS

O Happy Dream

Dhuvyansky!

Dhuvyansky, indeed!  That is a name?  A name!  An obscenity.

Very good.  Cigar...very good.  I must...tell Olga.  She will get more.
Dhuvyansky, indeed.  A poltroon, he is.

Meersman, I will say to him.  I will go to him today...

Watch!  Idiot, watch.  Have you no respect?  A 1937 Packard automobile, do you not see me?  To have respect, you should watch.  Watch.
Where are you going?  Ah, fools.  Well...

Should.  Ha.  Should.  An obscenity.  Truly, an obscene thing.  Yes,
Meersman.  You cannot for vileness match that word.  This should.  Out of
my own mouth!  Feh!  Almost, Meersman...

I will say to him.  Meersman, I will say, you are a...Now the machine
again.  He comes at me again, with his machine.  The police.  Yes.  I have
had a time or two, the police.  And that is a help?  You...you Meersman.

Ah, Meersman, I will say to him.  I will say to him, Meersman, you are
wrong.  Dhubyansky.  My name is Michael Paul Dhubyansky.

Olga is sweet.  To buy cigars....

Unnameable one.  Your machine is not fit to be on the avenues.  Get it
hence.

Olga.  My little bouquet of morning flowers.  Yes.  A lovely cigar.

That building again.  That building in which that doctor is.  I call
him butcher.  Michael Paul Dhubyansky, I, an old man, call him butcher.
I call him not a doctor.  He is butcher.  Butcher, you are not a doctor.
You are a butcher.  But...I should say he means well, Dhubyansky, you are
an old man.  You have mercy.  Once, once when you are a man, ah, then you
have not mercy.  The sword!  Then, for the butcher, the sword, Dhubyansky.
Michael Paul Dhubyansky, swordsman, cuts down the butcher with his own
instruments.

Your machine, your machine!  Nameless one, your machine.  Watch where
you steer it, headless idiot.  Watch.

Beautiful 1937 Packard....

Ho.  The bushes are trimmed.  Ho, ho, gardener, you have trimmed your
bushes.  At last.  Ho, we will pause here...Stop, 1937 Packard automobile,

stop here. We will stop here to observe the trimmed bushes.

Hah, Meersman. Observe the bushes. They are trimmed. Were you here, Meersman, would you equate yourself to such a task? No, I answer. Not equal, Meersman. You are not. I answer without cavil or hesitation, Meersman, you are not. You are a mispronouncer of names, that is what you are.

Allons. Yes, allons. Oui. Eh? How about that? You are speaking to Michael Paul Dhubyansky.

Olga. Dear Olga. I must teach her. The child. She will spend substance on these dear cigars for Grandfather Dhubyansky. And never will she address me as that other. Never. It is written. Dhuvyansky! Never!

Meersman, I will say....Beautiful Packard automobile. From 1937. A vintage year. It is not written....Meersman, in all respect. In all respect, you must pronounce my name with correctness. It is what you can do. The least. It is to say, after all....

Ho, what have we? Cigar, this is no time to go out. Ho, yes. There well, I flick your ashes. There. Does that satisfy?

What here? Building? Is it possible to imagine? How is it to suppose? I wonder, is it that they are doing this thing? Well. We will have to see. Building here, in the green meadow.

Yes, Olga. I will say to Olga. Olga, my child, Olga, dove, granddaughter of my limpid heart, I embrace you and invite you. Kneel here, little Olga. Here, beside my chair...

Fool. Errant wild one. Watch the automobile. The white line, blindness, watch white line. It teaches who is to stay on each side. I on mine, blind one, thou on thine. Let us so manage it, and we shall both grow old. Only with less ire on my part, fool. Let us proceed. I drive a 1937 Packard automobile....

Yes. Olga. So sweet you are, little Olga. Yes. No, Olga, no beard. Never do I have beard. No. It is not right. Not Michael Paul. We will not talk of that, eh, little Olga? You are sweet. Let me describe to you how it was then. You will know. And then, how the cigars will be for you, then, little Olga!

And he will say...I will say to Meersman, you are a mispronouncer... and he will say...Feh! That is what he will say...he being Meersman. He being like me, an old man who will give nothing. Give nothing, Meersman, old man. Give nothing. They will take it. Take it soon enough, Meersman.

Good cigar.

Yes....yes, Meersman, make them take it. It is like this....

By the feet of Olaf.....Ah, he is an old one. It is a police? And so old? My son's age. My son is younger! A police? What will they do here? Well....

I know, Meersman, ah, how I know! And when the children come, Meersman....When the children come, make them take, also, Meersman. Give nothing, old man. Give nothing.

Michael Paul Dhubyansky, you wander! You are an old man, wandering. You cannot keep the course. You and your cigars. And a palsied arm to smoke it with, old one.....They will "should" you to death, old man.

Do not mind, little Olga. The grandfather one talks, eh? Well, it is to talk a little, nothing more. Only the talk. We will continue our talk another time. Perhaps another time. Yes, then.

Yes, I will show you the buildings, eh? Oh, like these I passed on my journey today. Only greater, far greater. Of a height which makes the ears ring. The entrails hollow out at the height.

It is certain, Olga. I shall except you from the others. I, Michael Paul, Grandfather, shall find you singly and leave the others to their times. They are the children, Olga. They will....

I will give them nothing. Nothing. Michael Paul Dhubyansky will give the children nothing. They will take enough, and soon enough. I shall give nothing.

Tell them, Meersman, old adversary. Tell the children. I give nothing. Dhubyansky resists to the end.

Perhaps it is another time, eh, 1937 Packard automobile? Faithful machine. Here, this is the place. Pull in here. There, there. You purr like....

I cannot understand that. An old man police. They are insane. They are beside themselves. They are doted.

Sweet Olga...I shall ask her to get me more of these so fine cigars.

And perhaps one for Meersman, eh?

DICK GANCI

## 1

eddie leonard is a humburger
house
where they yell "next"
when you're the only one in line
the food is good
and the juke box is better
but i'll bet eddie's
a real bastard

## 2

do you know the wind
i mean  do you really
know the wind
do you know the rain
do you
the ocean
do you know the ocean
stillness of night
and what of stillness of night
do you know the ache
*there* it is
do you know the ache

## 3

i died once
in an auto wreck
(just had to laugh
to hear purcell
so angry at my driving)
you know
it's a very lonesome business
to miss
and how i missed
the giraffe stooping to board the bus that day
and the 8' 3" old lady who couldn't make up her mind
                    just who to vote for

4

```
        there comes a time
        when we
        in turn
        must forgive
        jesus
```

GAIL WAECHTER


The Convention

And I saw the connectedness of all things unconnected
On flypapers grocery store just to the left of sweating summer
And I went running on to nowhere fast
Tripping now and then on carnivorous toenail
Did you see me then

                entering gates of national convention
                                con
                                concept
                                con

            with velvet sleeves and lace cowboy boots
          head hitting either side of Liberty Bell
        shouting om om om
            splitting White House crystals
                talking slowly to Old Man River
            on the road to nowhere fast

    faded old photo of you whoever whenever and however you are
Backpocketed    to share in past remembering
      did you see me then
            walking backwards down Chicken Creek Hill
            feathered hat and striped hair
            silken underwear
                saying clearly under my breath
          whats already been said

    whistling on the side God bless my country

                        my planet

                    and my dog

TED ENSLIN

from *The Maine Journal*

November 7. A misplaced moth wandering around November, as I go out for
my usual woodcutting stint, and by the corner of the shed a misplaced goldenrod in bud, somewhat blasted by frost, but with a hint of possible flowering.
November, always the month of heart-eating--a confluence of the seasons--its
gray skies its only personal quality.

November 8. The heavy autumn rains have taken us from drought two weeks
ago when the first snow fell, to near spring freshet conditions now. The
roar of water everywhere. On my return walk today, depressed and sodden as
I was, I followed two pair of fresh moose tracks in the mud for nearly two
miles--the whole distance to Little's field. A presentiment, as I can have
them, that I would actually see moose this time, as I never have before, no
matter how fresh the tracks which I have seen. As I reached Little's field
I saw two--an old bull and a young one grazing as calmly as any cow. They
looked at me for a moment and returned to the alders which they were chewing,
and I approached them--within fifty feet--before I was aware of how foolhardy
I might be. Finally, both of them moved off slowly into the woods, still un-
disturbed by my presence. At this season? Two bull moose together and not
fighting? The whole thing seems very strange.

November 10. Looking up from my work table this morning. Who is that
man carrying a ladder past the windows? Why should a man be doing that here?
And then I realize that is is no man, but a moose. Going outside, I see as
large an animal as I am ever likely to see in Maine. His bulk fills the entire road, while his antlers spread far out to either side--the "ladder."
This must be the old moose of whom people talk--gray at the muzzle and flanks.
Again, he is not disturbed by my presence, though I am more careful than on
the former occasion, lumbers off down the road and into the woods, rolling
his great weight as if it were boneless, and after he disappeared into the
underbrush an occasional click of the antlers was all that I could hear.

November 23. Stopping by Mary Dalrymple's, Johnny Grant once more:
"When I was a young feller I worked for a feller in Wilton--combination
livery stable and undertaker. Well, part of my job was to go fetch the
bodies with a horse-drawn hearse. Usually had a man with me to help, but
like as not he was usually drunk, so I'd have to help *him* as well as myself.
We was sent up to Weld one day to bring a body down to the depot here. Cold!
Well, I guess prob'ly it was cold, and we was sitting up in front on the box
the whole way across the plantations. You know how the wind funnels down
through there. Well, this feller was so drunk that he'd fall off first one
side and then the other, and I'd have to climb down and prop him up again.
It was worse than handlin' a dozen coffins-full. Well, it started snowin',
and I was scairt he'd freeze to death, so I hauled him off the box and shoved
him in behind. He stayed there all right--dropped right off to sleep. We
got up to Weld, and the feller there helped me with the coffin, and I sot my

238

"helper" up on the box again. Once we got out on the road again, I got to
thinkin'. I'd give that miserable so-and-so somethin' to remember. I got
him down, opened up the back of the hearse, got the lid off the coffin and
put him in with the other one. 'Course he was dead to the world and didn't
know what was happenin'. Snowin' like hell and gettin' dark, but I figured
if he was to lay in there with no air at all he might smother, and then we
would have two dead 'uns. So I left them doors open, rattlin' to and back
the whole way home again. It was late by the time we got back, and the
train had gone, so we'd just have to wait until mornin'. I drove the hearse
into the barn and left it—left him right in the box with the corpse. I was
on call that night, so I was sittin' up to the house in the office. Guess
I must have dozed off. All of a sudden I heard the god-damnedest racket you
ever, and my "assistant" come runnin' in like the devil was after him. He
come to and found out where he was, but he didn't come the whole way, though
I guess he was sober as a judge by the time he landed in the house. He was
shakin' like a leaf, says, 'John, I was dead, but the good Lord brought me
to life again. I'll never touch another drop so long as I live.' Well, he
lived better'n thirty years after that, and so far as I know, he never did."

November 26. Out by subdued moonlight this evening, gathering wood,
singing, chuckling, a moon-mad man, laughing about karma and reacting vehe-
mently to every weather sign—to the moon itself—the slight snow underfoot.
A high time.

December 3. Whenever I talk of walking in these hills, it is usually
*toward* the mountain—the place where I live, of which others ask me incre-
dulously, "What do you find to do there?" I cannot ask them that question—
of what *they* find to do. In a way I am removed from them, but in such a
way that I am probably far more closely concerned in their lives than I
could expect them to be in mine. But I don't come back to a mooseyard or
rabbit warren. My concerns are small by some lights, but by others they
include far more than simply making a go of it. The fact that my house is
hardly a house at all by most standards allows me a freedom in action. I
suppose that a certain number of acres more or less with the buildings there-
on, are credited to me in the registry of deeds. At times it pleases me to
think of that, but usually with a feeling that I must not fail what I occupy
for a little time. I must not slaughter its timber, even though I may cut
some of it, nor foul its water. My place of habitation (high-sounding and
old-fashioned, but more accurate than "my house") becomes my friend. A
place that extends arms and a pleasure at my return—something to which I
return an embrace. If it were more a house, it would mean less to me. It
does not obtrude into my habitation, which includes the outside. I may bed
myself on grass or rocks or even under the snow. On the walk this afternoon, I see that the fox which I followed out last evening has followed my
tracks in and suited his gait to mine. Animals and men are alike in this:
they will take the easier way wherever it is available.

December 18. A bitterly cold morning, and well below zero most of the
day. The ice whoops and grinds in streams and marshes. A fine-seeding

snow which is hardly that--the final moisture wrung from unstable clouds into
a bitterness which is tonic if it is taken as itself and not as something to
be wished away.  So much that my neighbors miss, riding from door to door.
It used to be common coin when men walked--the subtle changes which one may
see in a road walked a number of times in a day, and yet a different road
each time.  The snow changes consistency now--the problems of footing are
different each time, and this is not due entirely to the walking which breaks
a trail.  The snow deliquesces, the wind packs it, ice wells up from the
springs below it.  There are places blown entirely clear--deep drifts in
others--the feel of surface below my boots can change completely.  Nor is
this simply a winter phenomenon.  It is so at all seasons of the year.  When
I travel to the village and back, in ostensibly the same and opposite directions, I travel over the whole earth in point of space and time.  It is a
little thing, but not less than the greatest concerns.  Coupled with that
precise and difficult act of "seeing," it becomes the pivot of what one lives
for.  I live through these continuous things, and not through surprises, the
*disjecta membra* which are accidents and destructive ones.

December 19.  I think I have rarely heard so much snapping in the trees
from frost as during these last few days.  They really suffer.  Sounds--all
the way from an ax-blow to a real explosion--as fissures open in old trees
which have wintered safely for years.  Hammering, the sound of engines, of
creaking as in the joints of an old building, whimpering, complaints as if
a child were crying.  It is at this season that we hear the suffering of the
woods, which is mute for the greater part of the year.  The lumbermen shake
their heads, but not in sympathy.  They think merely of the wood which will
be spoiled for another season's cutting.  It is the temper of a hard country
which hides behind the leaves.  The deceptive roundness of summer outlines
is stripped to bone starkness.  It is wrong, ever, to talk of the "dead" of
winter.  It is anything but dead--a vibrant movement of quick savagery, sometimes doom, though it is not certain.  We are caught in the midst of it, and
it is poor intelligence to complain.  The animal body hardens similarly, if
we listen to it--allow it to do what it will do.

```
amen zldm i say unto you
bfno ykcl i say unto you
cogp xjbk i say unto you
dphq wiaj i say unto you
eqir vhzi i say unto you
frjs ugyh i say unto you
gskt tfxg i say unto you
htlu sewf i say unto you
iumv rdve i say unto you
jvnw qcud i say unto you
kwox pbtc i say unto you
lxpy oasb i say unto you
myqz nzra i say unto you
nzra myqz i say unto you
oasb lxpy i say unto you
pbtc kwox i say unto you
qcud jvnw i say unto you
rdve iumv i say unto you
sewf htlu i say unto you
ftxg gskt i say unto you
ugyh frjs i say unto you
vhzi eqir i say unto you
wiaj dphq i say unto you
xjbk cogp i say unto you
ykcl bfno i say unto you
zldm amen i say unto you
```

```
       zenzen*
           i love you totally
           i love you entirely
           i love you quite
           i love you completely
           i love you [not] at all
```

*(The adverbs and the final adverbial phrase are taken,
in the order of their appearance in the definition of
zenzen, from M. Takahashi's Romanized English-Japanese
Japanese-English Dictionary, Taiseido Shobo Co., Tokyo.

ROBERTS BLOSSOM

1

My thoughts have died
Or erupt in dumb ghostly waves
Here I sit on an esplanade
Looking through bars at an ascending helicopter
Manhattan's beyond
With its bars and knaves
Tall zoos of behaving slaves
The ships are being prepared to go
(And one is already sailing away)
(More zoos?)
And the used Ten Commandments sit in our pockets
Waiting for our tears to fall.

2

A shore
Where the pier posts
Are elephant tusks

A girl walks slow
In afternoon sunlight

As she enters her cabin
The blue of the sky
Clings to her skirt

At night
Only the sea is heard

In dawn
The green of the woods
Opalesces

She walks to the edge,
Plucks a leaf
Puts it in her hair

As she walks away
Around her whirl
In gray mist
The sometimes white
Elements of dreams

Widening, slowing
The now faint red whirlpool
Dissolves the scene

3

Oh peoples the sea in your veins is red
As a mask to hide from the sun
One day a beautiful green flower will cover the earth
And the sun will see that your blood, people,
Is only a reflection of her noontime bliss.


4

The figure in the garden
The dance of sea
The bird flying
All
Think of God
In their daily habits
All
Think
Of death
In their daily
Nights
All
Think


REE DRAGONETTE


Samarkand

I   Atoms & Molecules

If I say love me, as we are
where we collide near dying;
I mean
we are spheres, phenomenal earth
poles and changes.

I mean that which is ourselves,
and that which is still
beyond us.

When I dwell with you
in dark,
I speak with habits of fire, of feathers.
And I mean we are


243

weavers;
are persons of rock who claw upward
        seedbeds.

When I ask you to love
I am telling you to fathom
the self of a bird:
story of grasses and foxes.

I am one who lives without knowing how.
We stand
falling
        creatures of water.
        None and many,
        we are those in whom
first cause flutters,
crumbles.
Drummed, we are luminescent survivors.

Sitting with you in storm,
I am without volition.
We move without stop, without
knowledge of transcendence.

Nerveless between star chips
real and unreal,
my red veins learn the cut of the axe.
Fruit center in my loins
        coils ripe, the sluiceways
                round you.
After length of omens, after glass hour
I rest.
Schism of my legs is no more:
I cease running.
My ribs welcome you.

We close in desire, sword on fruit-blossom.
            Yes,
            until no desire.

If I say, I am shadow;
thinner than air, a gleam:
I say I am a body of no
thing, except moons.
And I do not deny subject or object.

If you are a sexual blade,
worsening.
Rubbed breaking,
I can come to be flower.

Dual and worldly, we tilt.
We follow two ways at once.
Polarized
I let you pierce me.

In the light of heaven, we
are only as blind as we wish:
when we embrace.

## II   The Nuclear Realm

In Samarkand, will you be my brother?
The way for him
hard, when he drowned.

Did the sea urchins tear him?

He delved into weeds,
his brain
turned to sparkle.

All roads in his eyes pointed
              downward.
He was lax, he was scratched
        for the fishes.

Which trace of his life,
under blood's copper
was the one nugget so buried,
that
dorsal in sunlight, he dived?

Toward what cold and
immaculate meaning?

Trees are thick on our Samarkand road.
They are vivid.  Swirling
they spin on their leaves, among ignorant questions.
Hailstones hiss in the wind:
a rain grieves.

We sit in a room filled with oxen.
With men whose original eyes come between us.
Gray as lead
blue as iris
colors of seashells.

We sit
wearing weeds in our skin,
wearing doors never open.

With men eating meal on their haunches.

They are bearers of grain,
They drive over roads leading outward.

They are human: by halves
they are gods
and they mimic the oxen.

Haulers of iron, of salt—lust
Green tea
and the lamb's fur.
Purveyors of truth, by long slaughter.

They have knives in their thumbs.

They have eyes made of smoke
            and of foam.

We are sly.  Full of raindrops, we ponder
the men riding out.
Our eyes turn on wheels,
turn gray flowers.
We study the searoad.

From our thoughts, swirling amber:
from their sparks full of ignorant questions,
no light comes
to flush us to gold.
No fable to dazzle our bodies
which suffer as deadly as foxes.

Be my brother, I fear
as I ask you.
Be the one who has died in the sea.

On a road beyond Samarkand,
amber we sit in our gaze beyond image.

Wearing hatchets,
you gaze among leaves.

I gaze through my memory's fishes.

III   The Realm of the Subnuclear

Looking at you
where we spin
parallel and antiparallel;

I stop combing my hair.

It is the moment to pause,
to bend and study Sanskrit.

I gather into myself
   think of you.

We are manifest in love.  Unstable,
small as nuclei.
At the very least, vulnerable.

We are enormous:
                    molecular giants.

My heart breaks,
I turn and go as far as I can go.

To a river's edge in your eyes;
swaying through bluebells,
through clouds of jonquils.

Rested, multiple after love's death:
I pass through seawalls.

I climb toward a knowledge of branches;
over beanstalks which cannot end
or topple:
my tears hum and spill into pods.

Snow beads me.
   Beads the first foothills.

Always, you are just out of sight.
Far as I go, brimming with you.
My ears bombarded,
with wind.
With ions,

wavering sunspots.

I am magnetized on low slopes.
Slopes high, unreachable as your eyelids.

They gape,
scarfed green
              they taunt me.

I see you with the frozen mandibles of birds.

              Under the sky's mountain,
              at the next sheer
              face:
              are leopards.
              They lie on their sides, etched
                    and not breathing.

We are clear, who love one another.
So baffled.

In your sight, silk showers touch me.
I glisten.
I caress your hammer-fires.
Stung by you, I want enlightenment;
knowing there is no time to learn.
No watery conduct, no
ribbon on which, strand by strand,
we fall free.

No luminous, precise alphabet.

Only at the interior of stars
is all truth.
In multibillion cataclysmic events;
which we cannot conceive.

At our last ultra-energies
beating
with flares in our wake when we
enter each other and burn
                          away
    there is more...

More under the crisscrossing,
after our rage toward exotic kiss:
toward the trance state.

We have been bound in quanta.
All that we know of the nature of love's life
is old.  Will never suffice.
Coins, hexagram
flashes.
judgments thunderous with steep forms.
                                  chaos

248

Familiar, I lean on your breast.  Curl myself
lonely into your thighs.
We are new.
Once again, released, we are excited.

Chargeless, after a time, not perceiving
we wait
remembering the first behavior of atoms.
Until gamma

until lepton pairs;

      our leaping and puzzling.

All our minute instances.

When our souls sleep together,
at ground
at passion of joy and sorrow;
we are most transitory.

Near to wholeness, we are heavy
massive as mesons.

We are torn apart;
stranger than quarks doubled.

Loving, I lean.
You are momentous on me as silk.
You speak in exact shower of Sanskrit.

Always, we fail one another.

Only in quasars
is the vision we seek.
In alphabet
at the center of matter.

Far in your eyes,
I sit at the river's edge:

    combing my hair.

GUILLEVIC

## Walls

(translated from the French by Anselm Hollo)


walls are companions
they always accept the weight of your elbow or palm
they always face you

they have a little earth
to fertilize with their excess of virtue

they appear to have proved their innocence
finding themselves in the air
though they live off the dark


.


it is in the walls
the doors are
by which one can enter

and by one of them
arrive


.


it wouldn't be so bad

to become the wall at the corner of the square
where the children play among the old men

the one who knows nothing of the town
except its anger

one could also become
a country wall, hidden by leaves

for happiness


.


some walls
are ugly

they're not
themselves

made to conceal
to prevent

armored at times
with broken glass

they won't be able to stop
the triumphant mob


there's a man
has become envious of walls

hard as he tries, the roots
won't let go of him any more

so he sits, at some distance
a familiar body

shuts out the doors
shuts out time

stares into the dark

and says: love


ENRIQUE LIHN


Christmas

(from *La Pieza Oscura*, translated from the Spanish
    by William Witherup and Serge Echeverria)


Will we have the courage to meet again tonight
fathers and brothers, the bride with no place to go,
    the friendly neighbor?
And the good childhood friend--what would become of her
    without him--will she find tonight
the good road between her heart and ours?

The thistle has overthrown the children we were and lost ghosts
    in the kingdom of the thistle
we are looking for a street in the desert, the street of childhood,
the good road between the dust and us,
our tears in the pools of swampy water.

NICANOR PARRA

(from *Versos de Salon*, translated from the Spanish
by Arlene Ladden and Anselm Hollo)


Long Live the Andes Mountains

I have a crazy desire to cry out
Long live the Andes Mountains
Down with the mountains on the coast

Reason would never allow it
But I can't help it:
Long live the Andes Mountains!
Down with the mountains on the coast!

It's been forty years
Since I've wanted to smash the horizon,
To go farther than my own nose,
But I didn't dare to.
Now, gentlemen, enough;
The decisions are made:
Long live the Andes Mountains!
Down with the mountains on the coast!

Did you hear what I said?
My mind is made up!
Long live the Andes Mountains!
Down with the mountains on the coast!

It's obvious I won't respond
If my vocal chords snap
(In a case like this it's quite probable they'll snap)
Very well, if they snap,
It means I have no resources,
That the last hope is lost.

I'm a storekeeper
Indifferent to the settings of the sun
A professor in green trousers
Who fades out in drops of dew
A petty bourgeois is what I am
What do rosy skies mean to me!
Anyway, I'm going up to the balconies
To shout what I give out to the whole world:
Long live the Andes Mountains!
Down with the mountains on the coast!!

Excuse me if i'm losing my reason
In the garden of nature
But I have to shout until I die
Long live the Andes Mountains!!
Down with the mountains on the coast!!!


Three Poems

1

There's nothing left for me to say
All there was to say
Has been said who knows how many times.


2

I've asked who knows how many times
But no one answers my questions.
It is absolutely necessary
For the abyss to respond just once
Because time's already running short.

3

Only one thing is clear:
The flesh grows full of worms.


Moais

No one's quite sure
Are they spirits or tombstones
The smallest are twelve feet high
The largest (which lean) are almost thirty

No one quite knows if they're stone
Those enormous cloudbursts of stone
Those venerable ancestors
From a distance they look like cardboard

Carbon 14 will tell

But O may they never determine
The nature of these mysterious rocks

253

The Master of Nan-ch'uan: Humorous Discourse
of Early Chinese Zen Masters (1)

(paraphrased from the Chinese by S.Y. Chi)

The Master addressed the audience in the assembly hall. "Gentlemen.
I have mastered this technique (2) since I was eighteen. Now, speaking of
'technique,' if there is anyone in this assembly who knows the ropes (3),
please come forward and let's talk about it. Of course, he should be an
old hand!" (4)

He paused for a long while, looked around the audience, then folded
his hands. "Good day, gentlemen. Obviously there is no business to de-
tain us here today. Why not retire; let us discipline ourselves." The
audience did not disperse. The Master continued:

"It is really an awesome task to direct people to reach an enlightened
stage! (5) On this point even the Supreme Master (6) was completely hog-
tied. Every individual is different, with his own identity; how could anyone possibly do the enlightening on behalf of anyone else! (7)

"The Scripture scholars say that the 'Universal Body' (8) is the ultimate aim, and call it 'the *samādhi* of supreme reasoning' or 'the *samādhi* of
supreme doctrine.' I myself had been taught long ago to 'retrace the source
and to return to the fundamentals.' But if you took these words literally,
it would be utterly disastrous!

"Gentlemen. Nowadays there are so many "Ch'an masters,' it is difficult
to find fools. Fools are now rare, if not altogether extinct. If there are
any here today, by all means step forward. Let us discuss such problems as
'Whether or not there is a hermit in the 'Aeon of Complete Emptiness'?'

"Well, yes or no? Speak up! What? No volunteers? Ordinarily everyone babbles easily enough. Why, then, when a question is raised, is there
always stunned silence? Are all of you tongue-tied? Now, please, don't
start giving me all that claptrap about the life of Buddha on earth and that
sort of nonsense! (9)

"Gentlemen. Nowadays people go about wearing their Buddhas on their
sleeves. (10) Once they heard me say, 'Mind is not the Buddha; intellect
is not the Way,' they immediately put their heads together and tossed it
around. (11) My dear fellows, don't expect me to leave you an out, unless
you can squeeze a stick out of thin air and knock me over the head with it,
only then will I let you play this game of yours."

Then a monk put a question to the Master:

"Our patriarchs, including the Master of Kiangsi (12), unanimously
agreed that 'Buddha is nothing but your own mind, and the Way is nothing
but the normal state of mind.' Now Your Reverence says, 'Mind is not the
Buddha; and intellect is not the Way'; we are very much confused. Please

be so kind as to point out the correct way to us."

The Master raised his voice. "In that event, sir, you must be a Buddha already. My congratulations! Then why on earth are you still 'confused'? And why ask me, a humble old monk, for instruction? Could there be such a thing as a 'confused Buddha'? I am afraid that I am no Buddha, nor have I had the honor of meeting a patriarch. Since you are so well-blessed, why not look for a patriarch on your own?"

The disciple: "If Your Reverence so instructs us, how could we disciples hold up our faith?"

The Master: "Quick! Hold up the empty space in front of you!"

The disciple: "How is that possible? The empty space is certainly not something which can be either moved or held!"

The Master: "When you say, 'It is not movable,' you have already moved it. How could empty space itself know that it's not movable? This is just your subjective speculation."

The disciple: "So even the view that space is not movable is just my subjective speculation. Very well, but just a moment ago I was instructed to 'hold it up.' Why?"

The Master: "Because you now realize how absurd it is to say that you 'uphold' anything. Why all this talk of 'holding up' in the first place?"

The disciple could only change the subject: "If it is wrong to say that Mind is the Buddha, would it be more correct to say, 'It is Mind which becomes the Buddha'?"

The Master: "It does not matter whether 'Mind is' or 'Mind becomes'; both are subjective speculations arising from sheer imagination. Buddha is a source of insight (13), while Mind is the repository of information, both of which start their intricate function as soon as they face their object. My dear fellow, please do not just recognize 'Mind' or 'Buddha'; you have not actually grasped them; they still belong to the object of cognition. This is precisely the so-called 'cognitive ignorance.' (14)

"This is why the Master of Kiangsi said: 'It is not the Buddha, nor Mind, nor object!' This is how he instructed the future followers to conduct themselves. Nowadays people just put on a robe, wasting time in doubts over irrelevant and trivial matters. What nonsense!"

The disciple: "Apparently the teaching is, 'It is not the Buddha, nor Mind, nor object'; yet Your Reverence has re-formulated this to 'Mind is not the Buddha, intellect is not the Way.' Would you explain this?"

The Master: "You do not accept 'Mind is not the Buddha, intellect is not the Way.' Very well, sir, I don't even have this 'Mind' with me. Now what are you going to clutch at?"

The disciple: "It seems that nothing at all is graspable. Would it, then, not be identical with emptiness?"

The Master: "Since 'it is not an object,' how is it comparable with emptiness? Furthermore, what exactly do you mean when you speak of 'identical' or 'not identical'?"

The disciple: "One cannot deny that there is something which is the subject of the sentence, 'It is not the Buddha, nor Mind, nor object'!"

The Master: "If you recognize this 'something,' again it is either Mind, or Buddha, or object." (15)

The disciple: "Pray instruct me, Your Reverence."

The Master: "I am afraid that I do not know either!"

The disciple: "Why not?"

The Master: "What on earth do you want me to tell you?"

The disciple: "Might I not be permitted to understand the Way?"

The Master: "What sort of thing do you wish to understand? Furthermore, how could you understand the Way?"

The disciple: "I really do not know."

The Master: "If you don't know, so much the better. If you just borrow my words, you would be called an 'intellectual parasite.' (16) Even if you were to meet Bodhisattva Maitreya out in the world, he would pull out your hair from your head!" (17)

The disciple: "But what would Your Reverence teach future followers to do?"

The Master: "Look to yourself only. Don't concern yourself with successors-to-come !"

The disciple: "A moment ago you precluded me from understanding the Way, but now you tell me to look to myself. Why is that?"

The Master: "I wish you to understand only by appreciating the essential. Does this mean anything to you?"

The disciple: "How to 'appreciate the essential'?"

The Master: "Good heavens! Once again you are echoing my words! Whatever I tell you is mine, not yours. Did it ever occur to you to try to work out something on your own?"

The disciple: "If I could understand by my own effort, naturally I would not have bothered Your Reverence. Be so kind as to instruct me, sir."

The Master: "It is wrong to conceal your ignorance by pointing here and there. Why did you not ask me this question when you were babbling on and on? Evidently you are wising up; now you admit you don't know. What were you up to a moment ago?

"Obviously you desire to become a Ch'an master some day. If you do become one, you might say, 'I left my home and became a Ch'an monk, ... I would then ask you: 'What were you before you were ordained?' Let's discuss that!"

The disciple: "'At that time,' I would have said, "I did not know anything about this matter.'"

The Master: "If you were completely ignorant then, are you sure that what you know now is correct?"

The disciple: "If 'knowing' is not correct, is 'not knowing' correct?"

The Master: "What the hell do you mean by 'knowing' and 'not knowing'?"

The disciple: "At this point I am totally lost."

The Master: "If you are lost, I am even more so!"

The disciple: "I am just a pupil, it is quite natural for me to be ignorant. Your Reverence, being a great master, should be otherwise. Am I right?"

The Master: "What a funny fellow! I was merely telling you that I just do not know. Has this anything to do with masters and pupils? Do not be so smart! When the Master of Kiangsi was alive, a scholar asked him about the meaning of the couplet:

> Like water, it is without bone or muscle,
> Yet supports ships of a hundred thousand pecks.

The Master answered: 'In my position, there is neither water nor ship. Why speak of muscle or bone?' My dear fellow! The scholar immediately achieved tranquillity. Is it not simple? Therefore I have repeated several times: 'Not even the Buddha could understand the Way. I discipline myself.' What is the use of knowing?"

The disciple: "But how to discipline oneself?"

The Master: "Certainly not by speculation! It is a most difficult thing to tell people how one should discipline oneself!"

The disciple: "Will you allow me to discipline myself?"

The Master: "Have I ever prevented you?"

The disciple: "But may I ask you how I should discipline myself?"

The Master: "If you want to, go ahead by all means! Only don't try to find out from others!"

The disciple: "The trouble is that without instructions from a master, it is hard to understand on one's own. Even Your Reverence has told us: 'Before one disciplines oneself, one should have some understanding. A blind discipline without understanding would lead one to the vicious circle of causation; consequently one could not achieve liberation in this way.' Would you be kind enough to tell us how we should discipline ourselves so that we might break the 'cycle of causation'?"

The Master: "You need not deliberate any further! Speaking of discipline, how have you ever been forbidden to proceed?"

The disciple: "But exactly how should I 'proceed'?"

The Master: "Oh, my dear fellow! Would you be kind enough not to keep following me around like a shadow? You'll never get anywhere by this persistent pestering!"

The disciple: "The fact is that so far Your Reverence has not told me anything yet. How could I possibly find my way?"

The Master: "Even if I told you, where would you find it? By the way, while every day you go to and fro from dawn to dusk, have you ever considered which is the right way and which the wrong? If even you do not know, how could anyone else know better?"

The disciple: "Do you mean that while I go to and fro, I should not think at all? Am I right?"

The Master: "At the time when you do not think at all, could you possibly tell whether something is 'right' or 'not right'?"

The disciple: "Your Reverence usually instructs us: 'Whatever I do I had no intention of accomplishing anything. Consequently I am not entangled in anything. Such a discipline is called 'the *samadhi* of omnipresence' or 'the universal manifestation of the Body.' Isn't this it?"

The Master: "Speaking of discipline of mind, which way are you not allowed to pursue? You need not talk of 'entangle' or 'not entangle,' nor of *'samādhi'*!"

The disciple: "I have learned that there exists a correct path leading to enlightenment. Does Your Reverence deny its existence?"

The Master: "I have neither denied nor asserted it!"

The disciple: "It seems that your way of discipline is far different from that of Mahāyāna. May I ask why?"

The Master: "I don't care whether it is 'different' or 'not different' from anything! Obviously you are interested in ecclesiastical questions. Why not approach the scholars of Scripture? They are quite, quite remarkable!"

The disciple: "Is it at all possible that I might understand through your instructions?"

The Master: "Judging from your questions, I can see that your consideration has so far been related to objects external to you. You are always puzzled just because you recognize nothing but the knowledge acquired through the channels of six senses. You might discuss it with me again when you are able to comprehend the truth from a different point of view, namely, that of the enlightened."

## Footnotes

1) His name in the Buddhist Order was P'u-yuan (A.D. 748-834). He was among the third generation after Hui-neng, the founder of the Southern School of Ch'an.

2) Literally, "the profession," which implies the training of Ch'an.

3) Literally, "those who understand the profession."

4) Literally, "mountain-dwelling hermits." In this context, the expression means those who are well-versed in Ch'an; whether "mountain-dwelling" or "city-dwelling" is of secondary importance. This is one case in which the implied meaning is more important than its apparent meaning.

5) Literally, "sagehood." The word is used here in a less religious sense.

6) It refers to the Buddha.

7) Literally, "I am not him, and he is not me. How could he possibly do anything for me?"

8) The ecclesiastical interpretation of the Buddhist Trinity is excessively complicated. The Sanskrit terms *dharmakaya, sambhogakaya* and *nirmanakaya* mean, literally, "the Cosmic Body," "the Recompense Body" and "the Transformation Body," respectively. The first is the body of true thusness, the second is the body to which the Buddha is entitled as a reward for his meritorious deeds in the past, and the third is the body appearing to sentient beings. The third body can assume numerous different forms depending on the potential of the observer. The first body is formless, and the second body seems to be his "private body," but many texts say that all three bodies are perceivable, also depending on the potential of the observer. In order to reduce the ecclestiastical flavor to a minimum, I have coined three terms, "the Universal Body," "the Consequent Body" and "the Apparent Body."

9) It implies that people are all very capable in quoting the Scripture, but become completely mute when Scripture is left out of the argument.

10) Literally, "Bearing their Buddhas on their shoulders."

11) The original word is *t'ui*, which means "to push," "to expel," "to investigate" or "to speculate."

12) He refers to Ma-tsu Tao-i (701-788), the teacher of Nan-ch'uan.

13) Literally, "Buddha is a man of wisdom."

14) According to the Scripture, there are two kinds of "barriers" which block the path to enlightenment. They are different in nature and so are their remedies. The "emotive barrier" is psychological, and it can be removed by mental exercise and moral discipline. The "cognitive barrier" is epistemic, and it can be removed by intellectual and intuitive insight.

15) The word "object" does not appear in the original; it is added here for the sake of congruence.

16) Literally, "One who always depends on another's understanding."

17) Maitreya is supposed to be the Buddhist Messiah, i.e., the future Buddha who is going to succeed Gautama.

CARLOS DRUMMOND DE ANDRADE


Death of the Milkman

(translated from the Portuguese by George Lensing)


There's little milk in the land,
It must be delivered early.
There's great thirst in the land,
It must be delivered early.
There is a legend in the land
that the thief dies by gunshot.

For this the young milkman
from morning darkness goes running
with his can, handing out
good milk to graceless men.
His can, his bottles
and his rubber-sole shoes
are telling all sleeping men
that someone rose up early
and came to the farthest district
to bring the coldest milk,
the whitest milk, from the best cow,
just to strengthen them
in the wild struggle of the city.

With white bottle in hand
he has no time to express
these things I say of him,
nor does the unlettered milkman,
resident of Namur Street,
employed at the outdoor market,
21 years of age,
know what can be the impulse
of human sympathy.
And he's in a hurry, his figure
leaving at the step of the houses
only his simple bottles.

And because the back door
might also hide people
who crave a little milk
available in our day,
let us advance through the alley
down the lane,
let us deposit the liters...
Without noise, of course,
for noise resolves nothing.

My milkman so subtle,
in the motion of his step so light,
he rather glides than walks.
Some rustling for sure
is always made: a false step,
that flower vase on the road,
the dog, in principle, yelping,
the puny cat.
And there's always a man who wakens
distraught, but soon rolls over.
But this one just woke in panic
(thieves infest the district),
he can think of nothing else.

From the drawer he takes
the revolver into his hand.
Thief?  it catches with a burst.
The shots of morning darkness
have liquidated my milkman.
If he was bridegroom, if he was virgin,
if he was happy, if he was good,
I do not know,
it's late to know.

Now the man is wide awake
and flees down the street.
My God!  I've killed an innocent.
The very bullet that kills the thief
serves as well to pinch
the life of a brother.
He who wishes can call a doctor,
but police will not lay hold
of this son of my father.
My property is saved.
The lengthened night draws on,
daybreak is long in coming,
but the milkman,
motionless in the morning air,
has lost the speed he ran.

From the shattered bottle
onto the peaceful cobblestones
runs a thickly thing:
milk, blood...I cannot say.
For among confused things
poorly ransomed from the night,
two colors try to blend,
softly touch,
lovingly entwine,
forming a third tint;
we call it dawn.

OTTO RENE CASTILLO

(translated from the Spanish by Margaret Randall)

Report of an Injustice

*For the past few days the personal belongings of*
*Mrs. Damiana Murcia, widow of Garcia, 77 years of*
*age, have been out in the rain where they were*
*thrown from her humble living quarters located*
*at 15 "C" Street, between 3rd and 4th, Zone 1.*
　　　　　　*--Radio newspaper* Diario Minuto, *first*
　　　　　　　*edition, Wednesday, June 10, 1964*


Perhaps you can't believe it,
but here,
before my eyes,
an old woman,
Damiana Murcia, widow of Garcia,
77 years of ashes,
under the rain,
beside her furniture,
broken, stained, old,
receives
on the curve of her back
all the monstrous injustice
of your system, and mine.

For being poor,
the judges of the rich
ordered eviction.
Perhaps you no longer
understand that word.
How noble the world
you live in!
Little by little
the bitterest words
lose their cruelty there.
And every day,
like the dawn,
new words emerge
all full of love
and tenderness for men.

Eviction,
　　　　　　how to explain it?
How know,
here when you can't pay the rent
the authorities of the rich

263

come and throw your things
in the street.
And you're left without roof
for the height of your dreams.
That's what it means, the word
eviction: loneliness
open to the sky, to
the eye that judges, misery.

This is the free world, they say.
What luck that you
no longer know
these liberties!

Damiana Murcia, widow of Garcia
is very small,
                  you know,
and must be very cold.

How great her loneliness!

You can't believe
how these injustices hurt.

They are the norm among us.
The abnormal is tenderness
and the hate of poverty.
And so today more than ever
I love your world,
                  I understand it,
                        I glorify
its cosmic pride.

And I ask myself:
Why do the old
suffer among us so,
if age comes to us all
one day?
But the worst of it all
                  is the habit.
Man loses his humanity,
The enormous pain of another
is no longer his concern
                  and he eats
                  and he laughs
and he forgets everything.

I don't want these things
for my country.

I don't want these things
for anyone.
I don't want these things
for anyone in the world.
                    And I say I
because pain
should carry
an indelible aura.

This is the free world, they say.

Look at me.
And tell your friends
my laughter
has turned grotesque
in the middle of my face.

Tell them I love their world.
They should make it beautiful.
And I'm very glad
they no longer know
injustices
            so deep and plentiful.


The One Who Is Always There

You,
      compañero,
the one who is always there.
The one who
never fell back.
Shit!
The one who never
played coward
with the flesh of the people.
Who stood up
against beatings and jail,
exile and shadow.

You,
      compañero,
the one who is always there.

And I love you
for your timeless
honor,

for your resistance
--little sensitive animal,
for your faith,
greater
and more heroic
than all the giants
of all the religions combined.

But, you know,
the centuries to come
will stand on their toes
on the shoulders of this planet,
trying to touch
your dignity
burning with courage
                                    even then.

You,
        companero,
who never betrayed
your people,
                        with tortures,
                        nor with prisons,
                        nor with graft,
you,
        tender star,
will come of age with pride
for the delirious
millions
emerging
from the depths of history
to give you glory,
                                you,
modest and human,
simple proletariet,
the one who is always there,
unbreakable
metal of the land.

# HAIKU

Pl. I.                                                          Décad. 7.

Gardenia florida Linn. sp. plant. 1679.
Jasminum ramo unifloro plano, petalis
coriaceis. Cohert. . T. 15.
Jasmin à fleurs doubles, de Malabar.

Cent. 2.
Prevost pinx.                                      Fessard Sculp.

NO. 67

CHRIS MEATYARD

We Flowers

We flowers
are here,
When TS says stop.

We flowers
are spinning the top,

Hawker here,
is drifting the breeze

We're
groping higher now
As TS sees:
        and you're goin' too

We
better go now--before we're
skipping the seas.

_____

TS means a group for
organized public (police)

WENDELL BERRY


Imitations of Haiku


1

I will never sleep:
the thought of the telephone
  ringing in the night.

2

Down the sunlit page
the shadows, again the shadows
  of the leaves falling.

3

The evening after
the dog died, her tracks are still
  fresh in the wet path.

4

When the pots were dry
she dreamed she was watering
    the begonias.

5

Bright frost adrift
in the morning air, light light
   drifting in the air.

6

Starting before dawn,
a long night, I saw the lights
   light in farm kitchens.

7

After a long night,
traveling, the locust smoke
  of country breakfasts.

## The Bees

Can the bees have lived
those cold days?  I knock on the hive
and I hear them hum.

Remember the bees'
lives: the order of the hive,
the freedom of the fields.

Or is my delight
after their freedom in the light
their order in the dark?


## The Snow and the Fox Sparrow

The fox sparrow sits
cold in the snowy branches
of the cherry tree.

Warm in the kitchen,
I look out--the fox sparrow
feeding in the snow.

Who came from the North
without baggage?  The snow storm
and the fox sparrow.

The fox sparrow, one
of my thoughts, flies through the snow,
a thought of his own.

Will the world survive
the snow?  No time for theory
says the fox sparrow.

He worries about
his feathers.  Let God worry
about the world.

Moon on the snow, all
the long night.  The fox sparrow
sleeps dark in the woods.

The morning returns,
glinting on the snow.  Again
the fox sparrow feeds.

MATTHIAS GINN


1

a frost-world
with the moon west
the sun east

2

in the morning
red-eyed and yawning
the April wind

3

the tiny bird
didn't sing a note
it came, it left

4

on the door
leading to the offices
a moth sleeps soundly



ANN JONAS


1

After the skaters:
Rice paper, calligraphy.
Scribes have come and gone.

2

Their constant squabble
over land rights.  Back and forth.
Sandpiper and sea.


[Should be MATTHIAS GILL]

271

RAYMOND ROSELIEP

Turkey

All the way home I
picked the best feathers for my
indian headdress

and so my mother
hadn't much of a fan for
her coming illness.


Among the Earth's Fragile

Among the earth's fragile
children
he makes out
a bronze

b                 f
    t
    u  e  l
    r
t                 y

on his door
just over

ƧꓘOOᗺ ƎᖈAᖈ
ᖇOTAᖇUƆ


PAT DINSMORE


1

The white horse lay
The windshield of the truck smashed
The ford skidded
I hope nobody is hurt
But don't think about it
It will only make you sick
She said


272

2

Red
    Angular
          Horse
Quivering in the wind
Cold
Alone
Will your wood
Always keep you there?

3

    probably sit
here the rest of
my life not caring

    while others
    keep moving

just sit until
I'm hard and
still cold

4

      sunset
between branches
I fall

everywhere

5

The pain of
seeing a
new moon
behind a
cloud.

6

creeping, giggling, trying
  to find out

the girl still sobbing
  when they brought her back

then leaving her

JOEL WEISHAUS

## Thursday Morning

thursday morning, cold & cloudy milk sky.
peanut butter sandwich & chunk of Monterey Jack cheese
in old army gas-mask bag.

Marin sun filters thru thin clouds & Dipsea Trail
begins its long uphill climb thru deep green forests,
bright Brueghel cow pastures ("a huge pissing," Snyder),
to the Ocean.

high above Pacific, cool sea breezes chill a sweaty body,
mild sun off playing somewhere else.
a lone hiker disappears around a bend in the road.
turning & strolling back, boots tied together & flung
over a shoulder, short mountain hairs tickling feet.

without missing a single cud-chew,
cows raise heavy dolorous eyes to watch a stranger
inspecting an army of ants.
old dung becomes petrified.
meadows become forests,
forests become meadows
and forests again, Muir Woods,
mostly downhill now....

a clearing off the trail, pine needle cushion to sit on
while devouring a slice of cheese.
then, left foot on right thigh, zazen....

all that remains is this poem--

*wind thru the trees,*

*one leaf*

*dancing.*

ALAN ABELE

# RELATIVITY
# RELATVITY
# RELTAIVY
# RELATIY
# REALTIY
# REALITY

DOM CYRIL v. K. KRASINSKI, O.S.B.


Excerpts from *Die Geistige Erde*

(translated from the German by Elsie P. Mitchell)


For the reader educated in an occidental Christian way, it is rather difficult to grasp the Tibetan conceptions of human character and health, the importance of the complex relationship that man has with his environment, and especially the sense of oneness with the earth itself. Our human role, as we in the West conceive it, our body-spirit dichotomy, conveys an unclear and incomplete picture to a Buddhist or to a Hindu. We rarely examine the dualism on which our understanding of the world is based. For the average westerner, the world, both visible and invisible, tends to fall into oppositions involving such notions as body and soul, content and form, material and spiritual.

On the other hand, Tibetan monk-philosophers have a superior sense of oneness as it is manifested in what may appear to be inexplicable relations and connections between widely separated organs and functions. Only a concrete knowledge of the relationships of these organs and functions, and the way in which the power of the spirit reveals itself in apparently unimportant phenomena, makes recognition of the "wholeness" of things possible. Consciousness of the great reality into which the smaller human reality is incorporated characterizes this world-view. Appreciation of the higher order which permeates man and determines his destiny as well as the fate of his world, is still a living philosophy in Tibetan lamaism. However, the values of this world, until recently hermetically sealed, are now being violently destroyed.

A science of nature originated in Tibet, a science not of the externals of the phenomenal world, but of the inner nature and character of all creation. For the westerner, the investigations of these contemplative naturalists who found the essence of things and of man in complex spiritual roots and principles, may seem pretentious and doctrinaire. Relationships as they are modified by endlessly changing circumstances and conditions, and as they affect the inner nature of each individual organism, are the key to man's psyche, his character and spirit. The medicine-philosophy of lamaism not only applies to man's body, psyche and spirit, but also significantly to all phenomena, and to man's social, economic and cultural environment. A wise man, a doctor-philosopher, always searches out the degree of disharmony in the greater environment. From this viewpoint, could we not contemplate the real root of the "malady" which torments the Occident today?

An especially interesting aspect of the Tibetan tradition of medicine, is the importance attributed to the control of the breath. Disciplined deep breathing is essential, and it is the vehicle of spiritual sound! Music is considered a vital source of spiritual transformation, and vibrations are recognized as cosmic manifestations of a spiritual

principle. The lamas skilled in medicine have developed a science as well
as an art of sound. They carefully cultivate a complex sensitivity to musical pitch and tone and to the moods thereby created, which they believe have
the power to heal, or, if misused, to sicken, according to the vibrations involved. The bells and giant conch shells used in Buddhist rituals are credited with particular powers of spiritual healing.

Another realm of the complex human psyche which preoccupies the Tibetan
doctors is the "magical" realm of the mood. The awakening and the spiritual
control of the senses to forms, colors, sounds and smells is the function of
the wise man, who is also artist and doctor. Such a master recognizes that
for each situation, time, sex, status, age and experience, there is a unique,
mysterious, sympathetic "bundle" of significant forms which is able to cap-
tivate a given individual--but also to liberate him from his physical, psychic
and spiritual fetters. Sensual experiences are dependent on their relation
to a superior spiritual principle, which resolves all conflicts and opposites:
the hard and the soft, the aromatic and the odorless, the irritating and the
calming, the intimate and the remote. The light-dark realm of psychic moods--
an elemental and therefore subhuman and often even demonic sphere--can be
spiritually transformed only by the art and wisdom of a master. This master
must be intimately acquainted with his disciple, his concrete circumstances
and his predisposition to certain harmonies.

A related but superior sphere of the senses is what our occidental tradition calls the realm of eros--in the widest meaning of that word. As long as
sensual experiences are only spontaneous creations of specific situations,
they are emanations of natural eros, and as such are bound to the physical
world. Their spiritual form develops only when man is secure not only in
subjective feeling, but also in his insight into truth. Psychic equanimity
is a hard-earned freedom, only realized when the transitory enjoyment of
pleasure is transformed by spiritual love and by good (including sympathy
for even the poorest creature) into the joyful security of spiritual beauty.
An accurate psychic diagnosis is arrived at only as a result of insight into
the different levels of being and an understanding of the difficulties which
may arise with the spiritual control of the various levels.

The transforming strength of the truth, of freedom and of kindness,
man learns only when he is able to realize the spiritual self, the true
self. Only then may a sense of the absolute, of the whole of creation unite
him with the world. Only then can be found final answers to the questions
of existence; answers to man's sorrow, his fate and his death. The wise man
who awakens to the wholeness of the world also discovers conversely in "the
all," a hypothesis that can not only be believed by a brave man, but also
experienced and suffered. At this point, however, there is no longer a
hypothesis.

Only the man in whom a synthesis has taken place between "the all" and
the individual, a spiritual fusion of body, psyche and soul on all levels,
can grow into the true Christian agape, the real Christian eros. It is im-

possible for such a man not to be interested in the whole of God's creation. He will learn to live in openness to all, with the strength given
to him by God, and the love in which eros and agape are inseparably
united.


ROBERT DESNOS


A Voice

(translated from the French by Jonathan Greene)


A voice, a voice that comes from so far
that it no longer rings in the ears,
a voice like a muffled drum
that is still able to reach us clearly.

Although she seems to rise from a tomb,
she speaks only of summer and spring,
she fills the body with joy,
she brings a smile to the lips.

I listen to her.  It is only a human voice
that walks through all this fracas of life and battles,
the crumbling thunder and the murmur of gossip.

And you, don't you hear her?
She says "the pain will last only a short time"
says "the good season is near"

don't you hear her?

ANSELM HOLLO

Four Love Poems

1

Louis Armstrong (68) says it's a wonderful world he loves it

2

easy to love bison and indian
see there they stomp through the sky

3

I loves you
but i can't find him

4

the world seen as a huge impenetrable granite arse
would Wallace Stevens have loved that for a title


Bear Poems


1  The Bear

it was an old dance, and he took a few steps
he was surprised to remember
then stopped        gazing at her
his body felt huge and warm
he did not want to go on      but he liked the tune
                          she was the tune


2  After You've Gone

the bear sat down
he felt weak      unable to move
his mind was going so fast
he fell asleep
his mind was going so fast

NELS RICHARDSON


I Voice


I voice
instructed in the arts
of motion and change
am sent to you with a certain
obscure silence.

I Mercury, Iris,
the sexless one
set before you
the sealed messages
which were entrusted
to my virgin ignorance.

I have not tarried.
There are no stations on my secret route.

I am no man
I need not sleep
No reward is either necessary or sufficient
to influence me.
I know no obstacles.
I am the perfect messenger of desire.

My winged feet
leave no marks in the dust.
The scrolls I carry in my dry palm
are never stained with the imperfections
of human effort.

Nothing that I undertake is lost
or fails,
nothing that I transmit
confuses itself in symbol or metaphor.
My memory has no logic of its own
to color and shape the images it retains.

I am the same arriving and departing.
My symbol is air
the undistorting medium,
the selfsame air that clothes both lover and
loved one,
the emptiness between two points of rest.

When I speak
I speak in no particular language;
when I think, I am
the absolute presence of everything
I think of.


281

I have nothing to give
and nothing to receive,
I alone am worthy of the faith
that men and gods have placed
in words and gestures;
I alone am honest, having no qualities,
no selfhood of my own.

I come to you naked
of all but the essential need I convey:
and that,
yours.

Open and read.


She Is the Quality

She is the quality of an awaited yawn
the sense of self-forgetfulness that crosses
books and scattered papers,
wreathing the smoker's head--
the gentle smoker of pipes:

he remembers her later,
after the moment when earth, her element,
was truly round him.
She is what being is backwards, the gesture
identified only after its effortless
doing.

She falls on his sleepiness
slowly, like snow
discovered on waking
formed in a moment
of fullness too full for reflection.

It is only later
her form appears;
the trees appear laden
with whiteness of form,
the light lifting gently
the darkness
up from their reaching
as she lifts a blanket
arises to wash
returning to gaze on him just
as he turns to her footstep.

Morning rebuilds the old
castle completely;
all that is truly important
comes of itself to his bedside
reminding him there
of the feats it was his pleasure to perform
daily and nightly
for her fresh unknowing.


Rain

Rain finds a channel,
the silence is furrowed
with gullies and rivers
formed to the nature
of what they conduct:

water, the past tense
withheld in clouds, and now
the voice and touch of it

Rain finds a channel


JOHN JONES


Christ Before Pilate: Hieronymous Bosch

That face has the cuirass expression.
It is Bosch we speak of,
the moment Christ's before Pilate,
no joke, but the faces are burlesque,
top banana, only Christ's without helmet
and that fawn-gentle, Persian.
The water in Pilate's basin's unseen,
yet everything breaks up, either in that water,
or laughing.
Why, there are rents all over these old wineskins,
old soaks. They smell the leaking vinegar,
the gush from the thorns. Touch us to wine, Abba,
Daddy. We are soured.

*John Jones*

### Museum Plainsong

("fragments, bronze head of Augustus, 100 A.D.")

The muscle under stone that moves in earthquake
shines in the breast of this Roman emperor:
Augustus, half his head gone, hangs like a firmament.

Christ, in the next room, is innocent
of the noble Roman.  Caesar mangers worms in his head,
this bronze cup with which I have communion.


### Gelded Monument

It is seen as a head,
hard homunculus, which the sun
melts down to Mammon,
our god of war.

A bronze stack of cash,
the laurel minted, its brow
(the thousandth noble one)
got from a stale template.

Ganymede is a one-armed bandit,
creature of affluent catamite.
The Sibyl, gipsy, fickle,
has her tin cup.

His magnanimous, beadling brow
is right here,
at the sun's usurous eclipse:
Please, sir, can I have more?


### For Hart Crane

1

*Fairy tales contrive even for their villains
euphemisms for death;* it is hard stone he is grown into,
*der treue Johannes,*
like the Fisherman's Prince all the bad part of him
                                      black marble;

that cave of thieves
his body was,
broke open like a pinata,
is geode, earth's gemmed center.

Ah Hart, it is difficult
to suffer sea change.
*I think constantly of you.*
I whistle for a metaphor
across the bus station.

2

I chip you out of a frozen sea
and study you.  Now you are near as autumn;
the world's in amber also.  Agony
is yours but not a martyrdom
though the sea's your chiseled reliquary.
Waves break at their middles and tent down,
a million caps for a dunce.  I
witness you here, landlocked and numb.

*In Sung scrolls pavilions are a shorthand*
*for the sage's efforts to know the beautiful:*
*angled pine, the view beyond the mountain.*

This pavilioned sea, arched like a skull,
bears your poet's brain, poor drowned Phoenician.
Now, Chinese and inland, I try to understand.

3

Here the sailors
turn to stone flowers or loose themselves
in the serge shrubbery.  You followed the ships,
white as an iceberg,
for your matchblack sailors,
mouth wry with the Cheshire question.
On Third Street you died,
little by little,
in mariners' alleys your moon broke through.
How can I see you except with your smile
on the dark pier,
like a dead anemone,
waiting, lonely, in the tide's pull?

I've brought out my lyre
once more under the trees
in the queer light
of this street.
It's Hallowe'en
and the moon,
*la vecchia strega,*
riding a saber
crosses my heart.
Lord Baltimore
shelters with a stone loin
the mumming fairies
and the sea frets
on its shore—
bloody Lesbos,
the lyric graveyard.
Now, masked in asphodel,
tragicomical,
rest, rest,
perturbed spirit.

5

In Corpus Christi
I watched the sea converge,
ash at the edge,
as if that confusion were fire,
tolling the bony rocks with blood,
salting your poems into my ear.

Ash, ash,
and the beautiful pale birds
crying.

*Hoc est corpus meum.*

At the candles
poor bees hum
around Antony, lilies waving in his hand.
Images from the sea
overwhelm me:
this waxen saint
and that lover broken at Actium.
Hart, old salt,
the miserable gall of heartbreak
breaks us all.

Waves netted with words,
your body taut in those meridians

by which the froward sea survives.
Hours, hours.
And this last mourning.
                              My sleeping prince,
make my words privy to your darkness.


EDWIN FORD


Once Under a Blue-Leaf

Once (under a blue-leaf) there was a rock
That said things to children and only it
made their hair red and their smiles sun

Now the rock is part of a school building
in the country and the little school
children are often found talking to all colors
and smells sing to them.

The once-blue-leaf rock smiles

You can hear them too if you leave your
eyes and their memories at the door

It is quite a thing to see and be at

Most who have done (or should I say gone)
So have lost their age and come back only
to do their parent-duty: to make more attendants
for the sun-eye-stone that is forever and good


Sometime

Sometime--place a small cold night-blue stone
On your head between your eyes and look at it.
If you are good and the stone likes you--
Slowly--you will begin to know what was before
Adam had a beard; and moreover if the blue is
The right hue and you are the right who you
Will get to know--someday--the thing that was
When the sun became the moon and the moon the sun.

## Childhead

Childhead comes back to you when the green
is smelled and good is violet--shoes that
tie into your legs to run to childhead are
only good when they're not said--so draw a
childhead with a melody pencil on fugueboard
yellow lyric locust sings for ears that you see
$\qquad$ with

## Lyrics

### 1

ringsom are good lights to carry me to the
where waters are in-you-waters *lilla lilla*
you can have a sun-bun to eat and be for
if your eye-waters is *lilla lilla*

### 2

soulshine is at the blue rim of manness--
only for findin' in your head church
*del rey is no flashlight* so trust your eyes
at blue-rim
*soul is round too isabella!!!*

## INSCRIPTION

MULL.BERE.BRAUN.C.MY.INSID-FLAEK:SAWT.SUCH.TO.TOD.
BUT.FAUND. INSTED.WER.UNBORND.FETHERS:THE.BLUE.
INSIDENT.BRAWT.OUT.ALL.SO.MULL.BERE.BRAUN.TO.BE.BETTER.
THAN.BORND.TO.BE.WOVEN.WITH.SUN.AS.WARP.AND.MOON.
AS.WEFT:MULLBERE.IST.BEFOR.FARB.

KEITH WILSON


The Rotting Hawser

Brightness.  & we must
die.  Darkening seawinds,
salt caught fresh on the eyelids,
young muscles under clean shirts
cleaner sails catching full

        --a tricky wake, but we
too slip away, full moon or no
moon at all, heavy with our loves,
our whiskied dreams, shouted lonelinesses
we pass

            --strand by strand, the
cables slip & with a snap! the
little craft we have, finally the sea
claims her loan, jiggers of island rum
caught in a brown light, a clink,
and the thrown glasses disappear,
winding their trails of bubbles,
sinking, move down, a few sharp glints
to leave a slender, laughing trail


Joy Song

        *Wem willst du klagen, Herz?*
                *--Rilke*

Out of this farcome light, the blue
flat mesa crisp-stern: moon
stars, land rushing in, in

    My son & I walk the ditchbank
in silence, warmed to the coldwind
by each other's nearness

    An Irishwarriorson he
carries his stiff bamboo spear
easily, the hills of distant loves lie
beyond the winter's light; this windless
flight of crying birds streaks the air
between our bodies

    *To whom, heart, would you complain?*


289

A waving sadness, grasping me
like a small hand, the pain
--that of being no longer along--
the warm smell of pinoned fireplace smoke
& hearths to rest all the spears upon


FIVE YORUBA PROVERBS

(adapted by Alfred Opubor and Jonathan Greene)


proverbs "are the horses of speech": when a word
is lost we go look for it with a proverb

here are five Yoruba proverbs
each of them seeking its lost words


1

the house that is built out of urine
we pull down by the dew

2

he that is being fed by another
does not know where there is famine fighting

3

all lizards have their bellies on the ground
but we don't know which of them has
a sick stomach turning

4

we call the owners of life: they do not answer
we call corpses: they cry out!

5

he who claps for the madman to dance
is one with the madman

AFRICAN RELIGIOUS MYTHS

(adapted by Thomas Merton)


Thonga Lament

Look the blue oxen
Come down from the altars
To your caverns O Fathers
We stay outside your tunnels
Do you see them coming
The Oxen
O Fathers?
Blue Oxen into the caverns.
You gave us life O Fathers
But now you are gone
Now you are secret
Alive in endless tunnels
(But where?)

Let us now eat together in peace
Let us never disagree
That I and my children
May live long here outside
Out here in the air
Without coughing or swaying
Or losing balance and falling
Into the long tunnels
Look O Fathers
The Blue Oxen are coming
May they find you
In your caverns


Hare's Message (Hottentot)

One day Moongod wanted to send a message to man. Hare volun-
teered to go to man as Moongod's messenger. "Go tell men," said
Moon, "that they shall all rise again the way I also rise after
each dying." But Hare the messenger deceived man, changing the
heavenly message to one of earth. "You must die," he said, "just
as I do." Then Moon cursed Hare. And the Nagama must now never
eat Hare's meat. They do not eat Hare the runner. For the runner
is death. And day by day he repeats his own message until all
others are forgotten.

RICHARD GROSSINGER

from *Ecological Sections*

The sun strikes the earth's cities like tinder, the bread that was
yeast at twilight, now a thin haze in the morning air, having been baked
and cooled, the haze rising like an odor from the swamp, from the underground factories, a thousand chimneys leading out crystal to the micro-
cosm, smoke, smoke, the river collecting dust, churning, the sun touching/
breeding on the kitchen table, a mold that is food itself, the moss on the
tree trunk, woman's garments on polished mahogany, fishing vessels on lakes
and rivers, tropical rains, chemicals of wet and blue light, smoke, water
through stone, face of a gargoyle, of a mountainside, ikon of a president
carved in a mountainside, digging up Lincoln just once more from micro-
organic time, and rust, to look at his face, fire through air, electric
current, the offshore current, hurricanes pursued by plane.  The earth is
a storm, and in that storm live lattices and crystals, live finely dis-
dected leaves and the path home, locally strewn stone covered with glyphs,
maps, the irrigated fields, the floating gardens of Mexico, the biblical
orchards, monumental architecture for both sun and moon, shrines for the
planets with known paths: the earth is a living conscious planet, tele-
vised electricity, consciousness in its clouds.  Special crews leave for
the North Pole to tag penguins and polar bears.  Crews leave for the ocean
to photograph the eclipse.  A jet plane in pursuit of shimmering lights.
Another crew to gather crocodile eggs.  A crew to dig up bones.  Posses
cross the African savannah to collect the seeds of *Welwitschia Mirabilis,*
the underground tree, a crew in Scotland to seek the Loch Ness monster:
is a planet conscious of its own dimensions, latitudes, mysteries, is a
semantic simultaneous planet, the baseball photographed and broadcast the
moment it is thrown--strike one!

And who would allow for the inhabitation of Jupiter: that poisonous
methane storm, that frozen giant of helium and hydrogen oceans and metallic
hydrogen continents, ammonia weather, ammonia winter and ammonia spring.
No food, no water, no air, no one can live in chemical hell, everything
crushed and lethargic, everything frozen and submerged without context.
Jupiter lacks a true archaeology, for no mass conceals a more subtle and
more ancient form; Jupiter is a planet of sheer moraine where even the most
occult markings are in lieu of consciousness.  Subtle tropisms fail to produce a mirror, the face of a woman combing her hair, fail to whirl, to repeat themselves, to know syntax, happen without friction or organic tangency.
Jupiter has no genetic code, cannot remember itself, cannot remember its
own body, or how large/how far, no proprioception, distal or proximal, no
nerves but violent and alert moves, as a cat moves, seeing sounds and fragments of sounds with her eyes.  Its flashing explosions are without history
or recall, instantaneous, one and then another.  Jovian cycles preserve the
essential chaos, the number of explanations never multiplied across the
vast geosphere, the number of causes without interior reference.  And this
is a lie.

We cannot imagine that Jupiter is inhabited.

Yet we imagine the ancient desert cities of Mars, as though Oaxacan or Egyptian, the canals bringing water from the polar ice caps to a dying empire. We can embroider Venus with dense jungles, an age of seeding ferns and lizards, rain forests and quaking bogs. Venus is our mythical past, Mars our mythical future. But what creature breathes ammonia and swims under tons of icy atmosphere? What creature could bear the sight of such a creation without screaming out in panic and dying? On Jupiter the universe is hardly getting down to something interesting; it is getting down to itself, what it is at this distance and pressure, as on earth. But we believe our own melodrama, hence the garden between fire and ice, between water and stone, between jungle and desert. Jupiter is a garden also. Life breaks like a crystal, grows outward, a bud shedding protective hairs, knows itself in sexual feedback; life is methane and ammonia, for methane and ammonia are children of the sun as oxygen and carbon, and are conscious but to other ends. Jupiter is now in the middle of its ammonia and methane history; the planet is mapped, its surface features of grave importance, their geology and weather known; there are many nations on Jupiter, and there are some places considered more healthy and fertile than others. The telescope on Jupiter reveals an historic age, a creature, an emblem of consciousness and commerce as surely as the globe of earth reveals to us our history, Alexander, Genghis Khan, Columbus' route, Cuba as Japan, Captain Cook, the Louisiana Purchase, Seward's Folly, cannibals, Amundson; the red spot, the bulbous landmass is surely a place of ceremonial and historical significance. To explain it by convection currents and atmospheric pressure is like explaining the forests by an extension of the science of stone. The map of Jupiter, belted in colored latitudinal zones like the forests and tundras and deserts of phytogeography, is an historical puzzle, a map left by unknown ancient sea-kings of another world of which we are dimly and always conscious, a map we cannot deny by reducing it to literal chaotic vectors. Wherever there is matter, depth is conscious and violence is history. Jupiter's history is as tragic as our own, as uncertain, as needy of saviors and wise-men, these ammonia-hydrogen life-forms assuming crystalline bodies as flesh but their own flesh, like being conscious, only conscious of themselves, accepting as harmonious and optimum the fever and climate of a planet which is their own body.

Hence natural selection is the law by which life exists everywhere in the universe, not just in farm country and on planets with soft evening rains. Inhabitation is a local phenomenon, a tense and rhythmic duplication of local fabric to whatever consciousness is warranted and whatever ends are implied. Inhabitation is like a word game which puns only on the resources it has, hence man a being mostly of water and carbon crystals, but each planet has a special chemistry, a chemistry of its consciousness which it calls organic. A creature arises on each planet out of the density and richness of material there, out of the froth; this is the true law of natural selection, of micro-niches; all ends are teleological because all ends are the most eloquent and vital expression of the material being touched. We must recognize all signs, all markings, not just those

293

that apply to ourselves; Jupiter leaves on kodachrome through telescopic
lens a signature of history, of use, of conscious dreaming to undo the
enigma, the vast astrology in which all of us softly reproduce and all
our bloods run in rivers around and feed themselves. Ecology leaves us
all at home, a dire product, a chemical necessity to make something too,
that we must hear the voices, the wailing tones that ring this planet in
and speak consciously from a body of meteors and moons, an anatomy of
electro-magnetic limbs, as the Jovians listen for the voice of their planet, listen from the North Polar Regions and the North North Temperate
Belt, listen from the Equator and the South Tropical Zone. They are not
Esquimaux and Polynesians; they are creatures of ammonia, and breathe
ammonia and love ammonia bodies, and the dreams are the eternal dreams
contained in ammonia crystal.


JUNE J. YUNGBLUT


Passage

I shall become
            an echo of my own name
                        in your hearing

there will blow
            the wind of my memory
                        past your life

and you will turn
            to watch the flight of bird
                        across the sky

Crying
            come the cranes

Time
            and space are one

*June J. Yungblut*

## Confirmation

tomorrow
hands will be laid on me
like the touch of that dying
apple tree
that tugs at my flesh
as I pass by

and I--
I remember those hands
one December night
I saw them suddenly
snatch at light
with palsied fingers
clutching the sky
are they asking
permission to die?

and now--
now it is I
who must suffer in my soul
their wintry grasp
cooling warm flesh
in the prelate's clasp

is it my body--
mine?
that kneels on the stone
and receives this sign?
no more the wheat, no more the vine
the mystery is left
in the lees of the wine

I look at the cup, I look at the bread
but I remember
the moment I fled
along the night
past the dying tree

Reverend Father, your hands on me
have signed my soul
to winter rites
clutching at stars
on December nights
like palsied old trees
which covet their light

my body kneels on a frozen road
and raises its hands
to a silent sky

        we are suddenly old
        the Bishop
        and I


            Magdalen

There!  Through the summer air
The first faint warning of the mowing scythe
Do you hear?

September's near.

The lifted jug has caught the midday sun
And holds it still
The harvester drinks his fill
The morning work is done.

Why do you fear September?

What was the crop that was sown this year?
Whose was the hand that harrowed the field?
Where will you hide the summer's yield
Of all you remember, now in September?

See her straighten her back
Heavy, heavy the harvesting sack
Mary, what do you carry
Now that September is here?

No one walks at her side
Where does she get all her pride?
Who plowed that field
By whom was it sown?
Mary, Mary, how you've grown!

She doesn't hear
Her time is near

September

*June J. Yungblut*

Te Deum

autumn's odor of decay
sweats the blighted woods
and all
who walk this way
must bear mortality
nor can they stay
the summer's
sun-smelt days
though heart and reason pray
to golden gods--
they turn away

and love was all
the spectacle of spring
that swept our gaze
when we were young
and raced the days
across the sacred hills
nor stopped to praise
the gods
nor stood amazed
to hear the music
of ourselves--
for we were young

the song
of pulsing blood
remembers still
the surging sea
within the shell
and all we dream
will come to be
the shading
of the twilight woods

the gods
will sing
in ever-present time
of sun
and shadow's
racing play
and from the gods
as they from us
we dream--
and turn away

Christmas in Vietnam

running children
wings of death
run to the tree
in the village square
faces like blossoms turn to the sun
motor metal molten bright
the tree is the target
of sound and light
the pilot looks back
at the Christmas tree
alight with living candles
Christ.

BOBBY BYRD

Seattle: Gone

I left Seattle & drove east,
the gray clouds & the first mountains
off the West Coast
                    were behind me:
headed toward Philly.

Paul M. had said goodbye
& walked back into that brown house on Wallingford,

a happy loneliness in Montana
the snow melting in a May spring,
a high plain,
a morning

three mornings until Pennsylvania,
& I had got away from Seattle, that university
where the day before
I had made quick remarks on Joyce for a piece of paper
& never read *Ulysses*.

The time changes.
Windows rolled up in the cold air thru
Anaconda, Butte, Bozeman,
Billings, Crow Agency, Lodge Grass,
Wyola & a quick corner off Wyoming
thru Sundance.

Leaving Seattle after two years.
There were other addresses
besides Wallingford,
                    people & times, but
what would I say about the loss of the sun,
the mountains
(a friend called them greedy)
forgotten except for a few clear days?

There in Montana on a sky-high plain
I was thinking all this
about a conservative city,
that mon-eyed American town,
& water all around.
& water all around.


        Mazatlan

    The sun to the west.
    They would have none of it.
    Two men, maybe three,
    against the rocks far down the beach,
    dressed in their summer suits.

    The beach ended,
    the rocks tore into the surf.
    One woman, arms & legs,
    sat stiff on a higher point,
    her dress the color of rock.

    The smell of salt,
    the men bent in slow motion
    to catch the crab,
    a fish.  The sand.
    I walked that way.


    The Road to Maroon Belles

       (for Lee Merrill)

One night when she slept easily
there was the rock station from OK City,
the porcupine in the road; Colorado, its mountains,
its moon is red now,
is halved now
in a Pasadena smog.

### The Directions

Sounds with meaning.
Here not like a river, fluid from its source,
the mountains to the sea,
brown perhaps,
               & flowing with the land,
the land & feeding, being fed,
a natural dance.

But this my own way,
like man's way: the way he gets, holds his land,
plots measured off by a paid surveyor's eye:
the damned plumb to the center, gets gravity
& holds.


### Poem: Returning

I cant explain the South--
its like in the fall

        those brown cottonfields
           stuck like picture postcards
              onto a long ago landscape
                always moving past them

the highways
are miles of the wrinkled boards of sharecropper cabins
the black kids on the porch with the old & humbled
still scratching
              loans for the big shiny red cars
              whizz

past those cottonfields spinning like a burnt-out sun


### MARGARET RANDALL

### The Dream

I keep saying there was nothing afterward, no trace,
nothing to follow, the decapitated man
was not in the papers, was not
there anymore.
You kept going back to the beginnings,

the film, the building that crashed
just missing the car
                        as we drove
the blowup tightening
in our heads.

The fact is
at twelve-thirty Wednesday night
or Thursday morning
there was a bright red light
a patrol car blocking the inside lane
two policemen standing almost alone
in the dark and the sparse traffic
turned out around and then
closed in and continued, a

body without a head
in pale yellow and very dark blue.
There was gut or esophagus or whatever
spews from a severed neck and there
was no head.
And there was the pressure, the imposed pain
of that man on our eyes in our eyes
as the past tense registered   our heads
becoming that act, that thing.

        The morning paper
        too soon
        the afternoon
        paper
        ,going through
        the pages and
        the next day
        and the next.

        And you kept saying
        did you tell her
        did you tell him
        about the man
        we saw
        and I kept looking.

Now I have dreamed about the yellow and blue
the pale yellow it was almost white
Now I have asked if these bodies are the same
as those others
                chemically, structurally,
Now I have asked and dreamed

Now I will know what colors mean.

ROBERT LAX

New Verse Drama

Cast

(in order)

man                          waiter from the
                                  plains
woman
                             waiter from the
maitre d'                         hills


## Act I

| man: | ow | waiter 2: | zow |
|---|---|---|---|
| woman: | oh | man: | zow |
| maitre d': | ik | woman: | zow |
| waiter 1: | ok | | |


## Act II

| man: | ow | waiter 2: | zow |
|---|---|---|---|
| woman: | oh | man: | zow |
| maitre d': | ik | woman: | zow |
| waiter 1: | ok | | |


## Act III

| man: | zow | waiter 2: | zow |
|---|---|---|---|
| woman: | zow | man: | zow |
| maitre d': | zow | woman: | zow |
| waiter 1: | zow | | |

Act IV

| man: | ow | waiter 2: | zow |
|------|-----|-----------|-----|
| woman: | oh | man: | zow |
| maitre d': | ik | woman: | zow |
| waiter 1: | ok | | |

THOMAS MERTON

Proverbs

(for Robert Lax)

1  I will tell you what you can do ask me if you do not understand
   what I just said

2  One thing you can do be a manufacturer make appliances

3  Be a Man-u-fac-tu-rer

4  Make appliances sell them for a high price

5  I will tell you about industry make appliances

6  Make appliances that *move*

7  Ask me if you do not understand what is move

8  First get the facts

9  Where to apply?  Ask industry

10  Do not expect to get by without Mr. and Mrs. Consumer

11  Man-u-fic-tion

12  I am wondering if you got the idea be a manu

13  MAKE FALSE GODS

14  Apply mind energy they will move

15  Mention one of the others see what happens

16  Now apply that to our problem

17  Try not to understand

18  Be a mounte-fictioner

19  Surpass all others in price and profit

20  Assail the public with lies

21  Home-spun-facts-are-more-fun repeat this

22  Prevent spreading on garments

23  Breathe more than others

24  Supply movement and traction

25  Our epidemix will exceed

26  A homemade appliance: no honorable mention

27  Now you can refer to garments and spread out

28  But there are still more facts

29  For excitement: say whose epidemic may be next

30  Apply this to the facts and see what happens

31  Wear dermal gloves in bed

32  Here is an appliance that will terrorize mothers

33  And fight the impossible

34  Man-u-fac-ture: wear it on your head

35  Beat it here come the mothers

*from* The Geography of Lograire

Prelude

Look out mumper lookout to shore. Coonsails! Conmix! Katzenjobber
Picnics! Yoyo Silver rushing into the shops. Tonmix riding into the
places of ownership. Momma Mudder for less than you'd pay. She has a
Zeiss under her left and stores information. She has a viewfinder and
finds the shapes. Can fashion be considered an investment?

1

THE NORTH AS EVERYBODY KNOWS IS VERY NORD.
It is Aquilonic.

2

Gare du. Money for Egypt. Way down in Old Cairo where the Virgin blesses
Copts and complains about the Holy Spaces. Visit Egypt with Thomas Mock.
Yoyo Lompoc rushing into doubt. They both deliver big. Gare du Garcon.
Hollow logs and tender bundles of love.

3

Nordsee chowder. Long shower past Ostende. Shimmer summer. Trawl away
over rocking Dutchland. Sick as Dover all over the sea is frailest pas-
senger swooning for the rails. (The missus can't take it. Well, keep her
under a bed for Class' sake! Keep her under glass for the Sea's sake!
Save her glass box for the British viewsem.)

4

Taupes are willing all the cheers this summer. Why pay more for the one
that is less? If you add one more accessory you can toptop the funnel-
box. You can smell the smokes all the way to Crete. Weeds out of London
trawl: Gravesend way. Serious Kent. Reedy showers. Seedy springs.
Conrad hunter lives over the beach: hunts editions. Captain Rugby seems
unfamiliar at landlubber tea. Major John with a field-size parralax cap-
tures the hunter. Funnelhouse sees with eyes. Madmen betting again on
the same walking kettle. Kettle's Yard where the paintings are. Funnelhouse meanwhile sees with pot. You can smell the deadly visions all the
way to Skete. You can go wrong in a Skete.

5

North is LNER wending off to Scotch Nero's in the dark. Aberdeen puddings
and cobbles. Scotch fisheries. Lake kipperies. The Loch Ness Mumps.
The Nordsee haggis. Cuthbert is on his rock warmed by the noses of seals.
Hilda on the Hilltower, Bede at his desk, Caedmon in the pub, and Grace

sings all her loudest alarms for Old King Cole.

6

Bridgelost. Bridewell. Basewall. Next to St. Andrews. Nord is Forth.
Bluegreen aquilons. Walking in a misty season to wink of water. Lighters
crafted like jewelry. Pickets like a rave. Cobbles under the Castle of
a lost queen. Nowhere to assemble even theaters. George comes out briefly
in pale sun. George is Easter sundown's Rex. Crimson boxes of deliverup.
Foghorn tempo with gulls. Live whitey, rule the frames. Live whiskey on
a thousand clippers.

7

Weeds black sound along gulls foot part waste pace foot way humming bridge.
Begin again the light of lemons in the little mother doors. Mines are
Nord. The Mine smokes blue. The minesweeper. Shimmer summer the Nord-
ling tree. Minereader. Coal from under the sea. Offside, you lemon!

8

Speaking of famous drinks there might be more and there is

9

O bell of blue flame from under the mind. Less than human phones. Celtic
masters leave aboard the barcraft. Tell it all to delicate feelers (you
ought to see with those ears!) Confessions into the eyes of flowers, fox-
gloves and bluebells. Telling it to the eleves' eyes, the diamond dews
of Uxbridge Foxbridge and Harrow. Sweet blue morning of Harrow (Easter)
from the Church and down there is Elaine's house. I confess it to the
bluebells. You ought to speak to the elms O browneyed Elaine. We are
bluebells to one another on the river. The great gray serious river of
Nothing.

10

Speaking of famous words. The Irish singers whirl the gaudy spokes of
Bejaysus all over the Islesoof Man Skye and Orkney. There Ezechiel comes
in a flaming hearse. Riding a green monument and announcing his swords.
Wheels, wings of Merkabah. Flaming Ottomans straight out of Dublin. The
jeweled teeth of a heavenly contraption. Come ye Evangels to the coasts
of Nord.

11

Run run Ezechiel you are on probation.

Special continuations: the Gethesmenai racetrack:
HELLO ARNOLD HELLO ROGER HELLO ISIDORE HELLO ODILO AND HELLO MEIN LIEBER
AUGUSTIN STOP HELLO WILFRID HELLO LEO AND HELLOFERDINANDAND ZACHARY AND
DONALD THE BRAVE GANG IN THE OLD BACK ROOM

Continuation for more races to the Gethsemani Track and acknowledgments
time out for customer identification:

HELLO CASSIAN HELLO CHARLES HELLO MARTIN HELLO RODERICK STOP THERE ARE
PLENTY OF OTHERS BUT IT IS A RARE SHOP

Hello all the boys in the barbershop

13

North 10.  Millways.  King of the postbus.  Comes with a Gainsborough
and puts a pillarbox under the tree.  I have drops in my eyes and can't
see the pictures.  Stunsun Newmarket morning.  I can't see the starters
because I am gated again.  Gated in Bridge Street with a pillar of pos-
tals.  Shred my letters and feed them to the birds.  Stunsun Newmarket
morning is wide wide all over.  Bookies in the lane.  Topfunner New-
mocker news.  Radios and signs.  RAF gleamers.  Cries of lonely Auden
there in the heights.  Lincoln fens are for the airmen.  I sit alone
under the mornings of Cambridge pylons and watch fliers.

14

Catch forties.  The Millways' Tale told to an autobus.  Running home from
Chesterton by night among the fences.  Stunsun and it is another morning.
Sunday down by the boatless river.  Goldilights of Northmorning see tell-
tale Maundies colder and older.  Gold February tells Millways' boat to
spill amid a calm.  Tall stands of Twickenham captains.  Baroque pieties
of a fine Anglican.

15

Winner take all Mondays.  Climates.  Emblems.  Surplices.  Twinkling
garden vision precision eyebeams strung on a string (Get thee to an eye-
doctor)  Excise management pouring into Pauls with innocent faces gleam.
Strike out Mazdas of John Dean oh great dark grinning deathshirt John
dumbstruck subway under a guilty city!

16

Stained stained to Henley Thames we go to tame the water with our
butterflies.

SISTER M. THERESE


A Hill Is for Celebration

With certain apologies to Juan de la Cruz

(for Tommie and Frank)


On a lucky night
(the lake meadow now at rest)
with no map but the spirit's pilot
we slipped through the valley gate
and scattered--one to the strict road,
a gay two at random.

When a leanbeaten path
outbranching held us--toward a sky-
hung light we three together
laddered that happy mountain.
At a stumblestair a door blazed
open and under

the icon light
we found our guru who thundered
us out of our sky with the parable
of his house: dance of the tea-mugs,
Beatle-beat, and a pocket of poems
thewed like girders, yet

gentle as first rain
weeping the world.  Onetwothreefour
together made up of one
another were five in Whom we
grew as we nudged the Pleroma
closer toward its

bright center.  Late we
left that singing hearth all in
a joy, as lit by the swami's
hand we shook out our cares lightly
under the great moonflower
along the downtrail pines.

You Sing from Islands

(for Robert Lax)

(You sing from islands--
Manhattan, and you came into my summer
lightly as Mogador
in the 'circus of the sun'
while a marvelous music sang
through all our conversation.

Then a dazzle
of sail up my greensea orchard, this sky-flown
song signed Mytilini
and I hear the wind harp through the olives
where low white houses shine like manna
on the Aegean's blue floor.

But you know islands
undefined by sea, at the mind's center
where the sun sets never
and the lyric bird broods monk-
hooded (lucky the poet
who has found his island!)

Now as the caique
boned like the skeleton of the *christoparo*
swims you to Kalymnos
scarped sheer from the sea--as the sponge-
divers plunge into the sun-bronzed
water so do you into

that singing darkness
at the quick of spirit where the *logos*
hides deepkenneled.  Dive into
that iridescent wave and snatch
the Word that sang through David's harp
and plumes and is your song.

Morro Castle


*This view shows the gigantic fortification known as El Morro, which
stands at the narrow entrance to San Juan harbor.  Although centuries have
passed since it was built, the edifice is still well preserved.*

*--from a post card*

*As is said of St. Francis, who used to apply his tongue to his lips
after pronouncing the Holy Name of the Lord to draw thence the greatest
sweetness therefrom.*
*--from* Introduction to the Devout Life


Force of madness;
The ham-red sun
Moves above the old wall
Approaching noon.

A fortress once conceived is
Forever the scene of violence.

In this glare
And in the visions
It prints behind the eyelids
Burn green outrageous shapes
Of cannons brought from another country.

Came they with hawk bells, swords and icons;
These stones raised from quiet earth
And cast in the form of a fortress.

A land that is once dishonored is
Forever the place of suffering.

Yet trace the lines
Of exhausted beauty
Cut in the breast
Of this city.
The faces that are dark
And broken, stone and water,
You will look hard in each
For answer.

Pieta.  It loves to happen.

Men are captive to nature
And dignity for the poor
Is upheld with urinating
At the foot of a statue.

Four photographs by Ralph Eugene Meatyard

Wendell Berry on his farm at Port Royal, Kentucky

Broken, the Green Stones

(note on a poem by R.M. Rilke)


The panther's trellised visions
Are lakes of dead fire;
Pacing the iron shadows
The lights have gone to nothing

In a dance of perished strength
Turned upon itself
A giant will remains
Submerged in black water.

Now,
An image pierces the eye
Shudders through each tendon,
Reaches the heart, to die.


MARVIN COHEN


The Speedy Reason Why

Do you like to ride on a plane?

No, but by a *boat's* leisurely pace.

But you recently *flew* back here.  Why?

The hurry I was in.  In a mad hurry.

Why?  What appointment was compelling you?

A plane I had to take, for quick results.

Why?--in earth, in air, by sea--why?

Nature's urge: the bathroom beckoned me.

Which Is Wronger?: Atrocities Weighed on an Uneven Scale

I accuse you of being violent!

Yes, I'm very violent--I even swallow the very germs that enter my mouth from the air. And what do *you* do?

Manslaughter.

*(Sarcastically)* Oh. Too trivial to mention.

Yes, things *are* as they *compare*.

Comparison identifies the two compared things?

Yes, comparatively.

Then whose violence is greater? *Mine*, consisting in swallowing germs from the air in the normal inhaling process--or *yours*, deliberate and willful, of manslaughter?

Yours, because of the *multiple* deaths you cause. I kill a big life, but it's only one man's.

I see. Degree by quantity, not by kind or size.

Yes. Gulp another mouthful, you murderer!

But don't *you* gulp germs in dyingly, too?

My lung capacity is smaller, my mouth tinier; you're a bigger man than me.

Yes, you comparative germ. I hope you don't cut me down to size.

How?

By reducing me to *death's* special nonentity.

*(Reassuringly by threat)* No. I want you, to win debates from. Talk some more.

## How to Counter Time's Speed

What are you looking at?

That clock.

Why?

To make sure the time doesn't go by too fast.

What if it does?

Then I'll die sooner.  Rather than that, I'll keep my eye on the clock.

Will that slow the clock down?

Psychologically, it'll lengthen the time.

Good: more time left, more things to do with it.

Yes; a lifetime is little enough: so let's extend it.

*Extend* it?!  You mean into death?

No, that's carrying time too far.

Right.  Only *vital* time matters.


## Using Euphemisms Moderately

### (How to Rephrase "I Don't Like You")

I really don't like him.  Not at all.

Yet you must regularly deal with him.  Can you suppress, or disguise, that sentiment?  To say "I don't like you" would be bad, for he's your daily business client.  How can you avert that revelation?

I don't blurt it out: I resort to a euphemism.

How guileful!  What words do you use?

"I like you," is what I say.

And does your hypocrisy succeed?

He requites it, with the same reply.  And we make deals, and mutually profit.

Insincerity's expedient device.

Advantage dictates it.  For our common interest.

Nicely explained.  I *do* like *you*.

You like *me*?  No euphemism intended?

No, the frank tongue of affection sped it out.

Good.  In *like* guise, may I reply the same.

Is this *deception's* artful practice?

No, outspoken praise, in your honor.

Good.  Your euphemism *discriminates:*  no need, with me.

None.  "I like you" by the literal sense, in simplicity's direct way; not that tortuous circuit deviously contrived.  You are the you for whom a euphemism doesn't apply.  A friendly "I like you" distinguished from disguised unfriendliness' resorting to those same words.  Necessity's sense varies the meaning behind identical words.

But what if *I* became your client, by entering an allied business? How would you *"I like you"* me?

Friendly habit won't turn crooked.  Let's *trust* in commercial gain and let fairness arbitrate.


An Encounter Consummated by the Joyous Concord of a Separation

What a coincidence that we should have met!

Unless prearranged, *all* meetings are to some extent coincidental.

How pedantic!  As for me, I'm spontaneously happy to see you again.

And I too.  Enough of these preliminaries.

Preliminaries to *what*?

Why, let's enjoy our meeting.

Naturally, and to that we shake welcome hands, my friend.

Gorgeous.  I'm stunned with delight.

Don't outdo it.  Your company has become tedious.

On that note, let's part, biding our next coincidence.

I'd tolerate only a coincidence as our next basis of meeting.  I don't pursue you actively out of my way, you bore!

Your reflections act adversely upon my regard for you.

That's excellent, if it discourages you from seeking an eager coincidence again.  Another meeting with you would incur my distaste.

Then deliberately, and not by coincidence, let's be bent upon avoiding it.

Good day, and bad coincidence to you, you leper!

Coincidentally, I concur in assessing *you* that way.

I boil with impatience to be parted from you.

Your feelings are generously reciprocated.  Let that be the last cue for our simultaneous mutual interaction.  No news from you would only be too welcome.

How *identically* I share your views!


## Time Brought to a Head


What an event has just transpired!

No, not an event: an *incident*.  It was an *incident* that expired.

*(Correcting angrily)* *Trans*pired, I said.

Yes, *that's* what happened.

What were you referring to?

Why, everything that just took place.

Yes, but what occurrence was it?

It's over.  So at least we have something to forget.

Yes, a memorable little incident.

Hardly an out*stand*ing event.

No, just a passing thing that happened.

Yes, it *will* get itself occurred, *won't* it?

There it was.  It *was* there, wasn't it?

Yes, so what are we left with now?

The most *recent* of our forgetfulnesses.

To open us, it jolted us--

And with impact it was taken in.

Well, that's that.

Over with.  And now?

*(Looking ahead)*  The *next* one to advance, to cover up *that* one's *(turning to look behind)* receding.

*(Peering ahead, to the near-immediate future.  Refers to advancing thing)*  Allow it.  I'm ready to forget.

*What* will you forego to remember?

The occurrence soon to happen.

About to take place?

The incidental event.

Eventually, the next incident.

*Now*, is it when?

Yes, it's being taken in.  *(Eyes follow the passing, keeping pace with the arc)*

In passing, there it goes.  *(Their eyes follow it out, in unison)*

What was it?

*"It"?* That's just the word to use, for what we failed to capture.

What *was* it that was failed to be captured?

The same thing.

Yes, my memory is vanishing under it.

And my recollection escorts it outside, into oblivion.

Well, that's that. *Now* what?

Now? There's an impending thing, something brewing in the air. Our reception is to meet it.

Is receptivity so alert that forward-looking anticipation is expecting what hasn't taken place yet?

So it is. The opposite, or other side, of forgetting, premature to the taking in of memory.

And the experience about to befall us?

Actively is in the wings.

Well, I wait. *(They wait)*

Not here yet.

Does it take long?

Yes, until it arrives.

*Then* what?

*Then?* Ah, *that's* when. Soon, but not now.

Is time triplicate?

With three parts, it is.

*Now* hasn't arrived.

But will soon be by.

And what's *passed?*

It clears the air, makes room, and what it vacates, the future moves over and takes up.

Movement. Where to?

What's arrived, is derived *from.*

Oh.  Where *from?*

Ah!  The source's origin!

Mysterious?

Being uncommonly unknown, it sheds mystery in long and lingering rays.

It beams out?

Yes, but darkly.

And when it comes to light?

Revelation!  Discovery!  Concrete experience!  Immediacy, straight before you, seen with the eyes' touch in actual realism that's undeniable, a sensation jabbing the mind into work, poking ideas out of us.  The excitement, the inspiration, the being stimulated.  It's Time, being active.

A high moment.

It is.  And lowly levels the usual plains before, and the dull lapse after.  It defines what's ordinary.


## With a Resolute Stride


Here we are, off to a wrong end.

Not very promising.  When do we get there?

Never, if at all.

Not exactly what I call success.  But still...

Still?  We're moving, we're not still.

I meant anyway.

Is *that* what we're headed for?

It's in the same direction.

Well, let's join it.  Or head it off.

We can, by arriving.

Starting from when?

From our earliest destination.

Yes.  Let's be steadfast.


AUGUSTINE WOLFF


Fifteenth Nisan

What a wonderful thing is Water!
The experts in various branches of Natural Knowledge
Will tell you, with astonishing exactitude,
To what an overwhelming proportion
Water
Enters into the composition of most created things;
Certainly of the most usual, the most necessary, the most familiar,
And even of our own selves.
How very fond God must have been
of Water.

Yes, indeed,
Even at the very start, we learn,
In that Beginning of all Things of the World,
The Spirit
Brooded over the face of the Waters.
There was also Light,
But that was made
After the Waters.
The Waters came first:
The Waters must be sanctified
By the brooding Spirit,
The Waters must wash and cleanse;
Then comes the Light.
The Light *is* before the Waters.
It must be so, or the Waters cannot be.
But it shines in a Darkness
And the Darkness cannot grasp it,
Cannot be illuminated by it,
Cannot be enlightened,
Until the Waters have washed the Darkness clean,
Clean and clear of all that is in the Darkness to impede the Light.
Then the Light shines,
Shines through the Darkness dispelling it.

[Should be AUGUSTINE WULFF]

323

Shines on the Waters,
The wonderful Waters
That God likes so much.

So much
That He has told us story after story in which Water is present
In overwhelming proportions.
Once, at the beginning,
Once upon a time,
All
Was covered by the Waters,
Till the overbrooded Waters parted
And the well-washed Earth hatched out.
But all too soon,
It dried, hardened
And became dusty and corrupt,
Unsavory,
Incoherent
Unable to hold itself together
For want of the Waters;
So God,
Who is so fond of the Waters,
Called to them that once had been gathered together
Called the divided Waters from their appointed places
And from River and Sea, from Spring and Fountain and Cloud
Through the Flood-gates they poured, upgurgled, inflowed,
Till the hard, dry, dusty Earth,
The Earth corrupted by Dryness,
Was wetted again by the Waters,
Was soaked and drenched, purged and revivified,
Was bathed and washed
By the pouring and roaring, the welling andswelling
Of the Waters.
O, what a wonderful thing is Water!

For the Waters mean Life:
No Life can be without the Waters.
Through them the Road led,
From strawless Bondage to Honey-sweet Freedom,
From the Arid Desert to a Land overflowing.
Out they sprang
From their secret chamber
in the heart of the Rock,
to assuage the Thirsting of the People.
Yet a King's battle-parched lips
Refused the Waters
Of far-off Bethlehem
And poured the libation
on the bloodied Earth

To the honor and glory of God:
"For the Water," said he,
"Was the Blood of Men
Who had risked their lives."
And from that age-old Well,
The Well of our father Jacob,
Updrawn were the Waters
To assuage the Thirsting
Of One of the People,
Of a Scion of David,
Who, in return,
Offered the giver the Waters of Life.
How very fond indeed is God
Of Water.

Always they stood,
For the anointed to wash in,
Before Tabernacle in Wilderness,
Before Temple in Sion,
Into which
No Iron might enter.
But when it broke through the Wall,
And ripped through the Veil of the Holy of Holies,
Then out rushed the Waters
From their secret chamber
In the Heart of the Rock
Where had gathered
The Bloody Waters of God's agony of Love
The sere and withered Man,
To bring refreshment, life and joy
Into the dried-up heart of Man.
How very fond indeed is God
Of Water.

So fond
He poured it out again
On all Creation
As in the Beginning;
and again the Spirit
Brooded and still hovers
Over the Waters of Life
Sweetened, strengthened and hallowed
By the Banquet-wine of Christ.
O yes indeed, how utterly fond is God
Of Water.

RON SEITZ

### Dear Jack

dear Jack you rise
for me ghostly each poem
there is

(heartwrung muse & poor
to die)        I'll not quit
you yet dear Jack


### In a Monastery

Opening the window
            (to let the night in)
the sounds were nice but
cold as hell

So closed the window and
lay down with
only the clock
ticking me
to sleep


### Girl

as you lean to the wood, writing
your hair falls
        hanging in space
and each movement of the pencil-point
swings the dark lock, its shine

and I am weaker because
the heavy walls of my cage
        give way
        come crumbling down
as a glacier wall does when
        the ice, cracked
        slowly lets go its hold
        & falls crashing, white
        a broken island
        sinking, then gone
        to the watery bottom
that is myself, truly

when beauty enters me

How Like a Movie

how like a movie          poetry is

slapsticking your soul with pie

the baggy pants          piano-tink
hero
          slips on banana peel
          sits wide-eyed
          jiggling mustache          &
          smiling          (to the ladies)
          tips a black derby

the sole-flap poverty of his fall
bares him          brings tears

the hold & heart of it          till
rising          a split-tail turn
he shuffles quick          away

only once          turning
to wave          then
out again          &
darkness

How sad          !

& funny          ?


              Mom

              1

visions of you lost
wandering among birdbath & roses
alone with your Blessed Mother stone statue
confused & tearless
surrounded by flowers

what it is about you that haunts me always

those old tobacco photos, Brown-Williamson
white dress on a lawn, 1938--
those pictures of you, Post & Paddock
niteclub check-girl, your
hair high in curls, that
bland painted smile telling me
other mysteries

what did you think of your son then, Mom?
your son of other photos

the baby face, white stars
on his shortpants--
to grow shiny-cheeked, hands folded
a First Communion boy--
then a young man (already troubled) holding
the high school basketball--
at 19, handsome
the whole world possible

did you know me then?
or now?

a man
growing old, skin hanging
still caught
by those tobacco shreds in your pocket
your workday making cigarettes
your streetcar ride away
leaving me to mud & a cellar door
the shed before the alley


but what is left in my growing old?

hair on the pillow
potgut & wobbly knees

will I fill the future with nervous laughter?
finally weep a God-forgive-me plea
a too late "I'm sorry"
in the name of a son who choked his love
who died a thousand times in the solitude of his shaking flesh
who could never quite crash the wall of his mind
break through, cross over
& reach the other side of silence
the simple quiet smile of being a son
to his mother

ah Mom, I can't stand it anymore!
I've battered that sad hulk your sorrowed face too long
when will I begin the pilgrimage?
knees kissing the pavement
to cry forgiveness on your shoetops

or will I go on
hurling blasphemy & curses to the breasts that fed me?
to finally lift you heavy to heaven
grass growing my palms


                        3

what's it to be, Mom?

my vision of your grave in the sun
come true
a hand out of the dirt
reaching


gone forever that lost Sunday
hurt beauty through a picket fence
that Mother's Day gift of tears
--the birdbath


life spare me, Mom
I've got holes to fill
roughs to smooth

but you're caught too--
nailed to the Church
the memory of my childhood
when (looking to your eyes for comfort) I
found love there

accepting it then
as never since

CLAIRE LIVINGSTON


Kaddish on the Anniversary of a Death

I hear America burning in
This town of silences and dreamless
  Sleepers walk among
Their houses in the dark-stained streets.
Their winds stalk down flat fields of corn
And slam the doors and windows shut
  against the light
Of sun
  of all the stars and crazy moons

This year-long night of Charleston
  Train whistles wail and
Mourn me into waking quick
  exiled in the tremendous arms
Cold with the answer to the sun of love
  That death of his

And I am caught in Illinois

The fire miracle of woman given
  generous for nothing since
There's no one left of him, such
Mortal choices men have made
  for man,
(Or what archaic god is dreaming us?)

Still in myself the keen ear
  Listening hears
America burn
The children in their beds cry ruin
  for want,
But in my waiting animal
  I know
How all my milky love was spilled;
How all the violent virtues force
  to freeze the blood and
Break the flesh to words
  that unkind man.

O fire singers, children
  I
Don't know the names of God
  alone
Cannot conceive the miracle that sings the woman whole
  Man Kind
    again


330

And I am caught in Charleston
  in Illinois
    in blind America

Left in this rain of ashes I'll not
  Mother you to death with lullabies,
But in the heat of sun and time
  alone
I'll sing
  myself the instrument;
Taut silver of the string
  And resonant wood;
The breath of bow
  And hand possessed by it,
The human
  Being miraculous

Love is the sudden answering
  Breath that wakes
From silences of death
  To birth

And while America burns
  I stand
And fiddle in the ruins
  sing loud the golden fire children
    Celebrate
      the sensuous dance
Of man and woman in their love
Of all the animals
  Man is
Most beautiful.


Winter Solstice

(for Ray)

If you would have me, do not only ask
For what you see, touch, hold, possess, but ask
To hear, beneath my nakedness, the promised son,
For I was born to give delight.

A woman is perennial, the seed
Within a naked shell.  Still, if the sun
Withdraws, the flower withers of winter cold
And under the earth's dark crust, the kernel dies.

This is winter's longest night. I wake to hear
The children cry out in their sleep, dreaming of
Dark, daytime passions drowning the song.
Then all is silence save the senseless beat of time.

Out of the dark, they say, and cold,
The sun is born. Will I too die to wake?
Will you remember who I am and warm
My nakedness? O river of the sun,
Come down, unprison me, let me be born.

Two Poems in Celebration of the End of the World

1

*But every one shall die for his iniquity: every man that*
*eateth the sour grape, his teeth shall be set on edge*

I cannot tell you what they said,
Since calculation makes me tired
I went to bed.

But when I shut my eyes, I saw
The world's death acted out in small
In faces raw
And narrow.

Silence is more a friend than friends
Whose voices, edged with sour wine,
Seek their own ends
When love is dead.

2

*If I forget thee, O Jerusalem,*
*may my right hand lose its cunning*

What if the summer never came?
A cunning hand, informed by a witless brain
Has split the form of forms into a flame
Whose radiant death falls where it will, like rain.

Why do we still expect the sun
To rise, give life, and teach us to aspire
To it, since we've forgot Jerusalem
And pant to possess and break its fire?

Can we forget you, O Jerusalem?
Can we forget the miracle of heart
That beats life-blood into the sensuous hand?
Is there an end to our infernal art?

When life is gone, Jerusalem shall stand
In the ashes of man's mind, and the last man
Shall stand against the wall.  He will not wail
When the first silence of the world prevails.


IRA C. LIVINGSTON


The Beast

We go into Vietnam like match-stick statues,
With weapons obviously too heavy for us.
We contaminate their rice-fields with war.
We shadow their land with our power.

When our bombs dent Vietnam
We see Vietnamese blood
For earth is made up of
The blood of these scapegoats.

The beast is a demon who destroys,
He hypnotizes man to carry out his dreams.
His dreams are destructive.
The demon is a bully who breaks God's toys.


The Desert

People are placed in the center of a desert.
Many people follow the tracks of others.
These people do not find water,
But merely see mirages of it.

If you meet a seed in the desert, give it water
And it will grow and produce more seeds.
If you stop giving it water it will petrify
And gritty dust storms will erode it
    Into indifferent pebbles.


333

If you place this water out in the sun
It will evaporate, and if there is a dust storm
It will rain and the dust will fall to the ground
But the wind may raise it up again--
After all, who can stop the wind?


The Iconoclast, or the Image-Maker

Water is truth, plant-killer.
Plants are the image.
The image-maker, a vegetarian,
Thrives on plants.
The plants are kept in his basement
In little blue flowerpots.
The image-maker constructs a dam,
For the snow is melting into water.
The water might flood his basement.
But the iconoclast clears the canal,
Water rushes speedily down--
So rapidly it breaks the dam,
Floods the basement and kills the plants.
Now the image-maker must change his diet to water.

After this happening
A million image-makers try,
Try to knock down the iconoclast,
But fail, for only an iconoclast
Can knock down an iconoclast.


The Prairie Wind: Charleston

Wind clutched the cardboard house
Groping for a victim in vain.
This house was different.
It had the scent of some
Far-off land.
Most of the others
Were victims of the wind.
Empty and flat
Like the land they live on,
Making no attempt to break free from
The clutches of the wind.

334

The house seemed as though
It would crumble
Under the wind's pressure.
But a green sprout
Broke the surface
And now it is blooming.

ROBERT STOCK

Hegemony of the Abominable Snowman

(for Edward Sause)

*These months of solitude & accumulation in the deepest jungles have impregnated me precisely in what I had already got to belly from those months of solitude & accumulation among the highest glaciers: what must be melted & extirpated from the failing soul, i.e., pride of will in the shaping of acts from objects, is no more deeper-than-higher than evil is hotter-than-colder. Besides, one's skin is neither thick nor thin; yet it is alive--and prickles!*
                                  *--from the Journals of William Selkirk*

The mountains, beetling and cold, of the fixed mind
give, like wintry panes, on those farther massifs
which, colder, steeper, more imposing, bind
the white-empurpling brunt of the soul's first griefs.
Yet we are seven--five men, one only woman--
five men calling her, five-named, his leman.
We call us: Christian, that true-born Englishman;
our bloods of love, Dons Quixote and Juan;
Faust Furioso, our craggy mind, our guide,
almost our will; and myself, the American--
and I alone returned of all who tried.

Yet never call me Ishmael.  Those whom
gods must adore are loved with a costive will.
How possibly, then, may changelings of hubris presume
divine devotion?  The bulk of our trip's uphill,
Ishmael's and mine; but whereas he
rises and sweeps with the far-troubling kestrel, my
consorting sprawls nebraskan, or must buy
dear passage to a far-fetched *jeu d'esprit*.
You read this only because, when I have done

with what I must rehearse, I'll not apply
for the just requites that my ascent has won.

1

Tattered, bedraggled, bearded, sane though tense,
for days we mount the baser slopes, hard eyes
engrossed by nearness (our unique defense
against the soul), which makes us realize
how purple heights observed from wooded trails
are seemings: feints of distance and atmosphere.
This fact pertains to Faust, who from it fails
to draw conclusions touching on the near
enigmas of the ranging soul...The noose
we choke in tightens: only Faust seems clear
on how to tell blue cedar from red spruce.

We shoulder our quest conspicuously unfit.
Don Quixote--that dreamer!--stares all day
into the midst of ourselves.  Are we some pit,
so to be gaped into?  Some costume play
pulling his gaunt face longer, the tragedy
to his melancholic angelical comic relief?
Noble and grave, he blinks.  What truancy!
Does he trust (in dream as in mind-stuff brief)
to multiply by spots before the eyes?
Some hold that Christian's name is really O'Keefe
And his ambition's Faust to aggrandize.
Our campfire, gauged against an unseen fright,
confesses our slyest comings and goings.  The girl
(I call her Helen) cindered all last night
in Don Juan's sleeping bag, yet seeks her pearl
of price in Faust, who craves the probe and pry
he puts to stars, which court the lunatic Don,
who loves whatever this thing he stares upon,
which may in turn hold Christian dear, who'd die
to swive her were she Mary Queen of Remorse,
and "Sonia! Sonia! Sonia!" grunts Don Juan.
So persuaded I can cloud from love's source,

I lean outside the flickering compass of light,
converse with the needy hazards, calling each
by name: Ah, Helen! Helen! Helen!  Night
hugs me closer, attending to my speech
and smothering my howls.  So now I stand
stretched to eternal forms: a woman spread
from peak to peak, shape clamoring for my hand.
But beastly breathing laps me round.  I dread
the Abominable Snowman's skulking might.
"Ah, Helen, Helen, Helen," graspless I said
and shrank back to the smoky lap of light.

Logomachy over the ontological
reality of the dead strives fruitlessly
where even edelweiss has drained its all
into the nearness of eternity.
Why, even Don Quixote knows that much!
Yet Helen, in all artlessness, persists.
Number, founded unnumbered in nature, as such
secures geology to alchemists--
or so we figure, contemplating our seven:
new tangles for fairy-tale apologists,
and, sorting with bivious odds, a trait of heaven.

As we approach the great snows, outburst brews
between Quixote and Christian over the packs:
each covets always toting all. We choose,
for discipline's sake, not to permit it; backs
must share alike, and martyrdom spring from us.
And yet that rake, Don Juan, indulges their scheme.
Oh, he and Faust have much, much to discuss!
While Don Quixote, in his discourteous dream
of honor, starts and stares, grows long and flat,
Don Juan, also taking to staring, would seem
in search of a far wench, yet waxes fat.

As for both bent and point of our expedition,
still no trace of them. Though snow packs deep
and timeless here, no tracks redress our mission.
Good God! Could it be those monsters leap
from peak to peak--or soar like spirit-cranes?
Helen's breasts bob in my bag at the witching hour
--at last! But nothing concurs. And she complains
that Faust lacks passion and rises soon and sour.
At daybreak we discover Don Juan dead,
heart strangled with one golden vise. A shower
of soft gold mists a glory for Helen's head.

The buttress Faust outflanked this afternoon
leaps straight to Pisgah, Christian alleges. "Well,"
Faust counters, "be that as may, didn't the chockstone
I sprained my thumb to budge drop plumb to hell?"
wedged in a chimney, verglas breathed away,
oh, it is hard thinking this icebound stem
earth's navel, this cord where world and heaven sway
to scuttering cloud, this distant strategem
the soul adopts to jump nerves to a frazzle,
oh, hard wearing this proud balance a diadem.
And on deadwhite fields, what a sovereign dazzle!

We scale sheer icefall.  Our surviving Don
turns out an edgy hazard on the ropes.
At noon, in an ice-cave, we were aston-
ished coming upon a naked hermit.  Hopes
he would conduct us to the Snowmen's lairs,
at least inform us, came to naught.  He would
not open mouth to us.  Yet Faust declares
him Zarathustra, whereas Christian could
conceive him only Christ in wilderness.
I neither think him wise nor find him good;
I say he's mad: such wills are sevenless.

3

Friday--date forgotten.  Bottom man
on ropes today was Don Quixote.  Who
cut the ropes?  As doubled-up he began
the plummet, lightning-craggy granite grew
to slack him, collapsing torn measures of cry
wrung from his windmilling maze--to tell us what?
Now glacier strokes what woman wouldn't--his thigh.
        Oh, weep for Don Quixote, butt
        of faith and puppet of a drop,
        oh, mourn the gape whose O was shut,
        for maybe he has gained the top.

After long default, we've come to convene
a querulous court where Christian, Helen, Faust
stand variously arraigned.  Despite know spleen,
the judge's robes are mine, the choice of Faust.
Each man of blood in turn attacks his dead
then trains his glibbest guns upon his neighbor.
My quick decision prickles my lips unsaid,
for shadow inside some snow, as if in labor
to bare an inchling melting of the cold,
intones an edge as keen as awe's own sabre:
*Until you all die, all is yet untold...*

Just now, and right before our gritted eyes,
Faust felled Christian with an alpenhook,
and then, spreadeagling him to groaning ice,
pierced feet and palms with tent-spikes.  Though I shook
with indignation, what am I to do?
We need this killer, and, as he repeats,
"You cannot mourn lost virtue."  Every few
hours he wrily rapes and searchingly beats
pure Helen, or, since he enjoins, I call
her by his name for Helen, Ova.  Bleats
of phrensy prevail upon this soul's last fall.

And watch how, now that bless blinks, cose appears
and closes eyelids. Was there ever a woe
that couldn't abide a misery? Through tears,
we tease Philomela's eternal no.
Faust, who conned the books and found them lacking,
invents exclusions, limits of his own,
do not include the Snowman. Hence his backing
preordains the quest to failure. Alone,
for all his undulating Venus, pain
assails, debates him to the thinking-bone.
His silent shriek breeds silence through her vein.

The one unusual incident today
was Helen's suicide. Now we are three
and one of us quite mad. The sun, gone gray,
still glares; glare-snows, drifting above the knee,
packing and countershifting, buckling to send
evasion sprouting the cut camellias of ice,
define our sleights-of-spirit, our space, and spend
our world to spare us what of permanence
we know, who know now nothing but to cling.
A single belay holds balance taut: our sense
the Snowman surely is no human thing.

4

I climb alone, although the record read
that we are two. For an accident befell
poor Faust--yes, poor! since now, he being dead,
such pride seems mortal fever, hardly hell.
And was it pride, that flurry into the sun?
Or was it terror drove him, much the same
as we went thronged, and made his daring run
to our destruction--till he staggered lame?
This minute, by dawnlight in newfallen snow,
while farthest ranges loom to stake their claim,
I step in their tracks; I stare. They overgrow

my Breathing-Space, my road's Emmaus that led
direction through my lungs; yet stand for whole
disembodied presences: those dead
unsubstantiated in the soul
at heights of will where any are seldom met
except the hermit of his sore temptation.
And always, since drowned paddies without let
or swerving, they have been our constant ration,
a truth beside us, like a pine's felt shape,
beyond us, like the inscrutable elation
that took and shook Quixote by the nape.

Time's clouds embodied our essential I
until soul-space, dehumanized and numb,
was choked with acts shaped by objects.  Why,
then, Snowmen are their own vestigial sum
whose acts possess no object, whose sole mode
of being is to penetrate *to be,*
while height and depth become a single node
that radiates my emptied ministry.
No need to mourn Quixote now.  Some vied
to pitch on summits, some for the bottom tried,
and I alone returned of all who died.


ALFRED STARR HAMILTON


Three Tickets to Georgia

Oh, a pink thumb
Ought to have been
For a pink blossom
That thumbed its way
From there to Georgia
On top of the Boxcar Express

Oh, a pink thumb
Was to have handed
One a pink peach
For a pink blossom
From there to Georgia
On top of the Summer Express

Oh, a pink thumb
Was to have Undone
An ordinary box of pearls
For a dumbfounded blossom
On top of a pink wagon
On top of the Georgia Express


Room Rent

That pulled at the bullrushes, That gasped for space

I never went to the back of the house that night
To know what was at the root of the matter

That went back to the sink
That went on like a suction cup
And came back for more suction
And came back with a rush to the pump

I went to the pump, I lit the hallway light
To the toilet

That went back for suction

I remembered I can never have called the turnkey
That night
To have cured the pump

Oh! and to have gasped for more war


At Camp Heart

and toppled my exultant heart over
everything here was to have been toppled over
on top of the wondrous wasteland for miles
everything here was to have been ground
to dust as of the desert
everything here was to have been destroyed


Basket of Apples

Here we are on a burning branch
  Here we are in the midst of the twilight
    Here we are to be your friends

Here we are off of the autumn fences
  Wherever more fences have been hammered
    By a carpenter to the approaching dusk

Here we are responsibly
  Hanging to the approaching dusk
    Here we are to have been your neighbors

Here we are for our autumn handiwork
  Here we are for a basket of gloaming apples
    Here we are to have been your good angels

*Alfred Starr Hamilton*

## War Threat

our municipal plant
  was for gainsaying its intense ivied strength

our municipal soldier
  was for spreading its wings higher to our swollen lips

our eyes
  were to have been tickled for our sties

our dragons for our fingers
  were to have been for tickling the immense dimensions of the moon

## Air Raid Siren

why, they even used the canary whip
to send us indoors, as often as they did,
that whistled and played in the branches
that whistled amongst ourselves mostly
that flooded our hearts with ecstasy
that whistled to the bluejay for clubs
that whistled to the scarlet tanager
who was the colonel at the station
that whistled back at our bloodstreams
that held us in check ecstatically

## Outpost

Why, I'd rather I had the mange
Why, I'd rather divine my socks
Why, I'd rather smell like an orange
Why, I'd rather live in a shack
Why, I'd rather smoke a pipe mixture
Why, I'd rather be a totalitarian
Why, I'd rather be tattooed
Why, I'd rather divine an asparagus stalk
Why, I'd rather be carved out of a totem pole
Incidentally, I'd rather I were a border incident
Why, I'd rather be a soothsayer
Why, I'd rather be a divinity of peace

## Crowded

What is this huddling on top of the frightening plains
Why are we crying out and baaing in the winderness
What is our bovine bewinderment
What is our helplessness
Why are we approaching our nemesis
Why is the lion upon ourselves
Why are we marching over the lion's paws


## Outcast

I'd rather I were a voyager
I'd rather I were a stowaway
I'd rather I were a stayaway at home
I'd rather take the philactery ribbon like this
I'd rather I were a printer
I'd rather I were a pale outcast
I'd rather I were wearing an inky cloak


## Think This Over

just before
you left

just before
you shouldered a gun

just before
you left

the thunder
there is in the grass


## Municipal Club

There is a game over a golden lawn
That protected a dandelion flower
And the moon was a wicket
And the moon is wicked

And the war is wicked
And the way they carved the moon
And a dandy yellow flower
Was for a bookmark
War is for protecting the buttercups
War is for a little yellow clover league
Why the moon is wicked for a Sicilian landmark
War is a clodhopper
War is municipal club


Iron Town

I carved this over your handsome iron hand
I drew you a graph of however you are meeting this fiery challenge
I drew you a graph of however you are firing the molten angels
I drew you a graph of however you are gasping for breath
I drew you a graph of your hand that is reaching for help here
I drew you a graph of a smokestack that is fondling over a cloud
I carved this for your handsome iron hand
I carved you an iron sledgehammer
That is gasping for breath here


Thanksgiving Day Again

Why, I didn't know there was to have been a crust
    of bread
When they paid me anything at all
Why, I couldn't have devoured my thumb
    over a piece of cheese
And called that my Thanksgiving repast
Little that I had expected
Why, I didn't know there was to be a piece of cheese at least
    to have noted of a word of peace
Next day, at all a small check arrived
And thanks me for my peace offering
But I'd walked as far as the Salvation Army
    for a cup of coffee and a little chatter
But last time I saw you people was at Kansas City
I'd walked a mile for a Camel
    and remembered the ad
At a park I read of lamb chops over my thumb
But a Thanksgiving gust of wind arrived just then
To have taken the news from an artist of peace.

WENDELL BERRY, a well-known Kentucky poet who has also written a novel, *A Place on Earth* (Harcourt, Brace), is teaching English at Stanford this year. His latest volume of poems is *Openings*.

WILLIAM WITHERUP lives in a cabin in the Sangre de Cristo Mountains, New Mexico. He has published in *Poetry Northwest, Northwest Review, Prairie Schooner* and other magazines. He has a full-length manuscript soon to be published and is at work on a new book of poems.

DOROTHY BECK was born in New Jersey, went to the University of Richmond (Virginia), works in the Archives Department of Dartmouth College and is at work on a volume of verse called *Coat of Flesh*.

ROBERT DAVID COHEN is a young American poet living in Mexico. He has published in *El Cornu Emplumado* and elsewhere.

BESMILR BRIGHAM lives in Arkansas. The poems in this issue, as well as in *Monks Pond 3*, are from her book *The Tiger*, which the publishers have not yet had the sense to buy.

PHILIP GARRISON lives in Ellensburg, Washington.

HALVARD JOHNSON has moved to Puerto Rico, where he teaches at the University at Cayey. The poems here are from his new book, as yet unpublished.

ROBERT BONAZZI is editor of *Latitudes* (Houston) and has two volumes of poetry about to be published in New York.

DAVID M. COLLINS is a doctor and a member of the Louisville Art Workshop.

DICK GANCI is a young poet living in Oakland, California.

GAIL WAECHTER is a young writer, hitherto unpublished, living in California.

TED ENSLIN lives in Maine and publishes poetry everywhere in little magazines. We are glad to present more of his *Journal*, an unusual document in the Thoreau tradition.

EMMETT WILLIAMS, whose concrete poetry appeared also in *Monks Pond 3*, is the editor of Something Else Press. His most recent books are *Sweethearts* and *An Anthology of Concrete Poetry*.

ROBERTS BLOSSOM is an actor and writer who lives at the Hotel Chelsea in New York. Some of his poems were included in *Monks Pond 3*.

REE DRAGONETTE is also a New Yorker.

GUILLEVIC is a contemporary French poet of the first rank.

ENRIQUE LIHN is a Chilean poet (born in 1929), in exile from his country. He has published four books of verse, and William Witherup's translations of him are to appear this year in *Northwest Review* and other magazines. Lillibulero Press will issue a collection of these translations in 1969.

NICANOR PARRA is one of the foremost poets of Chile; he came to New York this year for poetry readings with other poets from South America and Europe. New Directions recently published his *Poems and Antipoems*.

RICHARD S.Y. CHI is a Chinese scholar with doctors' degrees in philosophy from both Oxford and Cambridge. He teaches Chinese philosophy at the University of Indiana. His article in these pages will be included in a forthcoming book, *Humorous Zen Literature*.

CARLOS DRUMMOND DE ANDRADE is one of the most important twentieth-century poets of Brazil.

OTTO RENE CASTILLO joined the guerillas in his native Guatemala, was captured by the government army, tortured and burned alive on March 19, 1967. A book of his poems in English translation has been prepared by Margaret Randall.

In our HAIKU SECTION, which includes other poems of an innocent temper similar to haiku, we have the remarkable thirteen-year-old CHRIS MEATYARD of Lexington, Kentucky; WENDELL BERRY (see above); MATTHIAS GINN, a monk at the Abbey of Gethsemani; ANN JONAS of Louisville, who has published in *Colorado Quarterly*, *Latitudes*, etc.; RAYMOND ROSELIEP, Catholic priest in Dubuque and well-known poet; PAT DINSMORE; and JOEL WEISHAUS of San Francisco, who has a volume under consideration with the Zen publisher Charles Tuttle.

DOM CYRIL von K. KRASINSKI, a Benedictine monk of the Abbey of Maria Laach in Germany, is the author of an authoritative tome on Tibetan monastic medicine. The excerpt here is translated by ELSIE P. MITCHELL, a member of the Cambridge (Massachusetts) Buddhist Society.

ROBERT DESNOS is a modern French poet of international reputation who died shortly after being liberated from a concentration camp. Our selection is translated by JONATHAN GREENE, writer and publisher, whose third book of poetry is *The Lapidary* (Black Sparrow Press, Los Angeles).

ANSELM HOLLO is a Finnish poet living in England and writing in English. Some of his own poems and translations of Guillevic and Nicanor Parra are in this issue; earlier we presented selections from his translations of Paul Klee's notebooks and Pentti Saarikoski.

NELS RICHARDSON is a young poet who has published in *Io* and elsewhere and who was at one time in the novitiate at the Abbey of Gethsemani, after having been with the Camaldolese in Big Sur. He studied at Amherst and the Providence School of Design.

JOHN JONES taught last year in Gaziantep, Turkey, and has traveled extensively in Europe.

EDWIN FORD is a center of intellectual ferment in Louisville, where he is a student at Bellarmine College and a promising artist.

KEITH WILSON lives in San Miguel, New Mexico, and has contributed to many little magazines. He has several volumes of verse in print, and two more are scheduled to appear this year, *The Shadow of Our Bones* and *Lion's Gate*.

ALFRED OPUBAR teaches Yoruba to Peace Corps trainees at UCLA.

RICHARD GROSSINGER is editor and publisher of *Io* magazine. Quixote Press (Madison, Wisconsin) is bringing out a book of poems by him and his wife, Lindy Hough, who appeared in *Monks Pond 3*.

JUNE J. YUNGBLUT, who has a doctorate from Emory University, helps her husband in directing the Quaker Meeting in Atlanta. She also appeared in *Monks Pond 3*, with an article on Beckett.

BOBBY BYRD is twenty-six years old and a teacher in Memphis. He has published in *Tolar Creek Syndicate* and recently had a motorcycle accident with his wife in Plain Dealing, Louisiana.

MARGARET RANDALL, co-founder and co-editor of *El Cornu Emplumado* (Mexico), has recently completed a volume of translations of Otto René Castillo, to be published by Doubleday.

ROBERT LAX, a concrete poet of international fame, is recently back from Greece and is living temporarily in Olean, New York.

THOMAS MERTON is editor of *Monks Pond*. Excerpts from *The Geography of Lograire*, a long poetic work in progress; *Proverbs*, in honor of Robert Lax; and the readings in AFRICAN RELIGIOUS MYTHS are his contributions to this issue. His next book, *Zen and the Birds of Appetite*, will be published this winter by New Directions.

SISTER M. THERESE taught English at Marquette and other colleges. She has written many books of verse, including *Speak to Me, Sparrow*, from which we draw two selections. She lives in Milwaukee.

MARVIN COHEN's book, *The Self Devoted Friend*, was brought out this year by New Directions. His dialogue mini-plays, of which several were also included in our previous issue, have been produced in London and Edinburgh. He writes: "Perhaps half or a third of the books I ever read have influenced my own work, especially James Joyce, Kafka, Henry James, some French surrealists like Henri Michaux, William Faulkner and the eighteenth-century English prose style; many unconscious influences must have been at work, too...such as my rather isolated Brooklyn childhood, my semi-deafness from the age of three; my interest in major league baseball, art and music; early abortive love life, poverty, the cosmos of New York City, travelings and tattered abundance of jobs and idlenesses. My work, however, hardly ever touches *literally* on events, being rather surrealistically abstract."

347

AUGUSTINE WOLFF, a priest of the Abbey of Gethsemani, was born in England and worked as an engineer and a lawyer in Argentina before coming to the monastic life. He is an artist and a prolific writer.

RON SEITZ teaches English at Bellarmine College, Louisville, and is on a sabbatical leave this year to work on a biography. He is also the author of an unpublished novel, *Somewhere the Other Side*.

CLAIRE LIVINGSTON teaches at North Hennepin State Junior College in Osseo, Minnesota. She is on the board of editors of the magazine *Karamus* and has published widely. She is also a professional violinist. Her son, IRA C. LIVINGSTON, is eleven years old.

ROBERT STOCK is forty-five and his first book, *Covenants*, was recently published by Trident Press. He is, "to paraphrase Eliot, a classical romantic, a Christian and an anarchist...very much in the situation of Simone Weil."

ALFRED STARR HAMILTON has been one of our most generous contributors. Fifty-three and living in New Jersey, he has published in various poetry magazines. A book of his verse will soon be printed by Jonathan Williams (Jargon Books). He writes: "I have been on the road during the depression. I have been through forty-three states that way. I served (subservience) a year in the army. I have been a member of the Socialist Party ever since. I live on a budget of $80 a month today. I live in a big rooming house. I cook my own meals. I don't like money. I don't like more money. What would I do with more money? I spend all my time with poetry."

W.W. PEMBLE's interests include reading, writing and traveling, as evidenced in our selections from his poetry.

The CONCRETE POEMS facing pages 16 and 17 are the work of THOMAS MERTON; the one facing page 58 is by ALAN ABELE, who is Brother Carl, a novice monk at the Abbey of Gethsemani.

The four photographs between pages 92 and 93 were contributed by RALPH EUGENE MEATYARD. All the others are by THOMAS MERTON.


Correction: The poems in Monks Pond 3 (pages 40 and 41) attributed to ROBERT BONAZZI are actually by RON SEITZ. We apologize profusely!

Also we regret that in this issue Matthias Gill's name reads incorrectly as Ginn.

And our apologies to Fr. Augustine Wulff whose name appears as Wolff.


[The CONCRETE POEMS are pages 231 and 232. The work by Alan Abele is page 275. The above-mentioned photographs by RALPH EUGENE MEATYARD are pages 311-14. The poems by RON SEITZ are on pages 164-65.]

spring fever bear post-hibernation poem

          is it spring

          out of their fevers
          gaunt men come

          look      you new ladies
          they have

          a new thing

          *i*

          it was hot in the dream-hole
          there was light in the dream-hole
          there was smoke in the dream-hole
          music and dark and staggering dreams

          *ii*

          they have been in
          the within within the within

          *iii*

          staggering
          in their dreams they have seen
          the staggering dreams        and
          the staggering in the dreams

          *iv*

          it is spring
          and they are coming
          out of their eyes

          there is no thing
          not new to them now


                    --Anselm Hollo

# AFTERWORD

IT IS A DELIGHT to see *Monks Pond* made available again as part of the twentieth anniversary commemorative celebrations honoring the memory of Thomas Merton. When I was asked to write an afterword, I immediately thought of the summer of 1968, when I returned from an assignment in Rome. The abbot, Flavian Burns, informed me of my new work as Father Louis's secretary, saying that it would be a fulltime job since Merton would be travelling quite a bit. But in the summer of 1968 he was fulfilling some secret aspirations as editor of an avante garde journal of poetry and prose. Philip Stark was helping him with the typing, although Merton himself arranged the layout, chose the illustrations, and in general enjoyed himself immensely during this one shot at being editor. Brother Cassian Vigna, Gethsemani's printer, was responsible for the printing of it, and I recall Merton's pleasure at how well it turned out.

This special commemorative edition is making its appearance shortly after the first volume of *The Merton Annual,* which contains a hitherto unpublished article by Thomas Merton on the Chinese sage Shen Hui. Merton's article was originally intended as an introduction to some translations of Shen Hui by Richard Chi. For some unknown reason, these translations and Merton's introduction have remained unpublished all these twenty years. I think it is very fitting that this work should appear as a new edition of *Monks Pond* is being prepared, since the latter contains some excerpts from the writings of Shen Hui. I am sure that Merton would be pleased to see East and West united in this special publication of *Monks Pond,* and grateful to all who have made it a reality.